Coming in

Manchester University Press

★ ★ ★
★
★ **European**
★ **Politics**
★
★ ★ ★

Series Editors: Professor Dimitris Papadimitriou (University of Manchester), Dr Kathryn Simpson (Manchester Metropolitan University) and Dr Paul Tobin (University of Manchester).

The *European Politics* series seeks to tackle the biggest issues facing Europe in the twenty-first century.

Previously published under the *European Policy Research Unit (EPRU)* name, this long-established and highly respected series combines an important scholarly legacy with an ambitious outlook on European Studies at a time of rapid change for the discipline. Its geographical coverage encompasses the European Union, its existing and aspiring members, and 'wider Europe', including Russia and Turkey, and the series actively promotes disciplinary, theoretical and methodological diversity.

The editors particularly welcome critical scholarship on the politics and policymaking of the European Union, on comparative European politics, and on contemporary issues and debates affecting the future of Europe's socio-political and security outlook. Key areas of interest include Brexit, the environment, migration, identity politics and the ever-changing face of European integration.

Coming in

Sexual politics and EU accession in Serbia

Koen Slootmaeckers

MANCHESTER UNIVERSITY PRESS

Published by Manchester University Press
Oxford Road, Manchester M13 9PL
www.manchesteruniversitypress.co.uk

British Library Cataloguing-in-Publication Data
A catalogue record for this book is available from the British Library

ISBN 978 1 526 15934 2 hardback
ISBN 978 1 5261 9128 1 paperback

First published 2023
Paperback published 2025

EU authorised representative for GPSR:
Easy Access System Europe, Mustamäe tee 50,
10621 Tallinn, Estonia
gpsr.requests@easproject.com

Typeset
by New Best-set Typesetters Ltd

To all in Serbia fighting for LGBT liberation and justice for all

Contents

List of figures

Abbreviations

CARDS	Community Assistance for Reconstruction, Development and Stabilisation
CEE	Central and Eastern Europe
CEEC	Central and Eastern European Country
CeSID	Centar za slobodne izbore i demokratiju (Centre for Free Elections and Democracy)
CoE	Council of Europe
CPE	Commissioner for the Protection of Equality
DG	Directorate General
DS	Demokratska Stranka (Democratic Party)
DSS	Demokratska Stranka Srbije (Democratic Party of Serbia)
ECHR	European Convention on Human Rights
ECtHR	European Court of Human Rights
EC	European Commission
EP	European Parliament
EU	European Union
GLIC	Gay Lesbian Info Centre
GSA	Gay Straight Alliance
ICTY	International Criminal Tribunal for the former Yugoslavia
IGLYO	International Lesbian, Gay, Bisexual, Transgender, Queer Youth and Student Organisation
ILGA	International Lesbian, Gay, Bisexual, Trans and Intersex Association
ILO	International Labour Organization
IMF	International Monetary Fund
KPD	Koaliciju Protiv Diskriminacije (Coalition Against Discrimination)
LDP	Liberalno-Demokratska Partija (Liberal Democratic Party)
LGBT	lesbian, gay, bisexual, trans*
LGBTI	lesbian, gay, bisexual, trans*, intersex

MEP	Member of the European Parliament
MP	Member of Parliament
NATO	North Atlantic Treaty Organisation
NGO	Non-governmental organisation
NPE	Normative Power Europe
OSCE	Organization for Security and Co-operation in Europe
PM	Prime Minister
RSD	Serbian dinar
SAA	Stabilisation and Association Agreement
SDP	Social Democratic Party
SNS	Srpska Napredna Stranka (Serbian Progressive Party)
SPC	Srpska Pravoslavna Crkva (Serbian Orthodox Church)
SPS	Socjalistička Partija Srbije (Socialist Party of Serbia)
SRS	Srpska Radikalna Stranka (Serbian Radical Party)
TEU	Treaty on the European Union
trans*	umbrella term referring to different identities within the gender identity matrix, including but not limited to transgender, transsexual and genderqueer
UN	United Nations
US	United States of America
YiHR	Youth Initiative for Human Rights
YUCOM	Lawyers' Committee for Human Rights

Acknowledgements

This book has been a long time, about a decade, in the making, and has been a journey of self-discovery as much as a social scientific endeavour. Over the years, this research project developed and matured into this critical book where I have found my own voice, approach and queer power. I would not have arrived at this point if not for the people that I have encountered over this period.

My journey started in 2011 in a small office at the KU Leuven, which I shared with Heleen Touquet. During this time we enjoyed many moments of, what can only be described as, intellectual cross-fertilisation. It was through this meeting of minds that her passion for the post-Yugoslav region and my deep interest in all things gender and sexuality together sparked my curiosity for LGBT politics in the Western Balkan region. No words can express what these conversations – which still continue to this day – have meant for me, and still do. Not only did they provide me with a research agenda and the introduction to a region where I have felt a strong sense of belonging, they also provided a mentor and great friend.

The second leg of this book's journey centred around my research time at Queen Mary University of London. Here, I must first acknowledge that the research that ultimately translated into this book would not have been possible without the financial support of Queen Mary Westfield Trust Research Studentship. During this time, I was lucky to be supported by Paul Copeland, who not only kept encouraging me to push my arguments to their limits and make my mark with this book, but also became an invaluable friend.

During my time at Queen Mary University of London, I am also indebted to the excellent colleagues and friends with whom I shared an office space. Daniel Gover, Matheus Lock and Angus McNelly, in particular, stand out for the continuous and effortless support and friendship they have provided over the years. A particular thank you goes to Indraneel Sircar, whose shared interest for all things Balkan, coffee, biscuits, Eurovision and other talent shows have created wonderful moments of escape into absurdity and new scholarly avenues.

Living in London has not always been easy. At times it is a hard and difficult city, which I am sure I would not have survived if it were not for Jeremy Buckle. In fact, I am quite certain that without Jeremy's support – whether it was by helping me move, providing me with a place to live in times of hardship, or just having a night out in the Yard with gin and tonics – this book probably would never have seen the light of day.

Doing fieldwork in Serbia and living in a country where I did not speak the language was at times challenging. However, also here, I was never alone. Jovanka Todorović has been part of my fieldwork from the start. Not only did she dedicate an incredible amount of time to my research – I think we must have had conversations about LGBT activism and politics in Serbia which in total exceeded more than twenty hours of material – but she was always willing to help me out whenever I was stuck or struggled to reach other informants. Similarly, Agata Milan Đurić was another friend, who was always ready to help me out and provide me with a healthy dose of positive energy whenever I needed it. I also want to explicitly thank Isidora Stakić for her friendship and walks, dinners and drinks, during my fieldwork.

More generally, I want to thank all the Serbian activists for their inspiring work – there are too many to name, and I am afraid of missing people out. I am incredibly grateful to have become part of your community and being able to contribute to your important work, and I hope we will find many more ways to work together to improve the lived experiences of LGBT people in Serbia. Similarly, I want to thank Amarildo Fecanji and Dragana Todorović for their work as ERA, the newly established regional LGBTI Equal Rights Association. Their work has not only inspired me, but being part of their first annual conference in Kosovo in October 2016 means more to me than anyone can ever imagine. Indeed, at a time when I had lost sight of why I did this research, the incredible gratitude of all the LGBT regional activists I experienced at that conference, and the fact that they 'adopted' me as part of their movement, provided me with the motivation and inspiration needed to finalise the research project and ultimately this book. So I want to thank the LGBT activist community in the Western Balkans for all their support.

This book would also not have been what it is without Milica Popović, Jelena Đureinović, Franko Dota, Marko Jurčić, Tamara Pavasović Trošt, Danica Igrutinović and Filip Ejdus, who not only commented on parts of my work, but also provided hours of insightful conversation about LGBT politics, Serbian politics and everything in between. Similarly, there is the sexuality and politics research community whose work, input and ideas have greatly inspired my work and this book. I want to particularly thank Momin Rahman who introduced me to the Queer IR crew and provided me with an academic home. I am honoured to be able to share intellectual discussions with and continuously learn from friends and colleagues such as Philip Ayoub, Cai Wilkinson, Anthony Langois, Markus Thiel, Manuela Picq, Matthew Waites, Ahmad Qais Munhazim, Andrew Delatolla, Denis Altman, Emil Edenborg, Michael Stambolis-Ruhstorfer, and Francesca Romana Ammaturo, but also more widely with feminist colleagues and friends such as Katharine A. M. Wright, Annick Masselot and Roberta Guerrina.

Finally, while I consider all these colleagues my friends, there are two who deserve a special mention. Mike Bosia and Dean Cooper-Cunningham have become more than just colleagues and friends. Throughout the pandemic we continue to face, they have each in their own ways helped me survive – a thing to look forward to and a safe space to break down in. Moreover, throughout this time, they helped me to embrace my queerness, push me out of my comfort zones and teach me so much about what the power of my scholarship can be, about my politics and above all myself.

Introduction

On the evening of 15 June 2017, the news broke that Serbia would become the fifth country in the world to have an openly gay (in this case, lesbian) political leader. Following the election of Aleksandar Vučić as President earlier that spring, Ana Brnabić had been put forward by Vučić and confirmed by a parliamentary vote to become the new Prime Minister of Serbia. As the story developed, observers were quick to congratulate Serbia on the 'historic' appointment as it constitutes a double first for the country: the first female and first openly lesbian Prime Minister. Western news outlets highlighted the apparent progress made in Serbia by contrasting this development to the riots that accompanied the 2010 Belgrade Pride parade. To cite one example, the BBC News (2017a) stated that 'just a few years ago, the appointment would have been unthinkable. But EU [European Union] hopeful Serbia can present it as proof of increasing tolerance.' Although the BBC at the time remained cautious not to overinterpret the political meaning of the appointment, their Belgrade-based respondent argued that Brnabić's appointment did carry real weight. The reference to Serbia's EU candidacy in international reporting is no accident, as most of Serbia's improvements of lesbian, gay, bisexual and transgender (LGBT) rights have been linked to its transnational and European integration process.

As an observer of LGBT politics in Serbia, neither Brnabić's appointment nor the reporting on it came as a surprise. I recall that during a lunch break in April 2017, just after Vučić was elected President, I turned to my colleagues and semi-jokingly said: 'I bet Ana Brnabić will become the new PM. There would be no better way for the Serbian political elite surrounding Vučić to demonstrate their embrace of Europe.' Having previously witnessed how holding the 2014 Belgrade Pride had helped Vučić to become known as the reformer (see Chapters 4 and 6) – the man able to get difficult things done – the appointment of Brnabić seemed the next logical step. However, questions remain of how LGBT rights and politics became such a powerful symbol in Serbia's EU accession process, and how its symbolism has impacted

LGBT rights and lives in Serbia. These questions drive the research of this book.

Of course, the ideational linkage between what it means to be European and the advancement of LGBT rights is not something new (see e.g. Ammaturo, 2015b; Ayoub and Paternotte, 2014b) and has become subject to ever growing academic debate across multiple disciplines. For example, queer theorists such as Jasbir Puar (2007) and Rahul Rao (2020) have examined and theorised the structures of homonationalism and homocapitalism respectively, helping us understand how sexuality has become embroiled with modernity. Others have turned their attention to the role of activism in imagining Europe as an LGBT-friendly space (Ayoub and Paternotte, 2014b), how LGBT rights emerged as an identity marker within the EU (Eigenmann, 2022; Mos, 2014; Slootmaeckers, 2020), as well as how the EU promotes these values and norms abroad (Ayoub, 2016; Ayoub and Paternotte, 2020; Slootmaeckers et al., 2016b; Thiel, 2022). More recently, scholars have also started studying those forces opposing gender and LGBT equality, such as anti-gender mobilisations (Kuhar and Paternotte, 2017) or the use of political homophobia (Bosia, 2014, 2015; Bosia and Weiss, 2013; Currier, 2010; McKay and Angotti, 2016).

Taking a critical look at the sexual politics embedded within EU enlargement is vital, as over the last two decades we have seen the EU take an active role in protecting LGBT rights in the world, both afar and in its near neighbourhood (Thiel, 2022). For example, in 2013 the European Commission (EC) adopted its new Enlargement Strategy in which it declared LGBT rights a key priority in assessing fundamental rights progress in candidate countries (Slootmaeckers and Touquet, 2016). Following on from the observation that homophobia, discrimination and hate crimes based on sexual orientation remain commonplace in Turkey and the countries of the Western Balkans, the EC argued that there 'is an urgent need for *anti-discrimination legislation* to be extended ... *Hate crime legislation* will need to be introduced ... Countries must pursue a *zero-tolerance approach to hate speech, violence and intimidation* ...' and continued that '[f]reedom of assembly and expression should be protected including through the appropriate handling of Pride parades' (European Commission, 2013a, p. 11, emphasis in original). Such statements and monitoring practices contribute to the notion that respect for LGBT rights is an important signifier for what it means to be a modern and/or European nation. Indeed, the monitoring of these rights has turned out to be a powerful pressuring tool in the hands of international advocacy groups and organisations, a tool for politicians to manage their own countries international image and/or criticise other countries, but also a topic of direct political contestation, both within and among countries (see e.g. Bracke, 2012).

To illustrate such contestations, consider the diplomatic incidents that followed Uganda's adoption of the Anti-Homosexuality Act in 2014. When the Ugandan Parliament adopted a law that made engaging in the 'act of homosexuality' (broadly defined) punishable with a prison sentence of up to seven years and a life sentence for repeat offenders, the international community heavily criticised Uganda for doing so. Already in 2009, when the bill was first introduced to the Ugandan Parliament, the White House issued a statement stating that President Barack Obama 'strongly opposes efforts, such as the draft law pending in Uganda, that would criminalize homosexuality and *move against the tide of history*' (quoted in Eleveld, 2009, emphasis added). After the Ugandan Parliament adopted the law in 2014, President Obama repeated his criticism, stating:

> The Anti-Homosexuality Bill in Uganda, once law, will be more than an affront and a danger to the gay community in Uganda. It will be a *step backward* for all Ugandans and *reflect poorly on Uganda's commitment to protecting the human rights of its people.* It also will mark a serious setback for all those around the world who share a commitment to freedom, justice and equal rights. As we have conveyed to President Museveni, enacting this legislation will complicate our valued relationship with Uganda. (Obama, 2014, emphasis added)

Similarly, the European Parliament (EP, 2014) adopted a non-binding resolution wherein it not only deplored the adoption of the law as 'constitut[ing] grave threats to the universal rights to life, freedom of expression, of association and assembly, and freedom from torture and cruel, inhuman and degrading treatment', but also underlined that 'LGBTI equality is an undeniable element of fundamental human rights'. As such, the EP demanded an immediate reaction from the European Commission and EU member states, urging them to 'review their development cooperation aid strategy with Uganda' and 'consider targeted sanctions, such as travel and visa bans' (European Parliament, 2014).

These and other interventions of 'Western' actors in debates on LGBT rights across the world are an expression of the previously alluded to phenomenon in which nation states are increasingly defined and judged by their 'gay-friendliness' or homophobia. This phenomenon is most commonly conceptualised through Jasbir Puar's (2007) notion of homonationalism, which she defined as 'a facet of modernity and a historical shift marked by the entrance of (some) homosexual bodies as worthy of protection by nation-states, a constitutive and fundamental reorientation of the relationship between the state, capitalism, and sexuality' (Puar, 2013b, p. 337). Although over time, homonationalism has been interpreted and used in a variety of ways, in this book the concept is considered as an analytical tool 'for apprehending the consequences of the successes of LGBT liberal rights movements ... a way to track historical shifts in the term of modernity, even as it has become mobilised within the very shifts it was produced to name' (Puar, 2013a, p. 25). It is thus taken to describe a historical moment in which states can advance their exceptionalism or modernity by demonstrating their tolerance of homosexuality, in contrast to 'homophobic Others'. As it captures a historical moment in which LGBT lives have been embroiled in international power dynamics, homonationalism, like modernity, cannot be escaped, but only resisted or resignified (Puar, 2013b). While some countries and entities (including the EU) have increasingly embraced this facet of modernity by using LGBT rights as a symbol for what it means to be modern, 'Western', or even European (Ammaturo, 2015b; Ayoub and Paternotte, 2014b; see also Chapter 2), others have resisted this development by emphasising an alternative value system based on so-called traditional values (Kuhar and Paternotte, 2017), or engaging in what Cooper-Cunningham (2021) has labelled 'heteronormative internationalism' – the process of placing traditional family values at the centre of foreign policy.

On the global scale – the previously mentioned law in Uganda is but one example – and similar instances of resistance to homonationalism and geopoliticisation of LGBT rights can be found in geographical areas closer to the EU (Luciani, 2021; Shevtsova, 2020; Wilkinson, 2014). Within the European context, Russia is often taken as a prime example of such contestation as it has positioned itself as the defender of European civilisation from the perversions and demoralisation spread by the European Union – or 'Gayropa' (see e.g. Moss, 2017; Shevtsova, 2020). Since 2012, Russia has been engaged in 'a conscious and consolidated effort to build a "sexual sovereignty" of the nation' which has had strong implications for LGBT politics and rights in Russia and its sphere of influence (Makarychev and Medvedev, 2015, p. 51). Indeed, the 2013 'anti-gay propaganda' law can be and has been interpreted as an attempt to reposition Russia in the world by providing an alternative political and cultural model against the Western, EU- and US-led homonationalist interpretation of modernity. This alternative model of 'heteronormative internationalism' (Cooper-Cunningham, 2021) consists of promoting so-called 'traditional values' and defending 'authentic' national cultures, while actively resisting democratic and 'modern' values (perceived to be) imposed from abroad (see also Nuñez-Mietz, 2019; Wilkinson, 2014).

Instances of such resistance to the association between Europeanness and LGBT-friendliness can also be found within the EU, across most of the member states. Of particular interest for the argument of this book are the post-accession developments in some Central and Eastern European (CEE) member states, as they foreshadow the nature of sexual politics within the

EU enlargement process. Although the CEE EU member states have passed several laws regulating LGBT rights in one way or another (at varying degrees and mostly in the field of anti-discrimination) during the period leading up to accession (Slootmaeckers and Touquet, 2016), LGBT rights are said to have only entered the political agenda because of international (EU) pressure (Roseneil and Stoilova, 2011). Consequently, LGBT rights in some of the new member states became politicised after accession (O'Dwyer, 2012): whereas the pressure for equal LGBT rights was seen as a litmus test for modernity and Europeanness by those supporting the 'civilising mission' of the EU (Graff, 2006), it fuelled anger towards the EU among those who consider the pressure for LGBT equality a threat to the nation and local culture (Ayoub, 2014; Mole, 2011, 2016; Renkin, 2009; Slootmaeckers and Sircar, 2018). For example, Mole (2011) has argued that the pressure for equal rights for LGBT people was perceived as a direct attack by the so-called international gay lobby on the future of the Latvian nation. Similarly, in Poland, the Kaczyński government declared it had to combat the 'aggressive promotion of homosexuality' because it felt that 'although Poland may have joined the EU, they will have none of the "loose" attitudes toward sex' (Graff, 2006, p. 436). Although such contestations initially emerged after accession to the European Union in some Central and Eastern European countries, these contestations of an LGBT-friendly Europe are now a central part of wider anti-gender mobilisations across the European continent (Kuhar and Paternotte, 2017). The relatively recent events where Polish regions and communalities have been declaring themselves 'LGBT-Free Zones', and the European Parliament's resolution to declare Europe an 'LGBT Freedom Zone' (BBC News, 2021) – which sparked immediate objections from Polish elected officials (Catholic News Agency, 2021) – represents only one of many iterations of such normative contestations.

Although only touched on briefly here – each of these instances deserve their own books – together these examples do demonstrate how LGBT rights have become increasingly salient in relations between the EU and the countries in its close proximity, providing a fulcrum for political contestation. Association with the EU is frequently equated with same-sex marriage by opponents (in the case of Ukraine, see e.g. Shevtsova, 2021), while the EU similarly evaluates a country's modernity by examining its stance on LGBT rights. This is particularly the case within the EU enlargement process, as demonstrated throughout this book. For example, as discussed in more detail in Chapter 4, (former) EU Commissioner Stefan Füle (2014) called the 2014 Belgrade Pride a 'milestone in the modern history of democratic Serbia'. Similarly, Member of the European Parliament (MEP) Tanja Fajon said: 'After three last-minute bans over the last three years, this year, the Serbian government will have the opportunity to right these wrongs. The values of tolerance and diversity that will be highlighted this Sunday are European, and Serbia fully belongs in Europe' (quoted in Intergroup on LGBT Rights, 2014). Yet these sexual politics within the EU enlargement process are not without consequences. As I will demonstrate throughout this book, the way in which the EU instrumentalises LGBT rights as a litmus test for Europeanness has strong implications for the politicality of local movements and the potential for improving the lives of LGBT people.

Although the notion that the EU is a key player in the global arena when it comes to LGBT rights promotion has become mainstream, these practices remain somewhat puzzling. Despite the fact that LGBT rights have acquired important symbolic value in EU politics and discourse – e.g. Pride parades can now serve to illustrate a candidate country's endorsement of European norms (Slootmaeckers, 2017, 2020) – such emphasis remains in stark contrast to limited EU competences and EU's *acquis communautaire* in this field, not to mention the contemporary contestations within the EU as demonstrated by the attacks on LGBT rights in, for example, Poland and Hungary. As such, the aim of this book is to disentangle the symbolism of LGBT rights in the EU enlargement process by focusing on the promotion of, and resistance to, LGBT rights within it.

By considering the international context of homonationalism as a vital part of my analysis, I distance myself from a classical approach to Europeanisation in which the impact of the EU on a third country is examined and aim to develop a dynamic and relational conceptualisation of the EU enlargement process in which norms are inherently contested, and normative struggles between the EU and candidate countries must be resolved to advance the political integration process (see Chapter 1). As such, *Coming In* is not interested in examining the impact of the EU on LGBT rights in a candidate country per se, but rather asks 'How do the EU and a candidate country negotiate normative tensions in relation to LGBT rights which have been created as part of the overarching political integration process? And what political outcomes does this process produce?' These central research questions are answered by drawing on the case of Serbia's European integration process between 2001 and 2016.

Studying the sexual politics of EU enlargement

The literature on LGBT norm diffusion, and in particular Phillip Ayoub (2016, p. 48) in his influential book, argues that the international visibility of LGBT equality norms can contribute to change – although not in a linear way – in countries that originally demonstrated hostility to these norms, especially when these countries are 'embedded in international communities that champion an LGBT norm'. The scholarship on EU enlargement and LGBT rights tends to support this argument as it has highlighted that the EU accession process by and large contributes to the adoption of new laws in the candidate countries (Ayoub, 2014; O'Dwyer, 2012, 2018; Slootmaeckers et al., 2016b; Swimelar, 2016). In an attempt to summarise the literature dealing with the Europeanisation of LGBT rights, the first core finding has been that external incentives, i.e., EU conditionality, has played a key role in the adoption of LGBT rights in candidate countries (O'Dwyer, 2010; Swimelar, 2019). Other catalysts for change have been the role of transnational activism (Ayoub, 2013) as well as the new political opportunities (O'Dwyer, 2018) created by the process which contributed to increased norm visibility (Ayoub, 2016).

Although there is a general consensus that the EU matters for the development of LGBT rights in candidate countries, there have also been criticisms of its engagement with LGBT rights. A common critique, which this book also points to, has been that the EU has not been consistent, and its actions were subject to other priorities (Ames, 2004; Slootmaeckers, 2020; Slootmaeckers and Touquet, 2016). Others have pointed to the fact that domestic legislation is often introduced in a rather top-down manner, without public debate (Chetaille, 2011), which in turn has led to laws remaining under-implemented. Moreover, as already alluded to, the EU's promotion of LGBT rights has sparked resistance and state-sponsored and political homophobia within new member states (on political homophobia, see Weiss and Bosia, 2013). Such politicisation of LGBT topics has been linked to the interrelated phenomena of threat perception (Ayoub, 2014), nationalism (Mole, 2011; Swimelar, 2020) and Euroscepticism based on the rejection of so-called EU values (Slootmaeckers and Sircar, 2018). More recently, scholars have been highlighting how these hostilities against LGBT rights are part of a longer process of change. Ayoub (2016), for example, demonstrates that resistance and state-sponsored homophobia paradoxically make LGBT equality norms more visible, and therefore can contribute to further change in the long run. O'Dwyer (2018), similarly, argued that backlash can have both a unifying and professionalising effect on LGBT movements, allowing them to forge new alliances and coalitions.

While the importance and value of these findings are not to be disputed – and indeed, the research presented in this book supports these findings – there are two shortcomings in this literature that mean that the processes at play in the Europeanisation of LGBT rights are not yet fully explored and understood. First, it tends to approach EU enlargement as an asymmetric process in which candidate countries must (at least formally) comply with EU rules and, as such, focuses on the analysis of legal changes in candidate countries from an EU-centric perspective (for an exception, see e.g. Bilić,

2016c). Focusing on the top-down conceptualisation of Europeanisation (particularly relying on the impact of the conditionality principle), the EU's LGBT-friendliness is then too often taken for granted and, by extension, LGBT rights are considered to be a non-negotiable condition of EU membership (e.g. O'Dwyer, 2012). However, as this book argues, there is considerable room for political contestation and negotiation within the 'Europeanisation of LGBT rights', particularly because LGBT rights 1) play a symbolic role in boundary-making processes (Ayoub and Paternotte, 2014a, 2020; Slootmaeckers, 2020) and 2) are not deeply rooted within the EU *acquis* and thus remain ambiguous (Mos, 2020). Second, the literature is characterised by a rather optimistic 'progress' undertone, particularly when it comes to the international context in which the EU enlargement process takes place. Such optimism might be misplaced as the notion that the international visibility of the LGBT norm is a 'force of good' when states seeking to enter the LGBT-friendly international community might not accurately reflect reality. The international context is not just a scoping condition that determines how norm diffusion occurs, but is in fact fully intertwined with these processes, and is both actively shaped by and shapes domestic (LGBT) politics. Even though scholars, such as Ayoub (2016), have always remained conscious of the importance of domestic politics, there is a risk that by considering the international as a scoping condition, we end up unintentionally reifying Western sexual exceptionalism by demarking other regions and/cultures as pre-modern. To overcome these issues, the book adopts a more critical position that does not take the 'Western' position for granted.

Critical scholars, such as Kulpa and Mizielińska (2011) and Kuus (2004, 2007), have already argued that the EU's enlargement has ironically reinforced an East–West divide (see also Bilić, 2016c). With regard to LGBT rights, Ammaturo (2015b) has described the process through which this East–West divide is maintained as the 'pink agenda', which creates and promotes a fault line between presumably LGBT-friendly and homophobic countries and suggests that the EU is unique in its open-mindedness and tolerance to LGBT people. In other words, EU enlargement is a political process that contributes to the advancement and popularisation of the idea that the EU is exceptionally good at protecting LGBT rights (Slootmaeckers, 2020), and it does so by subjecting candidate countries to, what Kulpa (2014) has called, a 'leveraged pedagogy'. Through this leveraged pedagogy, which is crystallised in the conditionality policy, Western Europe condemns candidate countries as not sufficiently European or modern to be fully accepted into the European fold, but European enough to be offered redemption and to be aided in their attempts to 'Europeanise'. Within this framework, old (Western) EU member states are cast as the 'knowledgeable teachers of democracy, liberalism, and tolerance' (Kahlina, 2015, p. 74), while CEE countries are infantilised (Bilić and Stubbs, 2016) and rendered as permanently in transition, post-communist, yet to mature, and – especially important for this book – homophobic. The statements mentioned earlier by (former) Commissioner for Enlargement Stefan Füle and MEP Tanja Fajon on the 2014 Belgrade Pride illustrate this tendency.

Whereas the concept of homonationalism is extremely useful to critiquing how the 'West' reproduces its sexual exceptionalism on the back of other(ed) non-Western regions, it cannot fully capture that the resistance to LGBT equality in these regions is an important part of this reproduction process. In his work, Rahman (2014, p. 279) has eloquently demonstrated how 'Western' sexual exceptionalism is triangulated through a *homocolonialist* process in which homonormative nationalism is deployed 'within a dialectic of respectability/otherness in a classic colonializing mode, directed at "traditional" ["Eastern"/non-European] cultures as homophobic non-western "others" that need to be civilized or modernized but also constructing "home" western normative queer identities'. In other words, the resistance to the sexual politics of the West is an equally important piece of the homocolonialist process as it accepts the configuration of Western exceptionality. Or as Ayoub and Paternotte have reminded us:

> Even among the most random bedfellows – from the Eurovision pop diva and bearded drag queen Conchita Wurst to members of Vladimir Putin's government to activists across the globe campaigning for and against LGBT rights – there seems to be broad agreement that LGBT rights are part of European values. (Ayoub and Paternotte, 2020, p. 153)

Taking this important insight into account and applying it to the EU enlargement process, this book argues that sexual politics are located in the *relation between* the EU and the candidate countries, whereby the promotion of and resistance to LGBT equality produces political outcomes both at the international and domestic level. In order to analyse the sexual politics located within EU enlargement relations and the outcomes these produce, the book develops a *relational* and *transnational* approach to the 'Europeanisation of LGBT rights'.

Drawing insights from relational sociology (Emirbayer, 1997) and the relational turn in international relations scholarship (Jackson and Nexon, 2019; Qin, 2018), the book argues that the sexual politics within the EU enlargement process should be analysed through a focus on the relationality of the process of promoting and resisting LGBT equality. Such a relational approach highlights *transactions* over *interactions* – the main difference between these two concepts being that actors that interact are independent and unchanged by the interaction, while actors within a *transaction* are interdependent (Emirbayer, 1997, pp. 285–290).[1] A transaction is conceptualised as a dynamic and unfolding process, which does not necessarily need to be attributable to actors. The latter is crucial as it highlights that although it might be possible to define observable actors/entities shaping the process, when solely focusing on these actors/entities, one risks losing sight of the emerging effects of the process itself (Jackson and Nexon, 1999). In other words, the relational approach suggests switching from

> thinking about the world as a *noun* to understanding it as a *verb* – to focus on the effects of the blowing rather than the blowers. Doing this allows us to imagine that a process is mutable in relation to space and time, as are the mechanisms established to promote it. (Eyben, 2010, p. 388, original references removed)

By adopting a relational approach I am able to 'deconstruc[t] a taken-for-granted moral universe', and conceptualise norms and values not as givens that exist a priori and independently, but rather as 'by-products of actors' engagement with one another in ambiguous and challenging circumstances' (Emirbayer, 1997, p. 309). In other words, the relational approach taken in the book highlights that the so-called EU values are not fixed, but rather negotiated in the EU enlargement process through the transactions between the EU and candidate countries.

By taking a transnational approach the book is also able to focus on a single country without falling victim to methodological nationalism. This is the case because such an approach promotes supplementing the national with the non-national through shifting the analysis to 'linkages across cultural contexts [and political scales] rather than reproduc[ing] analyses of scale' (Kim-Puri, 2005, p. 143; see also Szulc, 2018). By embracing multiscalarity, the transnational approach takes the national and non-national as supplementary levels of analysis. Thus, rather than analysing a top-down impact of the international on domestic politics, a transnational analysis highlights, as Szulc (2018, p. 10) rightfully notes, that 'it is not those different scales separately but their combination and imbrication that created unique conditions, with unique opportunities and challenges, for lives and activisms of [local LGBT people]'. As such, this book asks what the configuration of international and national LGBT politics – as produced through the promotion of and resistance to LGBT equality within the European integration process – has yielded for LGBT rights and politics in Serbia.

Thus, in order to study the 'Europeanisation of LGBT rights', this book engages in a critical conversation with the canonical literature on Europeanisation via enlargement and presents a revised and updated conceptualisation of EU enlargement that allows for the analysis of the negotiations of so-called EU values as part of political integration process. It does so by disavowing the tendency of EU enlargement studies to take EU positions for granted and their predominant focus on a 'top-down' introduction of EU rules and norms in candidate member states.

As discussed in more detail in Chapter 1, this book reconceptualises the EU enlargement and Europeanisation process by drawing on the literature inspired by Ian Manners' (2002) seminal work on normative power in Europe, albeit the critical approach as presented by Thomas Diez (2005, 2013). This critical approach not only draws attention to the Othering patterns inscribed in the EU's external relations, but also challenges the taken-for-grantedness of its normative foundations. The latter is achieved by emphasising hegemonic struggles and normative contests both within the EU and between the EU and third countries. Thus, rather than taking EU values and norms as a pregiven, I consider them to be relational and forever contested, which in turn means that they cannot simply be 'transferred' to third parties, but 'need to be reinterpreted in the process so as to write out the tensions at the core of the integration process. [Thus, whereas] there may be competing norms within the EU ... these maybe especially come into tension if applied to a specific context' (Diez, 2013: 202–203).

This being the case, it no longer makes sense to simply focus on the outcome of Europeanisation, but rather one should foreground the process itself by studying the *politics* of Europeanisation. To that effect, I argue that the EU enlargement process should be analysed as a relational process in which different hegemonic struggles and normative tensions come together in a transnational (multilayered) normative struggle with its own tensions. Thus, instead of studying how norms are set within the EU and/or whether these norms are successfully 'transferred' to third countries, the book presents a more dynamic analysis and has as its central research questions: How do the EU and a candidate country negotiate normative tensions in relation to LGBT rights which have been created as part of the overarching political integration process? And what political outcomes does this process produce?

To conclude the conceptual background of the book, a few words on terminology are warranted, especially in relation to the term 'LGBT'. Indeed, it is important to remember that any term used to describe the politics that are at the core of this book represents an exercise of labelling and inevitably a process that shapes and defines the politics that can emerge from the usage of these labels. For example, 'gay and lesbian', along with the acronym LGBT (and sometimes LGBTI to include 'intersex') are now commonplace terms (Paternotte and Tremblay, 2015) and are widely used within activism and academia. In international politics, and particularly within the UN system, the rubric of 'sexual orientation and gender identity, expression and sex characteristics' has been used (for a critique, see Lennox and Waites, 2013). Yet others seek to simplify language and have opted to refer to 'gay' or 'same-sex' rights when discussing sexuality and sexual politics. While each of these terms have their place in scholarly analyses, they also each come with their own set of politics and drawbacks; nevertheless, a choice needs to be made to put words to the politics we seek to analyse. In this book, the term LGBT is preferred over other labels, not because I seek to align myself with the narrow identity-focused politics that often underpin these labels, but rather because this is the terminology preferred by the people and institutions I study. Indeed, the acronym is not only dominant in EU policies and documents, but, more importantly, is also the predominant label used by activists in Serbia.

Although LGBT will be used throughout the book, it must be noted and emphasised that this acronym, like other terms, is not without its problems. LGBT is described by Binnie and Klesse (2012, p. 445) as signifying a 'coalitional practice between different collectivities of actors … [It] is controversial because it insinuates a quasi-natural confluence of interests around certain gender and/or sexual subjectivities.' Furthermore, in EU policies and documents, its meaning is often somewhat reductionist – it is mostly used to refer to same-sex sexual orientations (often only referring to lesbian and gay people) while trans* and bisexual issues remain invisible. The acronym has further been criticised for being a hegemonic and homogenising term, and does not always allow for local expressions of identity; it may even oppose such expressions (for such critique, see e.g. Kulpa and Mizielińska, 2011). Considering these criticisms (which I fully agree with), the reader must remain aware of the different meanings attached to the LGBT acronym as well as its problematic nature. In fact, whereas within the European (EU) context the acronym has increasingly been adjusted to LGBTI to incorporate the concerns of intersex people, in Serbia LGBT refers predominantly to lesbian and gay people and issues. To date, bisexuals and trans* issues, although not absent, usually remain relatively invisible and under-recognized, and intersex politics are only just beginning to emerge. Despite such disparity, most local activists remain adamant in their usage of LGBT to label their cause.

This book's contribution

Overall, this book presents a 'queer' approach to the study of the EU enlargement process not only in terms of the topic examined but also in its theoretical approach (Cooper-Cunningham, 2021). Whereas the literature on EU enlargement tends to take EU norms for granted, the book argues that these norms and the exceptional position of the EU in defending LGBT rights are constructed and reproduced through its relationship with candidate countries. Placing power dynamics and hegemonic processes at the heart of the research allows for a more critical analysis of the enlargement process in which the negotiation and the reinterpretation of norms can be observed. Moreover, by considering the social outcomes of these political processes, this book draws attention to what the LGBT politics embedded within the EU enlargement process produce and how they do or do not contribute to the lived experiences of LGBT people in candidate countries. With my research I seek to contribute to both global sexuality politics (or queer international relations) and the Europeanisation studies.

With regard to the former, the book takes a queer approach to international politics as advocated by Cooper-Cunningham (2021), drawing on Cathy Cohen's (1997) formulation of a queer political project that is continuously challenging and critical – a ceaseless interrogation of power, even after 'progress' or hard battles are won. Here I seek to provide an analysis of the diffusion of LGBT rights that goes beyond the adoption of legal instruments to protect rights or the mere critical analysis of the way in which LGBT rights have been instrumentalised within so-called high politics. Indeed, I do not consider law and institutional change an endpoint of analysis, but rather view them as a point of interrogation as to what these laws, institutions and power dynamics that allowed them to emerge do for LGBT people (see Part III).

For example, in Chapter 5, I demonstrate that the impact of new anti-discrimination legislation in Serbia is limited due to persistent societal homophobia. This societal context is not to be ignored as it creates visibility regimes and power structures that prevent LGBT people who have experienced discrimination from reporting their cases to the relevant authorities because they fear the process might 'out' them. In other words, the homophobic culture of Serbia seems to act as an 'attitudinal panopticon' (Slootmaeckers, 2022), limiting the potentiality of the law for LGBT people to combat discrimination. These findings thus deeply question a commonly held assumption that legal change represents progress and that social change will follow over time. Similarly, in Chapter 6, I highlight how the instrumentalisation of LGBT rights and politics at the international level have real and harmful consequences for LGBT people and activism. Indeed, I argue that the EU's homocolonialist practice of what Rahman (2014, p. 281) calls 'pink testing', combined with domestic resistance to such practices, has substantially shifted the politics of Belgrade Pride. The violent opposition to Pride in 2010, and the superficial and inconsistent engagement with Pride by the EU, not only led to it being banned for three consecutive years, but also depoliticised the event, potentially foreclosing further successes (see Chapter 6). In particular, the bans and the need to connect to European arguments pushed Pride into the human rights discourse, making having Pride a goal in itself rather than a tool for LGBT politics. This allowed the state to co-opt and militarise

Pride, creating a 'Ghost Pride' (Slootmaeckers, 2017). This state-tolerated manifestation of Pride takes place in a militarised 'transparent closet' that keeps LGBT people's visibility strategies invisible and outside the public sphere, reinforcing traditional and nationalist conceptions of Serbian society. Thus, while the return of the Pride on the surface seemed a positive development, through a more critical engagement with the politics that underpin it we observe a strategy through which certain aspects of LGBT visibility are tolerated with the aim of reinforcing wider heteronormative structures within the country.

Thus, with regard to global LGBT rights and queer international relations scholarship, I advocate for critical engagement with the notion of LGBT progress and argue that we should recognise that laws and visibility (although important) are not a measure of progress. To fully understand the complexities of global sexuality and sexual politics, we must ask why laws are adopted, the processes through which LGBT politics are produced, and ask what their impact is for LGBT lived experiences. As such, I advocate throughout this book for an explicit embrace of the social justice project of queer liberation, and push for active engagement with society and people in our analyses, rather than just legal and institutional change. By analysing the disjuncture between legal rights and some high-level visibility tactics (such as Pride) and what they do or not do for LGBT people, I argue that, as scholars, we must recentre our attention on the people about whom we write, their experience and their realities, as progress in law without a change in their lived experience remains hypothetical.

I also seek to provide a new energy to the Europeanisation literature by emphasising the politics of the EU enlargement process and its relational and transnational nature. Indeed, as the EU enlargement process does not take place in a political vacuum, the analysis of the process cannot and should not be ignorant of its wider context. For example, EU enlargement is not only a process by which new member states are admitted; it also plays an essential role in the positioning of the EU within the wider international system as it produces the EU's international identity (Slootmaeckers, 2020). As such, conditionality, and political conditionality in particular, are not a technocratic or neutral process; they are inherently political. Indeed, throughout the book I argue that the EU enlargement process should be thought of as a political process in which the combination and imbrication of domestic and international politics produce outcomes that the dominant approaches in the Europeanisation literature cannot fully explain. Moreover, as EU policies and/or norms are neither given nor fixed, it is through their particular use within a transnational context, and the interaction between domestic and international politics, that the meaning of these policies and/ or norms are negotiated (re)defined and reinterpreted.

To analyse these politics, I provide a new definition of the Europeanisation process that recognises it is a process of *negotiated transformation* in which EU policies and norms are (re)defined, contested, translated and transformed, with both sides making compromises to further political integration (Chapter 1). I further provide an analytical framework that reconceptualises Europeanisation as a transnational and relational process – a multilayered normative struggle in which it is recognised that norms (and rules) are always contested and cannot therefore be simply transferred to third parties. This new framework further embraces the complexity of the EU enlargement process and is based on a more longitudinal, multiscalar analysis of the EU enlargement process that is sensitive to the interconnectedness of (policy) fields. Taking temporality more seriously, I argue that what the Europeanisation literature often describes as 'policy outcomes' are not fixed endpoints, but are rather outcomes-in-process – i.e. they are not only the result of the process but also contribute to the reconfiguration of relations within the field, thereby determining further actions within the process.

By recognising that EU norms are not fixed and that they are subject to a process of negotiation and reinterpretation, the new conceptualisation of Europeanisation also has strong implications for another often-present assumption within the EU enlargement literature. Much of the Europeanisation literature not only engages in a top-down approach analysis of legal and institutional compliance, it also seems to operate under the assumption that formal compliance with rules and adoption of institutions will eventually lead to social change. Just as the pathological turn within the Europeanisation scholarship criticises the EU for its outcome-focused analysis of domestic reforms (Mendelski, 2015, 2016), I argue that an outcome-focused research agenda is equally problematic as it remains unaware of the translation processes that are part of the politics of Europeanisation.

With the aim of studying these politics of Europeanisation, the presented relational and transnational conceptualisation brings new energy to the literature as it provides a framework which allows for a more critical study of the EU enlargement process which considers its wider transnational context. To illustrate, the current homonationalist historical moment has meant that the EU has begun presenting itself as exceptionally LGBT-friendly, which is contrasted with homophobic Others. This context, however, has also created the opportunity for Serbia to politicise LGBT rights for its own goals and engage in what this book labels *tactical Europeanisation* (see Chapter 1). Tactical Europeanisation, as defined in this book, highlights the differential instrumentalisation of reforms and European values in which reforms are being performed at the international level to demonstrate Europeanness, while domestically being decoupled from those values. Tactical Europeanisation captures the process of doublespeak in which candidate countries use the reforms to highlight Europeanness externally, while domestically the execution of the reforms actively undermines the aims of the reforms. Indeed, with reference to LGBT equality, I demonstrate how in recent years Serbia has engaged in doublespeak: internationally recognising and showing adherence to the LGBT-friendly identity of the EU, while domestically engaging in political actions that are in line with an opposite Orthodox national identity. This, in turn, undermined the politicality of local LGBT activism. Such processes only become observable when considering Europeanisation through the presented transnational and relational conceptualisation.

Notes on methodology

With its analytical focus that emphasises processes, the methodological approach of this book is guided by the principles of process tracing on a single case study (Bache et al., 2012; George and Bennett, 2005; Panke, 2012). The sociological roots of the relational approach to Europeanisation require rich empirical material to gain sufficient insights in the processes of promoting and resisting LGBT equality and the outcomes produced by such processes (Parsons, 2010). While process tracing is often used to either test existing theories or to inductively formulate new ones, the book moves beyond such binary engagement with theory. Instead, it uses process tracing methodology in line with Burawoy's (1998) 'extended case method' to engage in a critical conversation with existing Europeanisation via enlargement literature, and to improve/further existing theoretical thinking by means of detailed analysis of a single case.

To analyse the promotion of, and resistance to, LGBT equality within the EU enlargement process, the book focuses on the case of Serbia (2001–15).[2] Serbia has been selected as a case study for two main reasons. First, as an EU candidate country, Serbia exemplifies the current EU enlargement process and the challenges faced within it. Indeed, as Tanja Börzel (2013, p. 173) has proclaimed, the current EU accession process of the Western Balkans provide us with a 'real-world experiment' on the relationship between the EU and candidate countries. Moreover, the current enlargement process provides a perfect context to study tensions within the EU–candidate country relationship, as the conditions under which the enlargement process is taking place are much more challenging than before. Not only are the reforms Western Balkan candidate countries have to undertake expected to be much greater, but these countries are also dealing with added complexities resulting from, among other things, the wars in the 1990s (Börzel, 2013). In this context, Serbia is an exemplifying case. Although Serbia has a more or less consolidated sovereign state, the enlargement process is said to be constrained by Serbia's contested borders (cf. Kosovo), post-war ethnic tensions and nationalism, and limited state capacity (Elbasani, 2013b). Second, Serbia is selected because of its current state in the enlargement process. Of the Western Balkan countries aspiring to EU membership, Serbia, alongside Montenegro, is the most advanced candidate. Whereas Kosovo and Bosnia-Herzegovina (henceforth Bosnia) are potential candidates for EU membership, their membership prospects appear to be remote. North Macedonia and Albania, on the other hand, were granted candidate status in 2005 and 2013, respectively, but their progress has been slow until very recently. Montenegro (in 2012) and Serbia (in 2014) are the only two candidate countries that have entered the accession negotiations phase. Both countries, therefore, were identified as potential case studies. However, Serbia has been selected over Montenegro due to its particular relationship with the EU. Even though the early stages of the accession process were complicated, and slowed down, by Serbia's lack of cooperation with the International Criminal Tribunal for the former Yugoslavia (ICTY) and the issues regarding the final status of Kosovo (Kostovicova, 2014), Serbia has seemingly transformed into a front runner of EU enlargement. Furthermore, Serbia's progress and the speed of change is puzzling considering the country's ambiguous relationship with the EU, which is tainted by, among other things, the issue of Kosovo and the military intervention of 1999. Serbia's simultaneous display of increasing proximity and resistance to the EU, therefore, demands further investigations on how (these normative and political) tensions between Serbia and the EU are being negotiated, as this seems to happen in ways which are not 'expected or predicted comprehensively by [the current] rational institutionalism or sociological institutionalism' informed approaches to Europeanisation (Kostovicova, 2014, p. 69).

In the case of Serbia, two different themes are identified to analyse the sexual politics of EU enlargement. The first theme looks at the legal compliance of Serbia with regard to LGBT rights and analyses the adoption and implementation of anti-discrimination and hate crime legislation (see Chapters 3 and 5). While this legislation-based issue is situated in a field with formal codified rules of behaviour, the limited *acquis* and European standards in this area still mean that the 'rules of the game' are not fixed and can be subject to political contestation. The second theme looks at the Belgrade Pride parades (Chapters 4 and 6). Pride has developed as a globalised practice of LGBT politics, and has become, for the EU, a litmus test for human rights protections and Europeanness more generally.[3] Pride, as a practice of LGBT politics, however, is not considered a precondition for

EU membership due to the fact that there is no European standard on the matter. At the domestic level, the identity politics of such events stands in sharp contrast to the dominant, conservative, masculine and heteronormative values of Serbian society (see Chapter 2). This contrast makes Pride an ideal lens through which to examine the negotiations of these transnational tensions as part of the political integration process, and to what outcome.

Empirically, the book draws from a multitude of data sources. The three main data collection methods are semi-structured interviewing, document analysis and participatory observations at some activist events and Pride marches. Interviews were conducted with a variety of actors. At the EU level, these were with officials from the European Commission, the European Parliament (including MEPs) and the EU Delegation to Serbia. In Serbia, I did interviews with LGBT activists from almost all active LGBT organisations, other civil society actors, as well as with officials from independent state bodies (e.g. Office for Human and Minority Rights, the Ombudsman, and the Office for Cooperation with Civil Society) and state officials (e.g. officials from the Ministry of European Integration, Ministry of Justice, Serbian European Integration Office, and Members of Parliament).

A total of 89 interviews were conducted between 2012 and 2016, the interview length ranging from 30 to 150 minutes. Interviews were semi-structured, using a topic list which focused on the adoption of anti-discrimination policies, the implementation of these policies, the organising process of Belgrade Pride and the meaning of Belgrade Pride for LGBT politics in Serbia. The main aim of the interviews was to 'collect first-hand testimon[ies] from direct participants and witnesses regarding critical events and processes. [They were used as] a means to probe beyond official accounts [and] ask theoretically guided questions about issues that are highly specific to the research objectives' (Tansey, 2007, p. 767).

A triangulation strategy was employed when analysing the data and reconstructing the timeline of events to overcome potential interviewee biases. In addition to triangulation across interviews, the data of the interviews was also triangulated with data obtained through (qualitative) content analysis of several types of documents, most notably EU Progress Reports, but also official statements regarding the accession process, and documents produced by different actors, including activists' annual reports, as well as data obtained through participant observation of LGBT activists' events during two field trips (April–May 2015, and September–October 2015), with the 2015 Belgrade Pride being the most important one. The data analysis was also supplemented by insights and background information obtained through countless informal conversations with activists and other knowledgeable people during events in Serbia, and also during activist conferences throughout Europe (particularly those organised by ILGA-Europe).

Structure of the book

The remainder of this book is structured into three parts, each consisting of two chapters, a conclusion, and an Epilogue that pulls the research into the present. Part I, 'Rethinking Europeanisation and EU–Serbia relations', provides the theoretical and empirical background of the book. Chapter 1 develops the theoretical and analytical framework. Based on the observation that the EU enlargement process has undergone fundamental changes to highlight an increasing focus on promoting human rights, and democratic values to candidate states, the chapter provides updated theoretical and conceptual tools that are needed to analyse the process. The chapter first reconceptualises Europeanisation via enlargement as a process of negotiated transformation in which EU policies and norms are (re)defined, negotiated and transformed, with both sides making compromises to further political integration. Next, the chapter presents the theoretical framework that allows for a more critical analysis of the civilisational politics embedded in the EU enlargement process that goes beyond institutional changes to include an analysis of transnational configurations of politics and the complex (negotiated) outcomes they produce. Chapter 2 provides an overview of the normative struggles within Serbia and the EU, which together constitute the background of the book's research. Following on from the theoretical framework, it maps out the multilayered normative structure that governs and informs the promotion of, and resistance to, LGBT equality promotion in Serbia's European integration process. The chapter presents the most salient Othering processes and normative struggles that inform the Europeanisation of LGBT rights within the context of Serbia.

Part II, 'Adopting, resisting and transforming law and practices', focuses on the processes of legal and policy change in Serbia. Chapter 3 is the first empirical chapter and presents the adoption process and the implementation of the Serbian anti-discrimination legal framework between 2001 and 2015. It provides an overview of how Serbia's rapprochement with international society and its European integration process has led to the adoption of legislation prohibiting discrimination and hate crimes. It is argued that there were three distinct phases in the adoption of the anti-discrimination framework in Serbia, each with a particular configuration of domestic and international politics, and it has been these configurations that have been an important explanation for the observed outcomes-in-process. The chapter demonstrates the importance of a non-EU-centric approach to the analysis of the Europeanisation of anti-discrimination policies with regard to LGBT rights, as well as the need to include a transnational and relational awareness. It argues that the different phases in the process and the respective outcomes-in-process are the results of the changing relations between the different actors in the transnational policy field, as well as the intertwining of different policy fields. Chapter 4, on the other hand, focuses on the history of Belgrade Pride from 2000 to 2015. It argues that the organisation of Belgrade Pride has predominantly been a product of particular configurations of domestic and international politics, in which the context of Serbia's EU accession process has played an important role with diverging effects. Three phases are identified, which together present a story of engagement and disengagement of various political actors throughout the fifteen-year history of Belgrade Pride. As such, the chapter argues that one can only fully understand the political processes at one (e.g. domestic) scale by considering the other political landscapes (e.g. international scale) in which Belgrade Pride takes place. Although it is undeniable that the EU and accession process have played a key role in the three 'successful' Prides in 2010, 2014 and 2015, it is argued that a myopic view of these three Prides obscures the fact that the changing EU–Serbia relationship within the accession process has equally contributed to why Pride was banned for three consecutive years. Finally, the chapter argues that the return of Belgrade Pride is better conceived as, what I label, 'tactical Europeanisation' – i.e. a performative act to communicate the readiness to Europeanise by aligning oneself with certain 'European norms', while disengaging and undermining the underlying principles of the norm at the domestic level.

Part III, 'Looking beyond policy towards lived experiences', is the final empirical part of the book. It looks into what the policy changes and processes discussed in Part II mean for LGBT people in Serbia. Chapter 5 shifts the focus from adoption processes of legislation to their implementation and its consequences for lived experiences. Building on the existing Europeanisation literature which has highlighted EU practices, and domestic institutional and political barriers as key explanations for limited implementation of new laws, the chapter argues that these are insufficient explanations to fully grasp why the anti-discrimination legislation remains weakly implemented. It argues that scholarly enquiry into the Europeanisation of fundamental rights should not follow the EU practice of limiting fundamental rights and even democracy to its institutional incarnations, but rather recognise that the so-called European norms have an inherently normative and societal base. In particular, the chapter argues that the social environment in which these laws operate creates its own barriers for individuals to exercise their rights. The lack of social change becomes a disciplining environment in which people whose rights have been violated are prevented from seeking justice out of fear of further and more severe violations of their rights. Chapter 6 turns to the local meaning of Pride as an activist tool to change LGBT people's lived experiences. Although it has been recognised that Belgrade Pride, as part of Serbia's EU accession process, forced the topic of LGBT issues into the public debate and forced the state authorities to recognise the presence of LGBT lives, this chapter observes that these achievements might have been partly hollowed out by a problematic transfer of Pride as a (Western-originated) activist tool to Serbia, as well as Pride's turbulent organisational history. This chapter demonstrates how the history of Belgrade Pride has contributed to a transformation of Pride's politics in Serbia, by looking at the evolution of Belgrade Pride in terms of its achievements of the goals of Pride as an activist tool.

The conclusion summarises the main findings and arguments of the book and situates these in the wider context of the EU enlargement process and international LGBT politics. The book concludes with an Epilogue. As the book argues that any outcome within the EU enlargement process is always ongoing and part of wider processes, the aim of the Epilogue is to describe what has happened in Serbia since the end of the empirical data collection to demonstrate how the observed politics and processes have panned out since. It considers further evolutions in the anti-discrimination framework and its implementation, as well as the transformation that the Pride parade in Serbia has been going through since. In doing so, the book allows the reader to understand why Serbia now has an openly lesbian prime minister, who has not only denied the existence of homophobia within the country but has also become a parent while simultaneously presiding over a government that seeks to limit access to fertility treatment for LGBT people. Finally, the Epilogue provides the reader with insights into how activists have responded to the co-opting of Pride.

Notes

1 Transactions are more than interactions in the sense that the actions of actors in a transaction are relational (see Dépelteau, 2015: 55–56). This means that actors do not act based solely on their own predispositions or characteristics, but in large part in relation to the characteristics and actions of the other actor involved in the transaction. Consider, for example, a game between a father and his daughter. The daughter 'certainly influences the actions of her father, and vice versa, when they play a game. We could say that they self-act on each other, or that they interact with each other. However, the notion of transaction allows us to see, and reminds us, that if the child acts in *this* way, it is only and partly because the father is also there and he is doing what he is doing. They are interdependent, meaning for instance that do not simply act according to some pre-given, personal features – even if personality matters' (Dépelteau, 2015: 55, original emphasis).

2 This time period is selected to include the democratic transition of Serbia, which marked the reintegration of the country in the international system up to the

opening of the first chapters within the EU accession negotiations. The cut-off point for the analysis was set for 2015, because primary fieldwork was concluded in 2015, but more importantly because, towards the end of 2015, the first chapters of the negotiations were opened, which is expected to significantly alter the EU–Serbia relationship.

3 At this point it is important to note that Pride is not imposed on candidate countries per se. In fact, Pride only enters the international agenda after local actors express their interest in organising it. Pride, then, is not a foreign imposed event, yet it is also not void of an international dimension (as discussed in more detail in Chapter 4). Indeed, Pride events across the world remain deeply embedded in the history of 'Western Pride', as well as their current imagery. Acknowledging this reality, as well as the domestic origin of the desire to organise Pride, Pride should be considered a local, yet vernacularised, version of a globalised event (Thoreson, 2014).

Part I

Rethinking Europeanisation and
EU–Serbia relations

1

Europeanisation as negotiated transitions: towards a relational and transnational approach to EU enlargement

The EU enlargement process has undergone profound changes since its inception, developing into a tool whereby the EU seeks to actively influence third countries (Tatham, 2009). Whereas the first waves of enlargement were predominantly focused on the alignment of candidate states to EU policies and practices, the latter waves are increasingly concerned with the transformation of candidate countries into good democratic member states. Since the 1990s, human rights and democracy has taken a more central place within EU's identity up to the point that it started to consider itself to be a 'community of values' and guardian of fundamental rights (Sloot-maeckers and Touquet, 2016; Smismans, 2010). Against this wider development, the EU enlargement process equally transformed to increasingly focus on promoting human rights and democratic values to candidate states (Slootmaeckers, 2020). After what in hindsight can be called trial-and-error experiences with fundamental rights promotions during the 2004/7 enlargement and the accession of Croatia, the EU adopted the so-called 'fundamentals first' approach in an attempt to make the so-called EU's core norms and values the cornerstone of the entire process (Slootmaeckers and Touquet, 2016).

Given such profound changes to the enlargement process, wherein vaguely defined norms took centre stage, it is peculiar that a similar reflexivity has not occurred within the Europeanisation literature. With this I do not mean to imply that the literature has been stagnant over the last two decades, as the literature is producing a wealth of empirical findings on the process and the way in which it did or did not transform candidate countries – and several 'turns' have occurred to better understand when, where and why the process does not work (see e.g. Elbasani, 2013a; Mendelski, 2016). Instead, when I say that there has been limited reflexivity within the literature, I draw attention to its theoretical underpinnings. It cannot go unnoticed that the core theoretical tools and conceptualisations of Europeanisation via enlargement literature have not changed much since its inception, and arguably have not kept up with the changed nature of the process itself (Slootmaeckers, 2022). Building on a series of critical observations of the Europeanisation process from different disciplines, and from scholars studying what are (wrongly) perceived as niche (policy) areas (Ayoub, 2014, 2016; Bilić, 2016c; Gaweda, 2021; Kahlina, 2015; Kunz and Maisenbacher, 2017; Lombardo and Forest, 2012; Süleymanoğlu-Kürüm and Cin, 2021), I embark on a conceptual journey to incorporate these findings and arguments in a meaningful way into the theoretical foundations of the Europeanisation literature.

The study of the EU enlargement process remains dominated by the theoretical foundations laid out in the work of Börzel and Risse (2003), Schimmelfennig and Sedelmeier (2005b) and, to a lesser extent, Radaelli (2003). Although these theories have their continuing merits and produced a wealth of insights in the processes at play, there are at least three reasons why they are overdue a reappraisal: 1) these theoretical approaches have their roots in the Europeanisation process of member states, which is a fundamentally different process (Grabbe, 2003); 2) they were formulated at a specific time and in relation to a particular articulation of the EU enlargement process, which we know has undergone its own transformation; and 3) they were developed to analyse public policy and policy fields of a more technical nature, and thus are less equipped to deal with values and norms. In other words, applying these Europeanisation theories as they stand to the analysis of the 'fundamentals first' approach to enlargement – which emphasises values and political principles – would remain unable to deal with the specificities of these norm-based political areas (Slootmaeckers, 2022).

While the corrective turns within the literature (e.g. for the domestic turn, see Elbasani, 2013a; for the pathological turn, see Mendelski, 2015) have provided some relief in this regard by drawing attention to different empirical findings and challenges within the EU enlargement process, their theoretical basis does not divert from the wider Europeanisation literature. As such, I propose a theoretical reappraisal and reconceptualisation of Europeanisation. As feminist (Gaweda, 2021; Rawłuszko, 2021; Süleymanoğlu-Kürüm and Cin, 2021) and queer scholars (Ayoub, 2014; Bilić, 2016c; Kahlina, 2015) have pointed out, such a reappraisal is needed to allow us to actively consider the central role of norms and values in the EU enlargement process, as well as the fact that these norms are not neutral but play a vital political role in how the EU positions itself within the international arena (Diez, 2013; Slootmaeckers, 2020).

Foregrounding relationality and the notion that politics and norms are always located and operate within relations (Emirbayer, 1997; Jackson and

Nexon, 2019; Qin, 2018), this chapter develops a *relational* and *transnational* theoretical framework that is aware of, and avoids, the uncritical reification of European exceptionalism created by and through the enlargement process (Slootmaeckers, 2020). This conceptualisation departs from the notion that processes and the mechanisms established to promote norms and values are mutable in time and space. In doing so, it 'deconstructs a taken-for-granted moral universe' and highlights that values do not exist as an a priori, but are rather the 'by-products of actors' engagement with one another in ambiguous and challenging circumstances' (Emirbayer, 1997, p. 309). Additionally, rather than considering the impact of the EU (or the international) on the domestic, the national and non-national are considered as supplementary levels of analysis whereby the combination and imbrication of the politics at the different scales produce certain outcomes (Kim-Puri, 2005).

To develop this new approach to Europeanisation, the chapter will first provide an updated definition of the Europeanisation process that considers and accounts for the political nature of the EU enlargement process. Then it provides a brief overview of the existing approaches and their shortcomings. The next and main section develops the new conceptualisation of Europeanisation via enlargement, as well as an analytical model of how the new conceptualisation can be used for empirical research. In doing so, the chapter also considers how the field theoretical basis of the conceptual framework provides additional advantages to the study of EU enlargement. These advantages relate to 1) the logic of relationality which helps to overcome the duality between the logics of consequences and appropriateness; 2) the formulation of *outcomes-in-process* which recognise feedback loops within the process; 3) the recognition of the transnational nature of policy fields which allows for analysing new phenomena such as tactical Europeanisation; 4) the relationality of policy fields which allows us to specify EU-level outcomes-in-process.

Redefining Europeanisation via enlargement as negotiated transitions

In the broader European politics scholarship, Europeanisation has been used to denote a variety of processes and mechanisms (for an overview, see Olsen, 2002). The use of the term can be summarised as two overarching understandings of Europeanisation: 1) the building of the EU and European institutions – i.e. European integration; 2) a transfer from Europe's policies, institutions, rules, beliefs and values to third countries (and/or member states) (Bulmer, 2007). As EU enlargement fits squarely within the second category, the associated Europeanisation process has most commonly been defined as the:

> processes of (a) construction (b) diffusion, and (c) institutionalisation of formal and informal rules, procedures, policy paradigms, styles, 'ways of doing', and shared beliefs and norms which are first defined and consolidated in the EU policy processes and then incorporated in the logic of domestic (national and subnational) discourse, political structures, and public policies. (Radaelli, 2003, p. 30)

Despite its common use within the EU enlargement literature, the applicability of this definition – which has its origin in the Europeanisation of member states – cannot and should not be taken for granted in the context of enlargement. Nearly two decades ago, Grabbe (2003) made the convincing plea that Europeanisation via enlargement constitutes a process distinct from Europeanisation of EU member states, for at least two reasons: the scope of the process and the nature of the relationship between the EU and candidate countries.

First, the scope of the EU enlargement process far surpasses those processes that comprise the Europeanisation of member states. While the Europeanisation of member states is limited to the *acquis*, candidate countries have to comply with the broadly defined Copenhagen criteria. Indeed, the political Copenhagen criteria comprise expectations that remain outside the competences of the EU, that are not applicable and/or enforceable to member states, and as such are inherently contested in terms of their content and meaning. In other words, the norms and values that comprise the basis for the 'fundamentals first approach' often only reflect a set of vaguely agreed upon principles (Mos, 2020). This being the case, the process through which these norms and values are incorporated in the domestic realm of candidate countries cannot be the same as for the well-defined hard *acquis*. Empirical research has established that the enlargement process' impact in these 'soft policy' areas has been much less successful (Haughton, 2007).

Second, whereas member states can upload their preference to the EU during the policymaking process in order to reduce the adaptational pressure afterwards, candidate countries, by definition, are not involved in policymaking at the European level (Grabbe, 2003). In fact, candidate member states are solely at the receiving end of EU policies: 'consuming' EU policies without having the ability to influence them. Based on this observation, it has been argued that the ability of candidate countries to negotiate EU policies is limited due to their asymmetrical relationship with the EU (Grabbe, 2003). However, while this might be the case, it does not mean that candidate countries have no agency within the process at all, nor that they are passive receivers of EU policies/norms. As Webb (2018) has clearly demonstrated, there is considerable room within the process for contestation and negotiations on the meaning of EU policies and norms. Consider, for example, the fundamental values and their role within the enlargement process. Not only do they remain underspecified in EU policy documents (Mos, 2013) and subject to contestation within the EU (Mos, 2018), they gained their status and meaning through the relationship between the EU and its external others, including candidate states (Kuus, 2007; Slootmaeckers, 2020; Smismans, 2010). This being the case, the EU norms and values cannot be simply transferred to third countries but instead 'need to be reinterpreted in the process so as to write out the tensions at the core of the integration process' (Diez, 2013, pp. 202).

Based on these observations, as well as on research presented throughout the book, I argue that Radaelli's (2003) formulation of Europeanisation requires some modification. To account for the different, political and malleable nature of norms within the EU enlargement process, I define Europeanisation as:

> a political process of *negotiated transitions*, which consists of transnational processes of (i) construction (ii) diffusion (iii) contestation and translation and (iv) institutionalisation of formal and informal rules, procedures, policy paradigms, styles, 'ways of doing', and shared beliefs and norms which are in part constructed as part of the European policy processes and that, through the transactions of the political integration process, are further interpreted and (re)defined in order to be incorporated in the logic of domestic (national and subnational) discourse, political structures, and public policies.

Drawing on insights from norm localisation and norm translation research (Zimmermann, 2016, 2017; Zwingel, 2012, 2017) that has highlighted that the meaning of norms is continuously reconstructed within different contexts (Hofferberth and Weber, 2015; Poppe et al., 2019), this definition considers Europeanisation as *negotiated transition* not because enlargement entails formal negotiations, but rather that the content and meaning of the transformations demanded as part of the enlargement process is negotiated. In other words, both the EU and candidate countries are not only involved in formal negotiations that comprise the EU enlargement process, but in their relationship are also continuously negotiating – and thus defining and redefining – the meaning of those values and norms that the EU claims as its founding values.

From this perspective, it follows that existing models and conceptualisations of the EU enlargement process are not sufficiently equipped to incorporate these processes as they tend to take the EU norms and values as fixed and for granted, and tend to reduce 'fundamental rights to public policy measures and institutional change, [ignoring] their social and cultural underpinnings' (Slootmaeckers, 2022, p. 2). To overcome these issues, I reconceptualise the Europeanisation process to explicitly account for the political nature of the process as well as the normative tensions within, which are located in and produced by the transnational and relational nature of the EU enlargement process. I will present this conceptualisation in two stages. First, I will briefly review the most commonly used approaches to the study of Europeanisation – i.e. the top-down and bottom-up approaches – in order to demonstrate why they are not able to capture the complexity of the EU enlargement process as defined above. Next, I develop a new transnational and relational approach to Europeanisation. In this main section, I will demonstrate how this new approach creates the possibility of engaging with a whole new set of questions, as well as how such conceptualisation can be translated into an analytical model for empirical research.

The limits of top-down and bottom-up approaches to Europeanisation

The theoretical foundations of the Europeanisation via enlargement literature are situated in the work of Börzel and Risse (2003), Schimmelfennig and Sedelmeier (2005b), and Radaelli (2003), with the first two sets of authors having given rise to the so-called top-down conceptualisation of Europeanisation, and Radaelli the bottom-up conceptualisation. The first tradition, which has taken a dominant position in the scholarship, is (loosely) based on a linear three-step model of Europeanisation (Risse et al., 2001), which centres around the notion of goodness of fit and adaptational pressure. Misfit between EU and domestic level institutions and policies, in this literature, is theorised to be the main driver of the Europeanisation process. To explain why candidate countries adopt and comply with EU policies and rules, scholars within this tradition often take an EU-centred approach that understands Europeanisation as the emergence of new rules, norms, practices and meanings that candidate countries incorporate into their domestic structures (Börzel and Risse, 2007). The top-down conceptualisation of Europeanisation can be summarised as follows: it is a three-step model that has as its starting point the formal and informal norms, rules and practices at the European level that necessitate adjustments at the domestic level and considers the extent to which the adaptational pressure leads to domestic change to be dependent on the presence and/or absence of mediating factors that induce or inhibit change (Börzel and Risse, 2003; Grabbe, 2006; Schimmelfennig and Sedelmeier, 2005a).

One would be wrong to consider this literature stagnant, however, as there have been many 'turns' within it – the domestic and pathological turn perhaps being the most prominent (see Elbasani, 2013a; Mendelski, 2016) – that sought to take into account the different empirical realities, particularly of the Western Balkans region. Nevertheless, these turns have focused predominantly on redirecting the empirical focus of research and have not fundamentally challenged the core of top-down conceptualisation. Take, for example, the so-called domestic turn (see Elbasani, 2013a). Although pointing out the 'need to contextualise the impact of EU strategy and [to] bring in more prominently domestic factors as the key to explaining successful rule transfer' (Elbasani, 2013b, p. 8), at the core, its conceptualisation does not substantially differ from the top-down approach to Europeanisation. Whereas the domestic turn offers a much-needed corrective to top-down conceptualisation by highlighting the importance of domestic factors, it maintains that domestic factors are mediators in the process of Europeanisation. Similarly, the pathological turn has redirected attention to where Europeanisation can lead to negative unintended transformations (Mendelski, 2015), and focuses on how the top-down process reinforced negative patterns. As such, it draws attention to where the process goes rogue without challenging how we conceptualise the process in itself. In other words, while these turns constitute important ameliorative moves, they have so far not been able to fully accommodate some of the early critiques of the 'goodness of fit' approach (see Radaelli, 2003).

Three problems of top-down conceptualisation are important to consider here. The first concerns its explicit EU focus. By taking the EU, its policies and institutions as a starting point and tracking its domestic impact, the 'goodness of fit' conceptualisation of Europeanisation risks overestimating EU effects (Özdemir, 2014), or, perhaps even more problematically, starts from the assumption that there are EU effects (Radaelli, 2003). By treating EU policies and institutions as independent variables that cause domestic change (the dependent variable), the top-down model seemingly treats Europeanisation as an explanation: the explanans, instead of the explanandum – i.e. the problem that needs to be explained (Radaelli, 2004). Thus, although the EU enlargement process might contribute to domestic change, this is not necessarily through a linear process of cause and effect in which EU pressure results in domestic change. Indeed, existing literature on the Europeanisation of LGBT rights has demonstrated the complexity and non-linearity of the process (Ayoub, 2016; Ayoub and Chetaille, 2020; Bilić, 2016c; O'Dwyer, 2018).

Second, there is an implicit assumption in the top-down conceptualisation that EU rules and norms are foreign to candidate countries – or, when present, not European enough (see misfit). Whereas such an assumption can arguably be justified in technical policy areas where specific EU rules, procedures and standards have been well developed, it is far less the case with soft issues, such as fundamental rights, where EU norms or standards are either absent or weakly developed and expressed (see e.g. Mos, 2013). As fundamental rights have taken the foreground in the current iteration of the enlargement process (Slootmaeckers and Touquet, 2016), this is an issue that requires additional reflection. It is important to consider that although the EU has undeniably become a prominent promoter of these values – and certainly seeks to identify and present itself as such – it is, without question, not the only fundamental rights advocate in the international arena, nor does it have a monopoly on the promotion of fundamental rights. Also, the top-down model seems to operate from the notion that the EU norms and values have an a priori existence; they are taken for granted as inherently European. Such an implicit assumption ignores that these values are constructed and expressed through transactions of the EU with its Others (Diez, 2013; Slootmaeckers, 2020). Being unable to consider these realities, the EU-centric approach of the top-down model, then, appears immediately problematic for the study of the 'fundamentals first' EU enlargement process. Indeed, scholars studying the Europeanisation of LGBT rights have often pointed to the dangers of taking EU values for granted (Ayoub, 2016; Ayoub and Paternotte, 2014a, 2020; Bilić, 2016b; Kahlina, 2015).

Third, the top-down approach's view that adaptational pressure is the driver of change cannot account for domestic change that occurs in the absence of direct (EU) pressure (Woll and Jacquot, 2010). With its excessively structural focus with limited room for domestic agency (Radaelli, 2004), the top-down model – especially when conceptualising the EU as a 'teacher of norms' – suggests that the values underlying fundamental rights are initially absent in candidate countries. By doing so, domestic fundamental rights advocates are (re)produced as unintelligible actors that only act in response to EU norms. This ignores the fact that they have often been present long before the EU came into play (Szulecka and Szulecki, 2013). With their actions and agendas considered to be subordinated to those of the EU, local fundamental rights advocates are – through the top-down lens – seen as either irrelevant or, at best, mediating actors that react to pressures from the EU (see Börzel and Risse, 2007); local agency is under-recognised within the top-down approach.

Radaelli's (2003) bottom-up (inside-out) conceptualisation has been an important response to these shortcomings, but remains underused precisely because of the implicit Eurocentrism of the literature that favours a hierarchical and asymmetrical conceptualisation of the EU enlargement process. As an approach to the study of Europeanisation, the bottom-up model does not start from the EU but rather considers the system of interactions at the domestic level as the main starting point (Radaelli and Pasquier, 2007). Europeanisation is conceptualised not as a linear process but rather as a complex process of transformation that occurs on the basis of a 'multitude of co-evolving, parallel and not necessarily tightly coupled processes' (Olsen cited in Featherstone, 2003, p. 4); and the bottom-up approach 'checks if, when, and how the EU provides a change in any of the main components of the system of interaction' (Radaelli and Pasquier, 2007, p. 41).

Such an approach opens up the possibility of going beyond the study of legal and institutional compliance, to include non-change (which also entails non-implementation) and resistance (see Saurugger, 2012). Although it has offered many advantages for the study of the Europeanisation of so-called soft issues, including the emphases on processes and possibility of integrating 'ad hoc explanations based on the peculiarity of the [domestic] political systems' (Radaelli and Pasquier, 2007, p. 40), the increased focus on the domestic has come at the expense of a thorough analysis of the complexity of the EU policy processes that inform EU enlargement.

Despite the fact that the bottom-up model recognises that the EU policy processes designate 'a political space with a distinct EU dimension wherein social interaction among elites (and in some cases public opinion) take place' (Radaelli and Pasquier, 2007, p. 37), this political space is not included in the conceptualisation of EU enlargement. The EU-level interactions and policy processes are within the bottom-up approach considered to be a *référentiel* (Muller, 2000) in domestic political action – i.e. it is only analysed as an ideational framework external to domestic politics which provides principles of action for the domestic. By doing so, however, one does not only ignore the interdependency of the EU and candidate countries but also leads to ignorance of the transnational nature of EU politics and how both European and domestic politics actively shape each other through transactions.

In order to address this theoretical caveat, I argue that the bottom-up conceptualisation of Europeanisation needs to be expanded with an additional layer of complexity that recognises Europeanisation as a process of trans- formation in which 'European-level, national and sub-national institutions and actors may change at the same time and in association with one another, as they try to find a place within a complex multi-layered and multi-centred system' (Olsen, 2002, p. 943). Thus, when focusing on the domestic system of transactions, it is important to consider the domestic as embedded in a transnational system of transactions, with the EU enlargement taking place in a wider field of political contention and contestation. The following section will expand on this new transnational and relational conceptualisation of Europeanisation by drawing on the critical normative power of Europe literature while using relational and transnational theoretical principles as guiding principles.

A relational and transnational approach to Europeanisation

Although the theoretical, analytical and empirical merits of the notion of Normative Power Europe (NPE, as coined by Manners, 2002) can be and have been debated (see e.g. Merlingen, 2007), the concept provides us with an important and valuable heuristic tool for the study of the EU's engagement with third countries. By drawing attention to how the EU projects its values beyond the borders through ideas, opinions and conscience, the notion of NPE has redirected researchers' attention to phenomena and questions otherwise left unexplored. Or as Jan Orbie (cited in Manners, 2013, p. 319) explains: the real power of the NPE is found in its ability to move 'the analytical focus from institutions, policies and cases towards a critical discussion of the EU in global politics'.

One of these new areas of attention and emerging realisation has been how the EU's identity is constructed through its relationality with the rest of the world, as well as the fact that the EU's external relations are 'crucially determined by the nature of [the EU's] international identity' (Manners and Whitman, 2003, p. 383). For example, Nicolaïdis and Howse (2002, p. 769) have argued that the projection of the EU's fundamental rights in external relations is not the projection of the EU 'as is' but constitutes an 'EU-topia'. This projection of a 'better than' Self plays a crucial role in the construction of the identity of both the EU (Self) and its Others 'in ways which allows EU actors to disregard their own shortcomings' (Diez, 2005, pp. 626–627). If norms and values are a fundamental part of EU identity formation, then the projection and diffusion of these norms through the EU enlargement process equally contributes to this process. As such, Europeanisation as a process is inherently bound up with and shaped by the political nature of the boundary construction and maintenance processes – or in short, EU identity processes – embedded within the EU enlargement process (Slootmaeckers, 2020).

When conceptualising Europeanisation, we should not only be aware of the identity processes and power structures they reinforce, but crucially also acknowledge that any identity, including the EU's, is not singular nor essential. In fact, one of the key points made throughout the NPE literature is that the EU's identity is better thought of as 'fluid, consisting of ongoing contestation of complex, multiple, relational identities' (Manners and Whitman, 2003, p. 397), which are constantly (re)constructed through transactions with its different Others (see also Slootmaeckers, 2020). Although identities have a relative and perceived stability that is 'ongoing accomplishment of practices that represent [the] self and other in certain ways' (Wendt, 1994, p. 386), the fluidity of identities in part being found in the different Othering mechanisms that underpin these identities (Delanty, 2006; for a more detailed analysis of these process within EU enlargement, see Slootmaeckers, 2020).

Once we recognise the multiplicity and plurality of both identities and Othering processes, the realisation that both are dynamic and context-dependent is not far removed, nor is the idea that these different identities and identity processes also exist in a tense interrelationship; they will inevitably clash as well as contribute to the (re)construction of one another (Diez, 2005; Kuus, 2007). Moreover, the tensions, hegemonic or normative struggles that produce identities and guide Othering processes do not only occur between the EU and its external Others, but are also the product and source of hegemonic struggles within the EU itself (Diez, 2013). Indeed, challenging and expanding the notion that the normative basis of NPE can be found within the principles of the EU treaties, Diez (2013) has convincingly argued that these principles of democracy and human rights are both the outcome and continued subject of hegemonic struggles with the EU's external relations (i.e. its Othering processes) as well as those struggles within the EU itself. Consider, for example, the current rise of anti-gender mobilisations and the challenges to gender and LGBT equality that are occurring across the EU (Kuhar and Paternotte, 2017). These movements are not to be mistakenly seen as backward, conservative moments celebrating ideas from bygone days, but rather as actively shaping debates on what it means to be European. As such, they are seeking to challenge, reframe and reinterpret 'the collective destiny of Europe, understood as a standard-bearer of civilisation' (Kuhar and Paternotte, 2017, p. 268).

With norms always being contested and situated within relations (Wiener, 2007b, a), they cannot simply be transferred, as the top-down Europeanisation model would have us believe. Rather, we would see a continuation of these normative contestation from within the EU and the transnational arena all the way through the domestic realm. In other words, the normative and hegemonic tensions embedded within so-called European norms not only occur at the European level, but continue as they enter the domestic realm of third countries. This process of normative contestation is further complicated and affected by the fact that different identity processes can collide and clash with each other (Slootmaeckers, 2020). Thus, the Europeanisation process does not only affect those norms the EU claims to uphold, but all the competing norms within the EU may come into particular tension when they start interacting with a specific (third country's) context (Diez, 2013). To borrow some of Diez's (2013, p. 203, emphasis added) words, Europeanisation via enlargement is best seen as a *'transversal struggle over societal norms,* in which different actors interact on different levels – as opposed to the unidirectional and uncontested imposition of norms, which would only replicate the problems of the old top-down models of Europeanisation'.

This added sensitivity for the local contestation of these norms in third countries also highlights the identity of third countries, which inevitably will be shaped through transactions with the EU. For example, with candidate countries being constructed as the EU's Other (Kuus, 2007), the candidate country's Self will also be formulated in relation to the ascribed Other position. Although nationalism and national identity have been recognised as key to understanding resistance to Europeanisation processes (see e.g. Freyburg and Richter, 2010; Subotić, 2011), more often than not, nationalism and national identity are preconceived as pre-existing and fixed. Such a perspective, however, ignores the complexity, relationality and fluidity of national identities, and therefore risks essentialising resistance. Instead, within the relational perspective proposed here, local resistance is not merely a reaction to EU pressure, but is based on past and future actions of both the Self and the Other. The local, then, is a 'complex arena often informed by contradictory ideologies, cultural filters and identities and by ongoing power struggles among different domestic actors. Consequently, the diffusion of norms or lack thereof in the targeted country is also determined by internal struggles over hegemony' (Gordon and Pardo, 2015, p. 424).

Following these reflections that emphasised the contested and political nature of norms, as well as their relational and transnational essence, I conceptualise Europeanisation as a process in which different hegemonic struggles and normative tensions come together in a transnational (or multilayered) normative structure – comprised of multiple fields. As represented in Figure 1.1, I argue that the EU enlargement process is as a multilayered normative process, in which hegemonic struggles take place both within the EU and the candidate countries, which each have their own normative tensions and Othering processes. The political integration process inherent to the enlargement process, then, creates a transnational field in which these internal hegemonic processes interact and may clash (see also Kauppi, 2018). In other words, EU enlargement is a political process in which these tensions need to be negotiated and/or written out in order to obtain the ultimate goal of political integration. Similarly, it can be said that Europeanisation does not just concern the changes caused by the EU in the domestic system of transactions but refers to a multitude of political processes by which norms are negotiated through the transactions between the European and domestic-level systems of transactions.

The advantage of reconceptualising the EU enlargement process in this relational and transnational way is that it overcomes the interest/norm tensions and inconsistencies found in empirical studies, but also that it

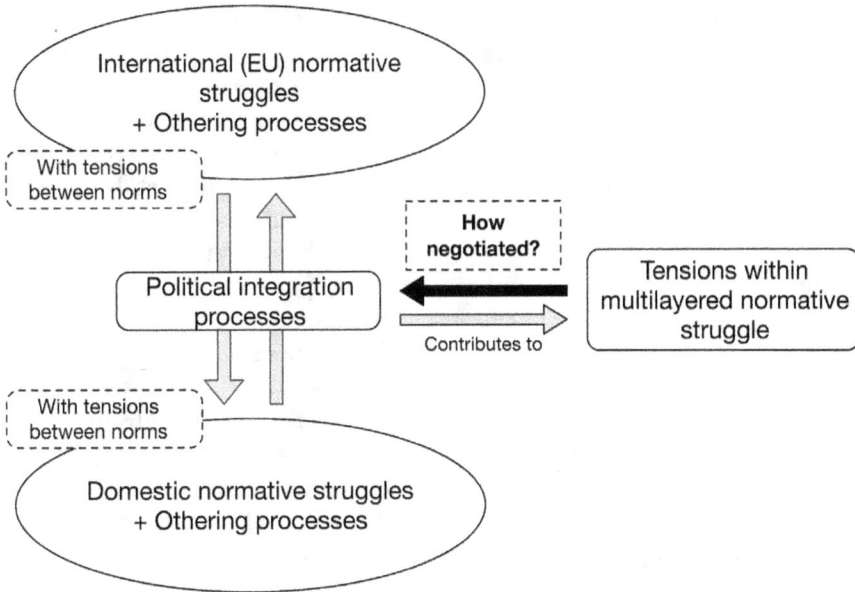

Figure 1.1 Schematic visualisation of the relational and transnational conceptualisation of the EU enlargement process

allows for what Youngs (2004, p. 431) described as the need to examine 'the detailed variations in human rights policies [to] transcend the unhelpful tendency to see human rights norms and strategic self-interest either as intrinsically incompatible or automatically commensurate'. By foregrounding relationality and normative tensions, the presented conceptualisation of the EU enlargement process no longer takes the asymmetrical relationship between the EU and a candidate country for granted and therefore draws attention to a multiplicity of new questions and patterns to study. The most interesting of these new questions relates to what can be called the 'politics of Europeanisation' – i.e. what happens when normative struggles and tensions occur as a consequence of the political integration process. Thus, instead of analysing how norms are set within the EU and/or whether these norms are successfully 'transferred' to third countries, this book argues that one should take a relational approach to Europeanisation and analyse how the EU and a candidate country negotiate the tensions within the multilayered normative struggle which has been created as part of the overarching political integration process. Fundamentally, by considering the EU enlargement a *process of negotiated transitions*, this new conceptualisation of Europeanisation highlights that, throughout the process, EU policies and norms are (re) defined, negotiated and transformed as both sides have to make compromises to further the political integration.

Having reconceptualised Europeanisation, the question remains: how can we translate this into an analytical model? How can one analyse EU enlargement as a process of negotiated transitions from a relational and transnational perspective? As the main focus remains on what happens in candidate countries – i.e. policy and normative changes (broadly conceived) – the domestic system of transactions remains the analytical focal point. However, the process by which domestic change occurs is considered to be the result of transnational political processes. As such, the bottom-up research design, with its focus on both agency and structure in the process of Europeanisation, presents the first building block for the analytical model to study the politics of EU enlargement. However, some modifications are needed to accommodate the new conceptualisation of EU enlargement.

Figure 1.2 presents a schematic overview of the analytical framework that expands the bottom-up model so that it can accommodate the transnational nature of the EU enlargement and Europeanisation processes. In short, the analytical translation can be summarised as follows: when normative tensions occur as part of political integration, they shape both the EU and its approach to enlargement (i.e. the EU system of transactions) and the third country's policies (i.e. the domestic system of transactions). From this point onwards, the tensions and their negotiation can be studied by looking at how the domestic system of transactions contributes (or not) to domestic change, and if, when and how the combination and imbrication of the domestic and EU arenas change the main components of the domestic system of transactions. Here it is important to consider that change flows in both directions – i.e. the EU and domestic responses to the tensions within the political integration process are transactional, inherently relational, and thus cannot be understood without reference to one another. Thus, the transnational and relational conceptualisation of Europeanisation provides an analytical framework that foregrounds the politics of Europeanisation and highlights the process through which the EU and candidate member states negotiate their normative tensions in order to advance the EU enlargement process.

At this point, it is important to note that what Figure 1.2 presents as 'domestic change' – and the Europeanisation literature often refers to as policy outcomes – cannot and should not be considered the endpoint of the process. In fact, as implied by the notion of negotiated transitions, the conceptual framework suggests that feedback loops are an inherent part of the EU enlargement process. The following section will expand on how the relational conceptualisation implies these feedback loops, the interconnectedness of different policy fields within the EU enlargement process as well as the different types of outcomes within the process at both the EU and domestic level.

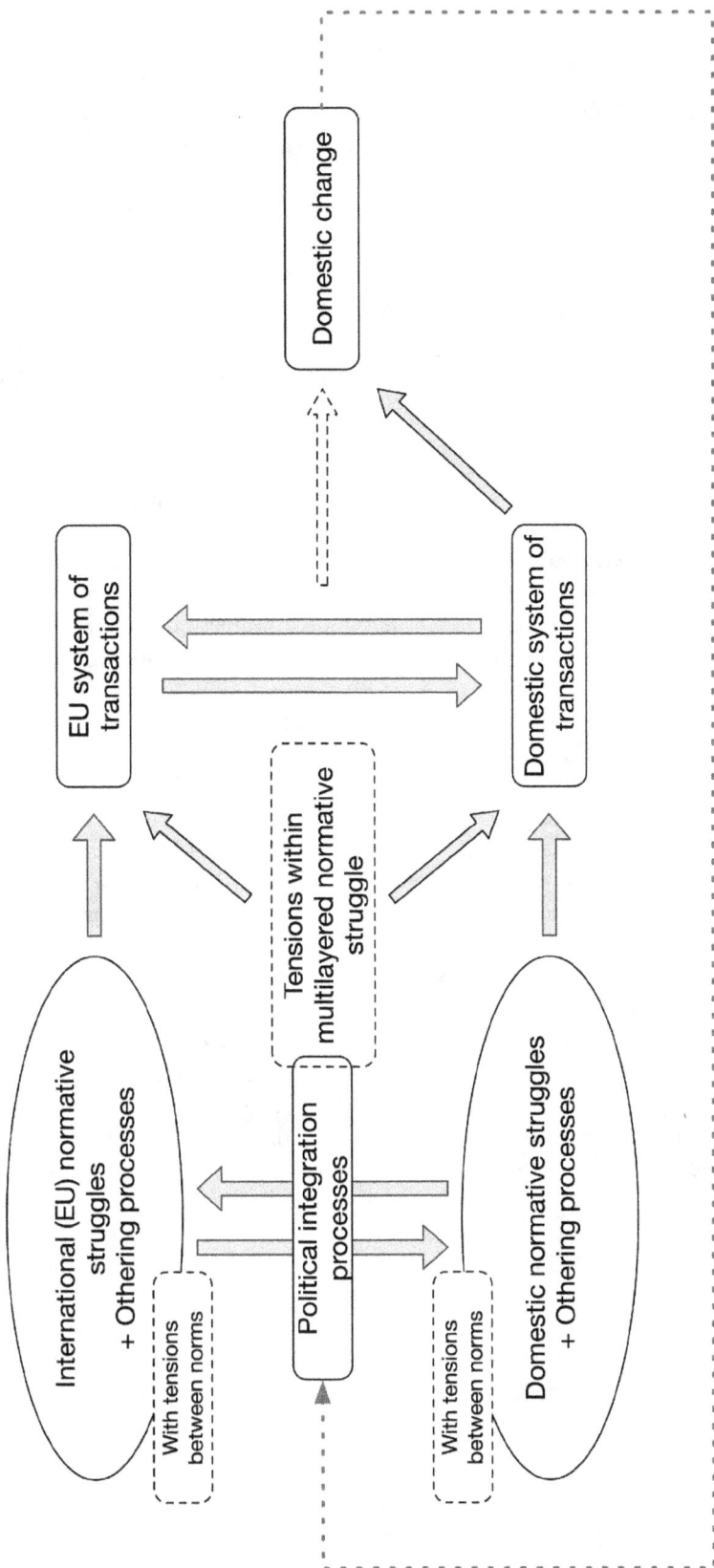

Figure 1.2 Analytical framework to study the EU enlargement process

Europeanisation's outcomes-in-process: the politics of relational policy fields and 'tactical Europeanisation'

The relational epistemology that underpins the proposed conceptualisation draws on a Bourdieusian (1985, 1989) field theory as it considers that actors are located within a relational field (for more on how Bourdieusian theory can be used in European politics, see Kauppi, 2003, 2018). Such a field can analytically be defined as 'a network, or a configuration of objective relations between positions' in which actors and institutions are involved in a constant struggle (Bourdieu and Wacquant, 1992, p. 97). The field theoretical underpinning of the presented conceptualisation has some key contributions to how we can understand and analyse the Europeanisation process. These relate to 1) the logic of relationality which helps to overcome the duality between the logics of consequences and appropriateness; 2) the formulation of outcomes-in-process which recognise feedback loops within the process; 3) the recognition of the transnational nature of policy fields which allows for analysis of new phenomena such as tactical Europeanisation; 4) the relationality of policy fields that in large part shape how the EU responds to normative tensions.

The first contribution that field theory has for the analysis of the Europeanisation process is the introduction of the notion of the logic of relationality. As a rationale for action, the *logic of relationality* serves as an overarching framework for the logics of actions that have thus far informed Europeanisation research – i.e. the *logics of consequences* and *appropriateness*. It is described as a logic of action in which actors 'make decisions according to the degrees of intimacy and/or importance of [their] relationships to specific others, with the totality of [their] relational circles as the background' (Qin, 2016, p. 37). Put differently, because 'relations select', one has to consider that an 'actor-in-relations takes action with the relational context as the background .... In this sense, the logic of relationality has priority over both the logic of instrumental rationality (consequences) and the logic of normative rationality (appropriateness)' (Qin, 2016, p. 38). This means that what is the rational and/or appropriate thing to do is defined by the relation through which the action finds meaning. Rather than having a priori conceptions about the rationale of actors, the relational approach suggests that actors' rationale for action is situated within the field of relations, in which the totality of relations acts as an 'intangible hand that orients an actor toward a certain action' (Qin, 2016, p. 38).

From this it follows that my conceptualisation of Europeanisation does not make any assumptions about how tensions are negotiated within the EU enlargement process and what approach is best taken to analyse this process. Thus, while the existing Europeanisation via enlargement literature tends to use either rational choice or sociological institutionalism (often positioned within an either/or dualism) to explain how formal and informal rules guide political behaviour, the presented conceptualisation allows for an analytical framework that overcomes this abstract and unnecessary dichotomy (see also Kauppi, 2003). The latter is important because the book's approach to studying EU enlargement does not discard the existing Europeanisation literature and its theoretical propositions. Rather, it acknowledges and integrates previous insights while simultaneously adding complexity to the analysis by drawing attention to previously ignored or understudied elements of the process. In doing so, the book also promotes a more flexible ontological position that allows actors to behave according to different logics depending on the relationships through which their actions are given meaning. As demonstrated throughout the empirical chapters, such a flexible position allows analysis and understanding of the seemingly contradictory empirical findings of the literature within one framework.

The second contribution of the relational conceptualisation of Europeanisation is that it makes feedback loops an inherent part of the analysis of the Europeanisation process. Indeed, as both field and relational theory emphasise processes and constant change (see Bourdieu and Wacquant, 1992), the same is true for the transnational field in which the EU enlargement process takes place as it is in constant flux – never settled. The existing Europeanisation literature, however, is unable to capture this fluidity as it seeks to explain seemingly fixed (policy) outcomes in the domestic arena in a rather static way – the notion of 'outcome' after all implies a fixed endpoint. The framework presented in this book, on the other hand, considers outcomes only a temporary part within the *longue durée* of the Europeanisation process, and are therefore in constant flux. In other words, the so-called outcomes mark both the endpoints and beginnings of subprocesses. They are in fact outcomes-in-process, which are temporary tools and moments within the negotiation process of the tensions that arise during the political integration process. Outcomes-in-process then are not only the result of the process, but also contribute to the reconfiguration of relations within the field, thereby determining further actions within the field/process.

To determine what these outcomes-in-process might look like, the empirical findings within the Europeanisation literature has provided a wealth of insights. In particular, it has highlighted that conditionality is more impactful for salient policy areas in countries with strong support for EU accession (Glenn, 2004; Haughton, 2011; O'Dwyer and Schwartz, 2010; Rechel, 2008); that compliance with EU conditions are often shallow and reminiscent of partial compliance (Czernielewska et al., 2004; Krizsan, 2009; Nancheva, 2007; Noutcheva, 2009; Vermeersch, 2004, 2007); that decisions on conditionality have been subject to geopolitical concerns which have limited the impact of the whole process (Grabbe, 2001; Haughton, 2007); that the Europeanisation process can have pathological impacts, reinforcing undesired practices rather than inducing change (Börzel and Pamuk, 2012; Mendelski, 2016); and finally that national identity processes have played a considerable role in how candidate countries respond to EU conditionality (Ayoub, 2014; Freyburg and Richter, 2010; Subotić, 2011).

Based on these findings as well as those presented throughout the book, a typology of at least eight outcomes-in-process can be observed (Figure 1.3 shows these outcomes-in-process schematically as part of the analytical framework). Two of them ('hierarchy of tasks' and 'perverted conditionality') can be discerned at the European level (which I will elaborate on below) and another six within the domestic system of transactions.

The outcomes-in-process within the domestic system capture different degrees to which transformation takes place in candidate countries, while also taking into account the different logics of action that underpin these processes. As such, we can make a distinction between the outcomes-in-process of *non-compliance*, *partial compliance* and *full compliance* which are based on the rational-choice-based model of action known as the logic of consequences. The other three domestic 'outcomes' – *identity divergence*, *identify convergence* and *tactical Europeanisation* – are guided by the logic of appropriateness.

These different domestic 'outcomes' can be summarised as follows. First, there is the option of 'non-compliance', which is in fact a non-solution in which neither party is willing to make the accommodations needed. Though this option might occur, it is unsustainable if the political integration is to remain on the agenda. Hence, it will either lead to some form of compliance at the domestic level or some changes in the EU's approach to the enlargement process (see below). Second, at the other end of the spectrum is full compliance. Here, candidate countries fully adopt the EU norms and rules, both at the institutional and implementation level. Although this outcome-in-process is the preferred 'outcome' of the EU enlargement process (at least from the EU's perspective), the empirical literature has shown this to be a rather unlikely outcome (Schimmelfennig and Sedelmeier, 2005a) as it implies a complete 'surrender' of candidate countries to the EU's position. The third 'outcome' has been described extensively by the Europeanisation literature and relates to the option of partial compliance or 'shallow Europeanisation' (Noutcheva, 2009). This outcome-in-process can be conceptualised as the neutralisation of normative tensions by which candidate countries produce formal changes without much commitment to implementing reforms. This 'talking the talk' outcome-in-process becomes an attractive option when monitoring is predominantly focused on the reforms themselves, rather than on the process of change.

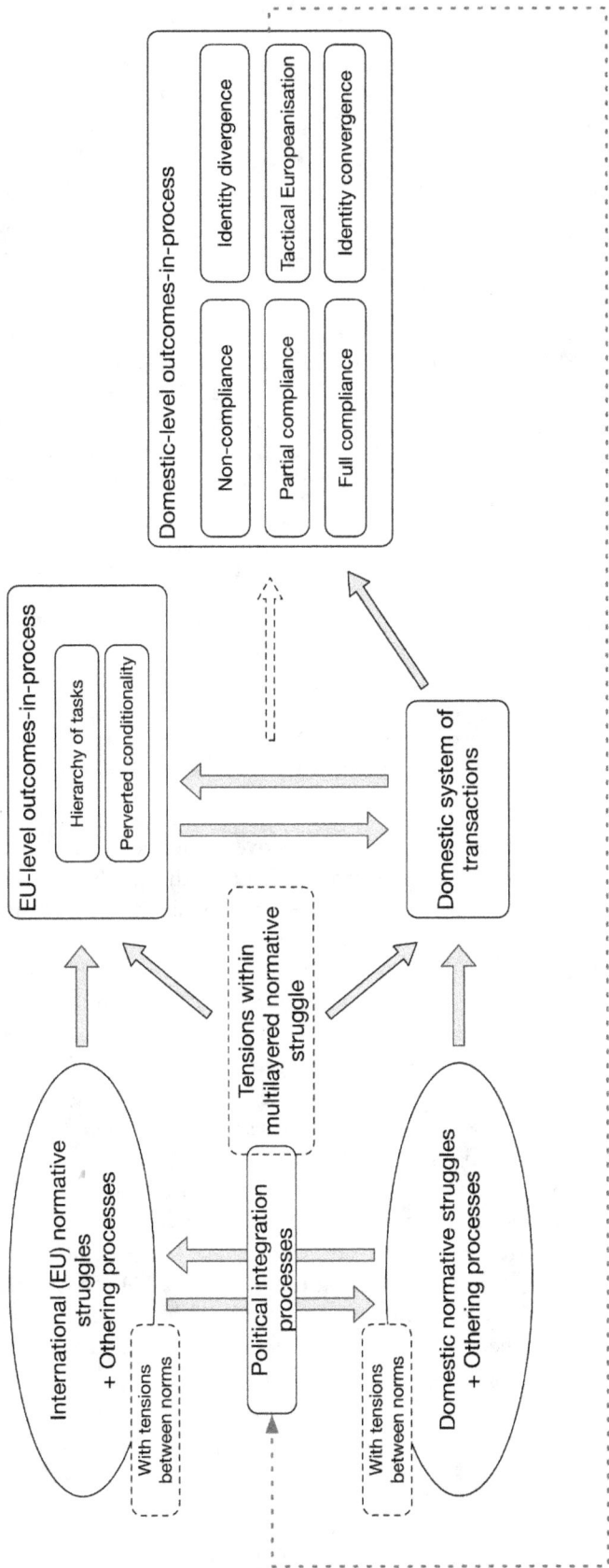

Figure 1.3 Analytical framework with EU and domestic-level outcomes-in-process

Domestic-level outcomes-in-process

Identity divergence

Tactical Europeanisation

Identity convergence

Non-compliance

Partial compliance

Full compliance

EU-level outcomes-in-process

Hierarchy of tasks

Perverted conditionality

Domestic system of transactions

Tensions within multilayered normative struggle

International (EU) normative struggles + Othering processes

With tensions between norms

Political integration processes

With tensions between norms

Domestic normative struggles + Othering processes

The 'outcomes' based on the logic of appropriateness are more attentive to the identity processes underpinning Europeanisation. Identity convergence and divergence (Subotić, 2011) are two outcomes-in-process through which normative tensions can be negotiated. They draw attention to the strategic use of identity claims by political actors in the course of the Europeanisation process, and have been defined as:

> *Identity convergence* is a dynamic process by which political actors strategically emphasize shared norms and values and disregard or omit contradictory ones in pursuit of particular political goal ... It requires direct political action and entrepreneurship of domestic political actors. Identity convergence is not simply a reflection of the normative environment of matching cultural values. It is a process by which domestic political actors nurture, reinforce, and promote a particular version of state identity that best serves their competitive electoral goals.
>
> ...
>
> *Identity divergence* is a mechanism by which domestic coalitions resist norms and rules of Europeanisation and instead define the national community in contrast to those European values or requirements domestically deemed illegitimate. Instead of reaffirming a state's European identity, Europeanisation produces a resurgence of nationalist and particularistic claims. The stronger the push for Europeanisation, the stronger the backlash. (Subotić, 2011, pp. 313–314)

In short, the identity convergence process overcomes normative tensions by emphasising shared values between the EU and the candidate country in political discourses, whereas identity divergence highlights the incompatibility of EU norms with the domestic culture, escalating existing tensions. However, as these two conceptualisations of 'outcomes' represent an either/or situation of acceptance of resistance of a seemingly fixed EU identity, I propose a third outcome-in-process that takes an in-between position, as it were. Whereas identity convergence and divergence processes are limited in that they seemingly conceptualise the candidate member state's agency as being reactive to the EU pressure to Europeanise, this third 'outcome', which I label *tactical Europeanisation*, acknowledges the transnational nature of policy fields that allows actors to use different logics of actions at different scales of the policy field. From this it follows that candidate countries can actively manipulate the multilayered normative structure for their own strategic advantage. Indeed, drawing on Youngs' (2004) observation that strategic interests have normative dimensions, I seek to emphasise that identity can also be a tool that can be used by candidate countries to manoeuvre within the multilayered ideational field of the political integration process.

Building on the multilayered normative environment of the political integration process, the outcome-in-process of tactical Europeanisation describes a process in which identity convergence and divergence occur simultaneously, yet at different levels and involving different publics. Tactical Europeanisation can be described as follows: at the international scale/level, the candidate country engages in actions (or policy reforms) that signal the 'recognition of the EU identity', thereby reducing the saliency of this EU Self-identity. Indeed, in line with the work of Rumelili (2004, pp. 37–38) on the construction of the Self/Other, the recognition of the EU identity is conceptualised as a performative practice of the candidate country in which it engages with 'identity discourses and performances' that reproduce the EU's identity. Because such performance reifies the EU's Self, the need for the EU to reassert its identity towards candidate countries is reduced (see also Slootmaeckers, 2020). As such, the performative recognition of the EU identity by a candidate country allows the EU to consider this country to become similar to (if not a part of) the Self, which promotes political integration.[1]

This international process of 'identity recognition', however, must not be confused with Subotić's (2011) process of identity convergence as the need to make changes at the domestic level is not justified by emphasising the shared values of the nation with the EU. Instead, with tactical Europeanisation, the justification for the domestic change is decoupled from the EU. This decoupling allows for subtle engagement with a process which is similar to identity divergence. In order to recognise and reinforce the national identity, the reforms are performed and discursively represented as foreign to the national identity, yet tolerable. Thus, at the domestic level, the EU's identity marker is reconstructed not as the Self's Other, but as a 'Stranger' that is best dealt with by ignoring it.[2] By moving the actions taken to recognise the EU identity to a domestic 'sphere of disattention' (Bauman, 1993, p. 154),[3] the potential threat to the national identity is neutralised, reducing the need to actively Other and resist the EU's identity markers.

In short, tactical Europeanisation takes place when a candidate country has to balance conflicting (normative) demands – it is committed to European integration but does not want to compromise its own identity – and can be described as act of 'liminal compliance' engaged in doublespeak in which at the international level Europeanness is communicated by performing an alignment with certain 'European identity markers', while at the domestic level opposite agendas are being pursued, albeit it subtly so as not to undermine the international (performed) alignment with EU norms. While at first glance, tactical Europeanisation resembles partial compliance, some important differences between the two are to be noted. First, as both are specified following a different theoretical approach, they envision reforms to be the result of different underlying logics (see *logic of consequences* v. *logic of appropriateness*). Second, and perhaps more importantly, shallow and tactical Europeanisation have a different analytical focus. Although both concepts capture limited implementation of sorts, partial compliance is more institutional and focuses on the limited penetration of EU laws in the domestic arena. Tactical Europeanisation, on the other hand, goes beyond institutions and actively acknowledges the multilayered nature of the Europeanisation process. It describes an instrumentalisation of EU identity markers, in which reforms are performed at the international level but are domestically decoupled from the identities, norms and values they are supposed to represent. Tactical Europeanisation is thus more than partial compliance as it discusses the liminal position in which one does not just 'talk the talk', but instead employ doublespeak in which political actions at the international and domestic level pursue different identities.

Although the balancing act captured by tactical Europeanisation constitutes a precarious position, difficult to maintain, there are two factors which make tactical Europeanisation more likely. First, as tactical Europeanisation is 'instrumentalisation of reforms' of sorts (see Mendelski, 2016), it can only occur when the EU measurement of progress is based on outcomes and not on underlying processes and meanings. Secondly, tactical Europeanisation is a viable tactic for candidate countries for those issues closely intertwined with the EU's identity formation and Othering processes.

Finally, when considering how the EU responds to normative tensions, it is important to note that the different policy fields of the Europeanisation process do not exist in isolation. And thus, in order to fully grasp the complexity of the Europeanisation process, one should not only analyse the intra-field relations of actors but also the inter-field relationality. To illustrate this point, consider the possibility that actors are parts of multiple (policy) fields, which therefore creates an interconnectedness of the different logics of fields. Alternatively, fields can be related not only through overlapping actors (e.g. actors engaging in multiple (policy) fields) but also through the relationship between the struggles that define fields (e.g. advances in one policy field might affect the possibilities for policies in another field). In other words, by considering the relationality of fields themselves, I maintain that one cannot analyse the developments of one (policy) field in isolation of other fields or scales, as actions in one field or scale might be inherently related to those (in)actions in another field or scale.

It is in this inter-field relationality that we see the outcomes-in-process at the EU level emerging. Based on the work of Grabbe (2006) that has drawn attention to the hierarchies of policy fields within EU conditionality, and the work Stahl (2011, 2013) that has shown how conditionality is altered when certain conditions are met with strong resistance, the two

EU-level outcomes-in-process are formulated: 'hierarchy of tasks' and 'perverted conditionality'. These two outcomes describe actions taken at the EU level in order to maintain the political integration process. Perverted conditionality refers to the fact that the EU can sacrifice (some of) its conditions for membership in order to keep the political integration process going – i.e. it produces a (temporary) sanctioned (if not rewarded) non-compliance (Stahl, 2011, 2013). Hierarchy of tasks, on the other hand, depicts the possibility of the EU to prioritise one area over another when two or more demands are received with resistance by the candidate country. Within this outcome-in-process, the multiple normative tensions are resolved by compartmentalising the issues – i.e. focusing on one issue at the time. As such, non-compliance in certain areas is left unmonitored or becomes 'strategically unnoticed' in order to first resolve a tension within a different field.

Conclusion

Starting with the observation that the conceptual tools of the Europeanisation via enlargement literature have not kept pace with the changed nature of the enlargement process, this chapter advances a new theoretical approach to Europeanisation via enlargement so that our analytical tools are more reflective of the changed reality of the EU enlargement process, its political nature and wider (international) political context. Considering that the political conditionality has taken a more central role in the entire process, I have argued that the EU enlargement process should be considered a political process in which the intertwining of domestic and international politics together produces outcomes. Indeed, rather than focusing on the domestic impact of the EU in candidate countries, the EU accession process is conceptualised as a *process of negotiated transformation* in which EU policies and norms are (re)defined, translated and transformed, with both sides making compromises to further political integration.

As such, this book presents a more critical analysis of the civilisational politics embedded in the EU enlargement process that goes beyond institutional changes to include an analysis of transnational configurations of politics and the complex (negotiated) outcomes they produce. Furthermore, through the increased complexity of the conceptualisation of the Europeanisation process, this framework demonstrates the need for a more longitudinal, multiscalar analysis of the EU enlargement process that is sensitive to the interconnectedness of (policy) fields. Taking temporality more seriously, it has been further argued that what the Europeanisation literature often describes as 'policy outcomes' are not fixed endpoints, but are rather outcomes-in-process – i.e. they are not only the result of the process but also contribute to the reconfiguration of relations within the field, thereby determining further actions within the process. Eight such 'outcomes' have been specified: non-compliance, partial compliance, full compliance, identity divergence, identity convergence and tactical Europeanisation.

By recognising that EU norms are not fixed and that they are subject to a process of negotiation and reinterpretation, the new conceptualisation of Europeanisation also has strong implications for another often-present assumption within the EU enlargement literature. Indeed, most of the Europeanisation literature does not only engage in a top-down analysis of legal and institutional compliance, it also seems to operate under the assumption that formal compliance with rules and adoption of institutions will eventually lead to social change. Just as the pathological turn within the Europeanisation scholarship criticises the EU for its outcome-focused analysis of domestic reforms, it is argued that an outcome-focused research agenda is equally problematic as it remains ignorant of the translation processes that are part of the politics of Europeanisation. With the aim of studying these politics of Europeanisation, the presented relational and transnational conceptualisation brings new energy to the literature as it provides a framework which allows for a more critical study of the EU enlargement process which considers the new political reality in which it takes place. One of these proposed new avenues is the notion of tactical Europeanisation, which highlights the differential instrumentalisation of reforms and European values in which reforms are being performed at the international level to demonstrate Europeanness, while domestically being decoupled from those values. Tactical Europeanisation captures the process of doublespeak in which candidate countries use the reforms to highlight Europeanness externally, while domestically, the execution of the reforms actively undermines the aims of the reforms.

Notes

1 In contrast, when a candidate country resists the EU's identity, it undermines the EU's identity, which 'creates a greater necessity to reinscribe the identity of the Self [the EU] and the difference of the other [the candidate member state]' (Rumelili, 2004, pp. 37–38). Thus, in the case of identity resistance, the EU will be forced to highlight the incompatibility of the candidate member state with the EU's values, which undermines the political integration process. This alternative process, however, is captured by Subotić's (2011) identity divergence process.
2 The Stranger represents an ambivalent actor in the public realm that threatens the operation of this binary. Or as Bauman (1991, p. 59) argues: 'unlike other "straightforward" enemies, he [the stranger] is not kept at a secure distance, nor on the other side of the battle-line. Worse still, he claims the right to be an

object of responsibility – the well known attribute of the friend.' The Stranger, thus, 'stands between friend and enemy ... the inside and the outside. He stands for the treacherousness of friends, for the cunning disguise of the enemies, for fallibility of order, vulnerability of the inside' (Bauman, 1991, p. 61).

3 Bauman (1993, pp. 153–154) further argues that as one cannot avoid meeting Strangers, the 'next best solution is a meeting which is not quite a meeting, a meeting pretending not be one, a ... *mismeeting* ...' This process of mismeeting 'relegates the other [stranger] into the background; the other [stranger] would be no more than a blot on the backcloth against which the action is set.' The Stranger is 'an irrelevant presence, a non-recognized being, a non-admitted existence'. Thus, '[b]y the technique of mismeeting, the stranger is allocated to the sphere of disattention, the sphere within which all conscious contact, and above all a conduct which may be recognized by him as a conscious contact, is studiously avoided. This is the realm of non-engagement, of emotional void, inhospitable to either sympathy or hostility ... and it must be ignored. Above all, it must be shown to be ignored, and to be wished to be ignored, in a way allowing no mistake.'

2

Mapping the multilayered normative structure of Serbia–EU relations

If we are to conceptualise the Europeanisation process as multilayered normative struggle, what are the normative struggles underpinning the relation between the EU and Serbia? What Othering mechanisms are at play and how do they potentially interact? In order to answer these questions and provide the political background for the research and arguments of the book, this chapter presents the core elements that constitute the multilayered normative structure that shapes the sexual politics of Serbia–EU relations, without claiming to be exhaustive (as such an endeavour merits its own book).

First, the chapter presents an overview of the evolution of the EU enlargement process and demonstrates how EU policy changed from promoting peace and democracy to an increasing focus on human rights (including LGBT rights). This shift in policy is also reflected in the EU's Othering mechanisms, in particular those employed to reinforce the (at times conflicting) EU identities based on either promoting sustainable peace (often based on geopolitical Othering processes) or the promotion of human (and LGBT) rights (based normative Othering processes) (see also Slootmaeckers, 2020). Next, the chapter presents two of the main hegemonic struggles within Serbia. Here, the point of departure is Serbia's involvement in processes of nation-building as well as a process of reintegrating within international society following the democratic revolution in 2000. As Serbia's politics remain informed by the legacies of nationalism and the violent conflicts of the 1990s, special attention is given to its victimhood complex (especially in relation to Kosovo) and the gendered and homophobic nature of nationalism in Serbia. As the empirical parts of the book (Parts II and III) touch upon the process of Serbia's identity formation in relation to the EU integration process, this section focuses predominantly on the role of Serbia's Othering processes in the late 1980s and 1990s, with references to how these processes remain active in post-2000 Serbia.

EU's changing patterns of Othering: the co-evolution of enlargement and LGBT rights promotion[1]

Since its foundation in 1957, the EU[2] has grown from 6 to 28 member states, before shrinking to 27 following Brexit. The process of incorporating new member states proved to be an ever-evolving process in which old rules and strategies for expansion are continually redefined, while new ones are crystallised. Whereas the first waves of enlargement were predominantly focused on the *alignment* of candidate member states to EU policies, practices and values, the subsequent waves are increasingly concerned with the *transformation* of candidate countries. For example, the second and third enlargement (the accession of respectively Greece, and Spain and Portugal) showed an increased focus on consolidating democratic processes in these countries (Meredith, 2013). These political issues, at first considered an informal part of enlargement, became a formal part of the accession process of the Central and Eastern European countries with the adoption of the Copenhagen criteria in 1993. In the second phase of the fifth enlargement (i.e. the accession of Bulgaria and Romania in 2007), home affairs and particularly justice and the rule of law became key issues. Finally, the accession process of Croatia (acceded in 2013) was characterised by increased attention on judiciary and fundamental rights reforms.

Every enlargement has provided the EU with the opportunity to evaluate, (re)consider and elaborate on the conditions for integration and membership. In doing so, the EU has transformed the pre-accession process from a passive leverage tool into a process that aims to actively transform prospective member states (Tatham, 2009). While these changing enlargement strategies and emphases have had an impact on the extent to which the EU can 'intervene' in candidate countries, they have also produced certain shifts in Othering mechanisms that are embedded within the EU enlargement process (Slootmaeckers, 2020).

Apart from the more general geopolitical East–West division that characterised the period, the EU's Other before the end of the Cold War and the fall of the Iron Curtain was not '"Islamic fundamentalism", "the Russians", or anything similar [but] rather Europe's … own past which should not be allowed to become its future' (Wæver, 1996, p. 122). Indeed, for as long as the Continent was divided by the Cold War, the European (Union) integration project took place in a 'definitional vacuum' – i.e. the 'founding fathers' and others could talk of the EU without ever 'having to confront the question of what Europe meant' (Crouch and Marquand, 1992, p. 1). Consider, for example, the enlargement article of the Treaty of Rome (1957), which simply stated that 'Any European State may apply to become a member of the Community' (Art. 237). Yet the taken-for-grantedness of the meaning of Europe came under enormous strain with the collapse of the Soviet Union and the fall of the Berlin Wall, and questions of the political meaning/boundaries of the EU could no longer be avoided (Wallace, 1992; Zielonka, 2013). This new geopolitical situation presented the EU with a double challenge to both 'reunify' Europe to avoid security threats and define its final borders (Smith, 2005).

In response to this political identity crisis, the EU's 'fundamental rights myth' emerged as part of the 'polity-building and constitutionalizing dynamics of the 1990s' (Smismans, 2010, p. 54). Against the background of the globalisation of the human rights discourse, which had lifted human rights to a standard of civilisation by which nations are being judged (Donnelly, 1998), the EU began to define itself as founded on the principles of democracy, later to be extended to include respect for human rights and fundamental freedoms (Article F, Maastricht Treaty [1993]). Although the concept of fundamental rights was occasionally mentioned and referred to in the EU's relations with the wider world and candidate countries as early as the 1970s (Williams, 2004), an explicit narrative on fundamental rights within the EU's external relations only developed from the 1990s onwards (Smismans, 2010).

To illustrate, after the fall of the Berlin Wall and the prospect of Eastern enlargement of post-communist countries with a questionable track record in human rights protection, the European Commission published its new Human Rights Democracy and Development Cooperation Policy on 25 March 1991. In November of the same year, the European Council and Member States responded by issuing a Joint Resolution which made the promotion of human rights a priority in the EU's relations with third countries – a commitment later codified in the Maastricht Treaty (1993). Furthermore, to deal and answer the question of what 'Europe' actually signifies, the 1993 Copenhagen European Council summit adopted a set of criteria for EU accession, demanding that candidate countries must 1) have stable institutions guaranteeing democracy, rule of law and human rights (political conditions); 2) have a functioning market economy (economic conditions); and 3) accept established EU law and practices (legal conditions) (Nenadović, 2012). Next to formalising the EU accession process, these criteria created much wider leverage on candidate countries, enabling the European institutions to guide transformations and developments in candidate countries during the pre-accession period (Slootmaeckers and Touquet, 2016). More importantly, however, the Copenhagen criteria 'specified an identity of the EU that had previously not existed as such ... specif[ying] its own values in the process' (Diez, 2006, pp. 244–245). This emerging European human rights identity was further developed by the Amsterdam Treaty (1999), which not only amended the Treaty on the European Union (TEU) to include the notion that the EU is 'founded on the principles of liberty, democracy, respect for human rights and fundamental freedoms, and the rule of law, principles which are common to the Member States' (Art. 6(1), TEU), but also enshrined the boundaries of 'Europe' by codifying the Copenhagen criteria as a condition for membership (see Art. 49 TEU).

In addition to enshrining the EU's 'fundamental rights myth' in the EU treaties, the Amsterdam Treaty also extended the legislative (human rights) competences of the EU to include, among others, LGBT rights (for more on how LGBT rights entered the Amsterdam Treaty, see Mos, 2014). Indeed, the introduction of Article 13 to the Treaty Establishing the European Community created the legal basis for EU institutions to combat discrimination based on, among other grounds, sexual orientation. These new competencies were consolidated a year later with the adoption of the Employment Directive (2000/78/EC Directive) and the EU Charter of Fundamental Rights (henceforth also Charter), both explicitly mentioning sexual orientation as a ground for non-discrimination. With these documents, the first steps were taken on the path to formally include LGBT rights in so-called 'European values', and thus EU human rights identity (for more on the linkage between the idea of Europe and LGBT rights, see also Ayoub and Paternotte, 2014b).

Thus, as the political Copenhagen criteria became a prerequisite for EU membership, the fifth (or Eastern) enlargement signalled a shift in how the EU defines its Others: from temporal and geopolitical Othering to normative Othering processes (Slootmaeckers, 2020). Indeed, Kuus (2007) convincingly argued that the enlargement rhetoric contributed to a geographical Othering of 'Eastness' against the 'Europeanness' of the EU's so-called founding values. For example, in an analysis of the European Commission's Regular Reports of 1997, Kovács and Kabachnik (2001, pp. 172–173) have found that the 'idea of an inferior eastern Europe, counterposed to the dominant western Europe, is embedded in the discourse between the EU and the applicant eastern European states … Eastern Europe has been constantly invented and reinvented as inferior to western Europe'. Similarly, Robert Kulpa (2014) has argued that the enlargement conditionality actually constitutes a 'leveraged pedagogy' through which candidate countries are positioned as 'less than'. Candidate countries are deemed not to be European and/or modern enough to be fully accepted into the European fold, but worthy enough to be given respite and help in their attempts to Europeanise. Old (Western) EU member states are then conceived of as the 'knowledgeable teachers of democracy, liberalism, and tolerance', while Central and Eastern European countries, and third countries more generally, are rendered as permanently in transition (i.e. not yet sufficiently liberal), post-communist and intolerant (Kahlina, 2015, p. 74).

Although this shift in Othering mechanisms is key in terms of the EU's identity formation, it only developed gradually, as the main process of Othering during the fifth enlargement remained predominantly based on temporal mechanisms of differentiation. Indeed, although the notion of the

Other that is 'not yet European enough' in terms of values made its entrance in the enlargement discourse, the need for enlargement was nevertheless discursively framed within the notion that Eastern Europe represented a potential reincarnation of the 'past Self'. Overcoming conflicts and maintaining peace and stability was the main 'legitimization for the European Union (EU) enlargement towards Central and Eastern Europe' (Diez et al., 2006, p. 563). For example, the 1994 Essen European Council conclusions stated that the accession of the CEE countries was to ensure 'the lasting peace and stability of the European continent and neighbouring', arguing that the enlargement of the EU makes an 'essential contribution to overcoming the legacy of past divisions, and promoting peace, security and stability in and around Europe' (European Council, 1994).

The continued dominance of the geopolitical and temporal Othering mechanism also becomes clear when considering the role of the Copenhagen criteria in the enlargement process (see also Slootmaeckers, 2020). Whereas the decision on which countries would be included in the first round of accession was, at the early stages of the process, based on the fulfilment of the Copenhagen criteria, this logic was sidelined following the war in Kosovo (1998–99) and the NATO campaign against Serbia. The Kosovo conflict was seen as an 'existential threat' to the region that could only be contained by pushing the enlargement process forward, even if that meant not upholding a hard line on the Copenhagen criteria. Or, as Higashino (2004, p. 361) summarises:

> Before Kosovo, the logical sequence of enlargement was that, as the first step, the CEECs should achieve peace and security within and between themselves, and then the EU could enlarge. After Kosovo, however, the EU completely changed the argument: the promises for future enlargement should be given to the CEECs in the first place, so that the EU could play a role in achieving peace and security in the CEECs. Initiating accession negotiations with those candidate countries which were seriously affected by the crisis came to be regarded as the most powerful tool to provide such perspectives, and thus to create security and stability in the region.

Thus, although processes of normative Othering started to take place during the EU's fifth enlargement, the main Othering mechanism within the process remained based on the 'past Self as Other', with CEE as the contemporary (potential) incarnation of the past Self (see also Diez, 2004). Indeed, that normative Othering was only secondary to temporal Othering is further evidenced by the fact that the 'EU considered reforms [in the areas of democracy, the rule of law, human rights, and respect for and protection of minorities] to be necessary to ensure stability and security in Europe' (Smith, 2001, p. 187).

Even though the idea of the EU as a peace project never disappeared, the EU's human rights identity became more prominent throughout the 2000s. In the enlargement process, human rights (and LGBT rights) gained more prominence after accession following political mobilisations within some CEE countries against, among others, LGBT people (Kristoffersson et al., 2016; Slootmaeckers and Touquet, 2016). Whereas LGBT rights were rarely mentioned during the accession process of the CEE countries (Ames, 2004), these backlashes helped to shape LGBT rights as a marker of Euro-peanness as they inspired the European Parliament (EP) to issue several resolutions to denounce homophobia in Europe. Although these resolutions called upon Europe as a whole, they singled CEE out as the EU's internal homophobic Other. This move, in turn, helped 'to crystallise the core of the West/EUrope as non-extremist, hence rational and middle-centred, and as non-homophobic, hence respecting human rights values of tolerance, equality, liberty, and individuality' (Kulpa, 2014, p. 437). In fact, these resolutions were only one way in which European borders were redrawn to define Others based on their violation of human rights principles both within and outside the EU, which enabled the EU to reinforce its fundamental rights myth and promote the idea that the EU has an exceptional record in protecting fundamental rights (Ammaturo, 2015b).

The second mode through which human rights identity has been promoted is the revised enlargement policy. Learning from these mobilisations against the EU's human rights identity and seeking to improve the enlargement process and its normative influence of the EU on candidate members, the EU sought to make the Copenhagen criteria a central feature of the enlarge-ment process of the Western Balkan countries. As the EU had initiated the stabilisation and association process for the Western Balkans as a 'preventive measure … to avoid ethnic conflicts like Kosovo to spread to the rest of the Balkan region' (Higashino, 2004, p. 359) and the implementation of Stabilisation and Association Agreements (SAA) were made a precondition of any EU membership application, the EU could shift the enlargement's focus back to the so-called founding values, which, as the EU experienced, are not easily transmitted to other countries. Hence, after the 2004 'Big Bang Enlargement', the European Commission amended the enlargement policy in 2005 by introducing a chapter that specifically deals with funda-mental rights to the negotiations (chapter 23, on judiciary and fundamental rights; see Nozar, 2012). This move upgraded fundamental rights from a precondition for membership, to a central part of the pre-accession negotia-tions, which, in turn, allowed the EU to focus on particularly critical areas of the political Copenhagen criteria (Neuman Stanivukovi, 2012). Moreover, in order to overcome the fact that there is only a limited amount of hard *acquis* in many of the areas covered by chapter 23 – the requirements mainly rely on general principles and so-called European standards – a benchmarking system was introduced. The European Commission (2006, p. 6) describes these benchmarks as

> measurable and linked to key elements of the Acquis chapter. In general, opening benchmarks concern key preparatory steps for future alignment (such as strategies or action plans), and the fulfilment of contractual obligations that mirror Acquis requirements. Closing benchmarks primarily concern legislative measures, administrative or judicial bodies, and a track record of implementation of the Acquis.

By introducing the benchmarking system, the EU further enshrined the complex pattern of Othering in which the 'clear distinction between "inside" and "outside" has been transformed into a more complex pattern of tendencies and proximities. The EU does not simply include or exclude; it communicates "inclusive" positions', thus making the whole accession process even more about 'shedding Eastness' (Kuus, 2007, pp. 158–159). In addition to these changes, the EU further strengthened its fundamental rights policy as part of the Lisbon Treaty (2009). This treaty, particularly provision 8, changed Article 6 of the TEU to give the Charter of Fundamental Rights the same legal value as the (founding) treaties – but without expanding the EU's competences. As the provisions of the Charter are directed at the EU institutions and only apply to member states when they are implementing EU legislation, the added value of a binding Charter can only be considered symbolic (Ficchi, 2011). Indeed, making the Charter binding strengthened the perception that the EU is a legitimate political actor founded on shared values that are codified in one (binding) document. In terms of the enlargement process, the new status of the Charter arguably increases the legitimacy of the accession criteria for candidate countries by somewhat reducing double standards.

A year later, the EU further strengthened its human rights exceptionalism by means of developing a strategy which could be labelled a 'pink agenda' (Ammaturo, 2015b) – i.e. a strategy 'which creates and promotes a fault line between presumably LGBT-friendly and homophobic countries, and [thus] suggests that the EU is unique in its open-mindedness and tolerance of LGBT persons' (Ammaturo cited in Slootmaeckers et al., 2016a, p. 6). Following up on the above-mentioned moves of the EP to denote homophobia as a non-European value, the EU introduced in 2010 a toolkit instructing EU diplomats to protect the human rights of LGBT people. The Toolkit to Promote and Protect the Enjoyment of all Human Rights by Lesbian, Gay, Bisexual and Transgender People aimed at helping 'the EU institutions, EU Member State capitals, EU Delegations, Representations and Embassies to react proactively to violations of the human rights of LGBT people, and to address structural causes behind these violations' (Council of the European

Union, 2010, p. 1). In 2013, and in line with commitments laid out in the 2012 EU Strategic Framework and Action Plan on Human Rights and Democracy (Council of the European Union, 2012), the toolkit was transformed into a set of guidelines which are said to be binding for EU delegations and provide 'officials of EU institutions and EU Member States, with guidance to be used in contacts with third countries and with international and civil society organisations ... in order to promote and protect the human rights of LGBTI persons within its external action' (Council of the European Union, 2013, p. 2).

The increased usage of LGBT rights as part of the normative Othering mechanisms can also be observed within the enlargement policy more specifically (Slootmaeckers, 2020). Learning from the fact that creating chapter 23 in itself did not yield the expected outcomes due to difficulties experienced in negotiating the chapter and the delayed opening and interruptions due to Croatia's lack of cooperation with the ICTY, the EC created a new approach for chapter 23 (Hillion, 2013). This approach made fundamental rights a key priority of the enlargement negotiations and is based on the principle that:

> [Issues related to the judiciary and fundamental rights and to justice and home affairs] should be tackled early in the accession process and the corresponding chapters [23 and 24] opened accordingly on the basis of action plans, as they require the establishment of convincing track records. The Commission would report regularly, at all stages of the process, on progress achieved in these areas along milestones defined in the action plans with, where appropriate, the necessary corrective measures. (European Commission, 2011, p. 5)

As part of this approach and following the newly formulated LGBTI guidelines, the 2013 Enlargement Strategy defined LGBT issues as one of three key priorities within the EU enlargement process (European Commission, 2013a). Based on the observation that homophobia, discrimination and hate crimes based on sexual orientation are widespread in the Western Balkans and Turkey, partly due to incomplete legislative frameworks and inconsistent implementation of the legal provision in place, the European Commission finds that:

> There is an urgent need for *anti-discrimination legislation* to be extended to include sexual orientation and gender identity within its scope in Turkey and the former Yugoslav Republic of Macedonia. *Hate crime legislation* still needs to be introduced in most countries. Training of law enforcement, ombudsman institutions, judges and media professionals is needed to raise awareness of new legislation, *to ensure proper implementation* and contribute to increasing understanding. Countries must pursue a *zero-tolerance approach to hate speech, violence and intimidation* and take steps as a matter of priority to address cases from the past and be prepared to react robustly to new cases in the future. Countries need to take measures to *counter stereotypes and*

misinformation, including in the education system. Religious or cultural values cannot be invoked to justify any form of discrimination. Freedom of assembly and expression should be protected, including through appropriate handling of Pride parades (European Commission, 2013a, p. 11, emphasis in original)

This excerpt from the strategy paper shows that the EU did not only identify LGBT issues as a key priority, but also demonstrates that the EC formulates demands that go beyond the hard *acquis* (i.e. with regard to a 'zero-tolerance approach', 'education' and 'appropriate handling of Pride parades'). The emphasis on Pride parades, in particular, has garnered a lot of media attention and has made, for example, the holding of them a litmus test for readiness for EU membership (as discussed in detail in Chapter 4). Hence, at this point, it becomes clear that the EU has fully championed LGBT rights as a symbol of what it means to be European, thereby embracing the 'homonationalist global moment' in which states are increasingly defined and judged by their 'gay-friendliness' or homophobia (Puar, 2013b).

In sum, this section has narrated a shift in the EU's Othering processes, in which there has been a gradual move away from a geopolitical and temporal differentiation focused on regional stability and the EU's peace project towards a more normative process of Othering based around human rights and democracy principles. Although this shift is presented, for reasons of clarity, in a rather linear way, it is important to note that due to the plurality of Europe's Othering processes – which are based on different types of identity and different interactions between the Self and Other (Rumelili, 2004) – one cannot and should not conceive the relationship between geopolitical and temporal Othering in terms of progressive linear succession (Prozorov, 2011), but rather that they exist in a constant tense relationship. Notwithstanding the fact that there has been a move towards Othering based on the EU's fundamental rights identity from the 1990s onwards, this identity can be sent to the background in moments of a potential threat to the 'EU as peace project' identity. Indeed, both in the fifth enlargement and during Croatia's accession process, this tension between the two EU identities has informed the politics of EU enlargement (Sloot-maeckers, 2020), and as this book argues this has also been the case for Serbia.

Serbia's Othering processes: the role of Kosovo and gender in Serbia's nationalism since the 1980s

Contemporary debates on Serbia's national identity and many of the current problems that inform Serbian politics can be traced back to the Milošević era (Ramet, 2011, p. 7), and the history of the 1990s, characterised by rising nationalism, retraditionalisation, wars and international sanctions against Serbia and the NATO bombing in 1999. It has been argued that 'there are fundamental elements of continuity between present-day Serbia and Milošević's Serbia' (Clark, 2008, p. 117). As the Serbian identity struggles in relation to the EU integration process are discussed in more detail throughout Part II of the book, the next section presents a brief overview of the rise of Serbian nationalism in the 1980s following Tito's death and during the Milošević era, focusing on the (religiously inspired) Kosovo myth, its reliance on patriarchal gender relations, and the oppression of alternatives. As this history is well-documented and well-researched (for an overview of this literature, see Bieber et al., 2014), it is beyond the scope of the book to present a comprehensive overview of the development of Serbian national history following the collapse of socialist Yugoslavia. Instead, the remainder of this chapter provides a snapshot of those elements that have spilt over to the 2000s and inform the processes analysed in this book.

With the gradual demise of communism and increasing calls for reforms following Tito's death, the political landscape in Yugoslavia moved away from what Zivković (2011, p. 1) calls the 'Socialist Dreamtime' to the 'National Dreamtime'. From the mid-1980s, and predominantly in the late 1980s, the 'dominant Yugoslav rhetoric of self-management socialism, brotherhood and unity, and non-alignment came to be increasingly upstaged by the narratives of national identity' (Zivković, 2011, p. 42). As ethnic relations became subject to political manipulation, discourses of nationalism (feeding on the exclusion of the Other) were increasingly promoted by political leaders in the region (Oberschall, 2000). Although Milošević was by no means the only political actor who promoted such ideas, his political rhetoric and rise to power were particularly characterised by ethnic nationalism which emphasised the need to end 'the suffering of Serbs' (Bieber, 2002; Ejdus and Subotić, 2014; Morus, 2007).

A key element in the rise of Milošević and his nationalist rhetoric was the Kosovo myth. This myth has its origins in Serbian epic literature and centres around a battle that took place between Serbian Christian forces and Ottoman Turks in Kosovo in 1389. This battle, although technically a military draw (Judah, 2008), is remembered as a 'fateful defeat, a loss of state sovereignty, and the start of 500 years of "Turkish yoke"' (Ejdus and Subotić, 2014, p. 164). The myth describes the Serbs' heroic struggle against seemingly hopeless odds, which, despite resulting in defeat, had a promise of rebirth and triumph. As Morus (2007, p. 3) eloquently summarises:

> According to the myth, on the eve of the battle, the prophet Elijah appeared to Knez Lazar, who was to lead the Serbs into battle. Elijah offered Lazar a choice between winning the battle and having an earthly kingdom or losing

the battle and instead having an eternal kingdom in heaven … Lazar chose the heavenly kingdom. To fulfill the prophecy, on the day of the battle, Vuk Branković, the traitorous Serb military leader, withdrew his troops at the last minute. This act of treachery left the Serbs badly outnumbered by the Turks, and so the Ottoman Turks came to dominate the Serbs for over five hundred years. Lazar's choice became the explanation for Serb suffering throughout history. Still, the myth implies that Lazar made the right choice. While the Serbs would suffer domination at the hands of the Turks on earth, they were the spiritual victors, and hence morally superior.

Throughout Serbia's modern history, the Serbian Orthodox Church (Srpska Pravoslavna Crkva, SPC) has played a crucial role in perpetuating the Kosovo myth, contributing to Kosovo's sacred status in Serbian national imagery. The Kosovo battle represents the moment when the Serb nation picked righteousness over earthly power, and made 'Kosovo the *place* of this ultimate spiritual sacrifice and, as such, sacred and untouchable' (Ejdus and Subotić, 2014: 164, emphasis in original). Whereas the Kosovo myth has been invoked in different ways throughout history and has known periods of somnolence, the myth regained traction in the 1980s (for an overview, see Ejdus and Subotić, 2014). The 1982 Appeal for the Protection of the Serbian Population and their Sacred Monuments in Kosovo – a response to several arson attacks on SPC sites in Kosovo – was particularly important due to the fact that twenty-one prominent Serbian Orthodox clergymen re-evoked the myth throughout the document by arguing that the Kosovo question is an 'issue of the spiritual, cultural, and historical identity of the Serbian People' (quoted in Ejdus and Subotić, 2014, pp. 166–167). Building on memories of Jewish suffering, the clergy also warned that taking Kosovo away from Serbia would be like erasing the nation's memories, and thus spiritually destroying it:

> [L]ike the Jewish people who return to their Jerusalem in order to survive, the Serbian people are fighting once again the very same battle of Kosovo that our ancestors began to fight in 1389 at the Kosovo field … And when it seemed that the battle had been won once and for all, Kosovo is being taken away from us and we are no longer what we are! (quoted in Perica, 2002, p. 124)

While the SPC reintroduced the Kosovo myth into public discourse, it was Milošević who capitalised on it, mobilising these religious resources and its symbolism for his political goals. From his first visit to Kosovo in 1987 – where Milošević announced, 'From now on, no one has the right to beat you again' (quoted in Edwards, 2015, p. 193)[3] – to the Gazimestan speech, Milošević used the Kosovo myth and concerns about the fate of Kosovo as his 'primary strategy of polarization … [which] served to greatly advance the cause of national homogenization' (Russell-Omaljev, 2016, p. 98). Realising the political potential of Serbian ethnic grievances, Slobodan Milošević rose to power by reinterpreting the Kosovo myth so as to emphasise the historical suffering of the Serbian people and present himself as the redeemer of the nation (Bieber, 2002; Morus, 2007; Russell-Omaljev, 2016).

This reinterpretation of the Kosovo myth is best illustrated by the Gazimestan speech that Milošević delivered on 28 June 1989 on the occasion of the six hundredth anniversary of the Battle of Kosovo (see Edwards, 2015; Morus, 2007). In his speech – which was delivered after the 1989 constitutional revision which abolished Kosovo's autonomy – Milošević (quoted in Edwards, 2015, p. 194) argued that Serbia had 'regained its state, national, and spiritual integrity', after six centuries of unjust suffering.

His representation of Serbs' suffering, however, diverted from the SPC interpretation of the Kosovo myth, as he presented a past–present continuum of suffering in which Serbs were not (only) subjugated by external foes, but were mostly suppressed by the disunity of Serbian leaders. Indeed, the 'disunity was a subtext that underwrote Serbian history. It was what united the Serbs of 1389 with the Serbs of World War II and the Serbs of the Cold War' (Edwards, 2015, p. 195). Or as Slobodan Milošević argued:

> The lack of unity and betrayal in Kosovo will continue to follow the Serbian people like an evil fate through the whole of history. Even in the last war [World War II], this *lack of unity and betrayal led the Serbian people and Serbia into agony, the consequences of which in the historical and moral sense exceeded fascist aggressions*. Even later, when a socialist Yugoslavia was set up, in this new state the Serbian leadership remained divided, prone to compromise to the detriment of its own people. (quoted in Edwards, 2015, pp. 196–197, emphasis added)

In his account of Serbia's history and through the lens of the Kosovo myth, Milošević positioned Serbia and its people as historical victims – always suffering at the hand of others, never in charge of their own fates, never the perpetrators. By reinterpreting the Kosovo myth as such, Milošević both promised redemption to the Serbian people – ending the needless suffering – and redefined the notion of heroism embedded in the myth: Lazar's choice for the eternal kingdom is presented as a grave mistake, which Milošević, the redeemer, would not make. In fact, Milošević implied that he 'would do what Lazar could not: make Kosovo a symbol of unity' (Edwards, 2015, p. 196).

Milošević's nationalist discourse resonated well with the people as it amplified an already present crisis frame which played on the 'fears of extinction as a group, fear of assimilation, fear of domination by another group, for one's life and property, [and most importantly] fear of being a victim once more' (Oberschall, 2000, p. 990). This crisis frame was first resurrected 'over the plight of the Kosovo Serbs' in the late 1980s (Oberschall, 2000, p. 990). Following the demographic changes in Kosovo, which saw a change in ethnic composition from 23 per cent Serbs in 1971 to 10 per cent in 1989, it was argued that Albanian Kosovars had been discriminating against Serbs and intimidating them to migrate (Edwards, 2015; Oberschall, 2000). Such allegations gained popular support and caused intense reactions by Serbs when several news media outlets accused Albanians of sexually assaulting Serbs. By labelling these instances of sexual violence 'an age-old weapon of Albanian nationalism ... "an act of genocide" and "an attack on the Serbian nation"' (Bracewell, 2000, p. 565), the nationalist discourse not only supported the crisis frame and Serbian victimhood narrative, it also played on an underlying 'crisis of masculinity', which was part of the decline of socialism.

Connell (2005, pp. 81–86) rightfully notes that this 'crisis of masculinity' should be understood as part of a crisis of gender order as a whole[4] that, according to Kimmel (1987, p. 123), occurs at 'specific historical junctures, when structural changes transform the institutions of personal life'. Such a 'crisis in masculinity' is therefore, inherently related to wider social and economic changes, including the crisis of socialism in the 1980s in Central and Eastern Europe and Yugoslavia. Most importantly, the rising uncertainty and increasing hardship during the crisis of socialism and the post-communist transition further separated the daily experiences of men from the expectations of hegemonic (traditional) masculinity (Eichler, 2008, p. 47). Within such a context where it becomes increasingly impossible to live up to masculine expectations, it is to be expected that men become particularly susceptible to 'manipulation by "identity entreprenneurs" [sic], i.e. state or military actors [but also nationalists] who use hegemonic constructions of masculinity ... to exert social control by actively enforcing a masculinity model that serves their purposes' (Seifert, 2009, pp. 27–28). The retraditionalising potential of nationalism, then, represents a pathway to gain masculinity for men caught in a crisis of masculinity, providing them with a sense of continuity, agency and belonging (Greenberg, 2006; Nagel, 1998; for a theoretical discussion, see Slootmaeckers, 2019).

The earlier-mentioned images of ethnic rape, then, were an important mobiliser because it 'linked assumptions and anxieties to do with gender (and especially masculinity) to a vision of Serbian nationhood under threat and to an aggressive nationalist programme' (Bracewell, 2000, p. 565). By linking the victimisation of Serbs to overarching concerns about the gender order, Bracewell (2000, p. 569) continues, the 'plight of the nation [became linked] to a putative crisis of Serbian masculinity'. By doing so, the redemption of the Serbian nation – as presented by Milošević and others – could only be founded on an aggressive political (nationalist) programme that would 'redeem both national dignity and masculine honour' (Bracewell, 2000, p. 569). Hence, the sexualisation of the 'Kosovo problem' became a catalyst for political mobilisation based on a (hyper)masculine form of Serbian nationalism – a form of nationalism that not only provides men with a vehicle to achieve masculinity, but also draws on and reinforces traditional gender role patterns inspired by the traditional, heteronormative and patriarchal pre-socialist past (Bracewell, 2000; Milićević, 2006).[5] Or, using Bracewell's (2000, p. 584) words, Serbian nationalism linked the 'ideology of the nation to ideas of motherhood and female submissiveness, of male dominance and power, and of uncompromising heterosexuality, marginalising men and women who did not conform to the imperatives of nation and gender'.

Both the reinterpretation of Serbian historical victimhood and the masculinisation of Serbian identity contributed to a nationalist discourse that was (and still is) reliant on a notion of defending Serbia from both internal and external enemies. Indeed, one of the central themes of the nationalism of the 1990s (often labelled 'First Serbia') relates to the 'subject of external and internal enemies and conspiracy' (Russell-Omaljev, 2016, p. 94). In this discourse, external enemies, such as international actors, other ethnicities and the other Yugoslav republics, were represented as oppressors of the Serbian people. Internal enemies, on the other hand, were those who did not support the regime, often described as rootless cosmopolitans, anti-Serbs and collaborators with external enemies, who were accused of continuing Serbian disunity and, therefore, Serbian suffering (see also Bieber, 2003; Guzina, 2003).

Such discourse became increasingly prominent when the wars broke out in the region. As warfare requires virile, strong men who are willing to kill and die for their nation, nationalism at war needs a specific kind – a militarised hypermasculinity (Väyrynen, 2013). Moreover, it has been argued that in armed conflict, these militarised men ultimately come to represent the nation; their masculinity becomes the symbol of what the nation is fighting for (Žarkov, 2002, pp. 189–190). As such, the hypermasculine rhetoric of Serbian nationalism helped to mobilise male Serbs to volunteer to fight (Milićević, 2006),[6] while the wars were also explained and justified by relying on masculine nationalist arguments – i.e. that 'Serbian men were defending variously themselves, their wives and children, their homesteads, the entire Serbian nation … and ultimately Christianity itself'. On the flip side, those opposing the war were branded traitors and enemies of the nation, again highlighting Serbia's victimhood. For example, the international isolation and UN sanctions against Serbia following the wars were interpreted by the regime as proof of Serbia's victimisation by the West (Gojković cited in

Russell-Omaljev, 2016), and internally, actors who opposed the Milošević regime (often labelled 'Other Serbia')[7] and opponents of the war were labelled 'traitors of their nation [and] traitors to their gender: cowardly, weak, *effeminate and probably homosexual*' (Bracewell, 2000, p. 580, emphasis added).

At this point, it is important to note that the Milošević regime and its nationalist politics were not uncontested. For example, in 1992 a non-governmental organisation, Belgrade Circle, was founded with the aim of being a critical voice against Milošević's militaristic, ethnonationalist and war politics (Russell-Omaljev, 2016). Belgrade Circle organised several public events in which intellectuals gathered and published several texts in which an 'Other Serbia' was envisioned, which was different and non-nationalistic. Indeed, the civil society that emerged in the 1990s, consisting among others of peace groups, women's associations and human rights organisations, was able to carve out an autonomous political space by organising debates, protests, demonstrations, sit-ins, etc. (Kostovicova, 2006). Although these groups were able to construct an alternative Serbian identity – the so-called 'Other Serbia' which 'opposed Milošević's policy of war, nationalism and isolation' and supported ideas of 'democracy, human rights, the rule of law and European integration' (Kostovicova, 2006, p. 27) – their impact remained limited due to Milošević's politics of destroying alternatives (Gordy, 1999; Kostovicova, 2006). As such, the dominant Othering mechanism in the 1990s was based on nationalist discourse, with nationalism as a vehicle for retraditionalisation in Serbia, in which Serbian society was '"coming home" to the true (patriarchal) values of the nation, previously erased by the communist regime' (Kuhar, 2013, p. 8). In this respect, the SPC, which had become the 'cultural and ideological "flagkeeper" [*sic*] of the state' (Ejdus and Subotić, 2014, p. 172), played an important part by presenting itself as the 'tool for re-building personal and collective identity in a rapidly changing social environment' (Štulhofer and Rimac, 2009, p. 7).

The pervasiveness of such rhetoric remains visible even after the toppling of the Milošević regime. Although support for Milošević had waned – which led to the Bulldozer Revolution in October 2000 – the Serbian public largely believed, and arguably still does, that Serbia was not an aggressor in the 1990s wars (Obradović-Wochnik, 2009; Obradović-Wochnik, 2013; Ramet, 2007). Although Milošević's war strategy was rejected as wrong and destructive, the public only opposed the economic, political and diplomatic consequences of losing the wars, not the wars as such. Indeed, it has been argued that people thought that 'Milošević was not wrong to fight the wars, he was wrong to lose them' (Judah cited in Subotić, 2011, p. 321). Such discourse and beliefs meant that the Serbian victimhood narrative was never really deconstructed in the aftermath of the Bulldozer Revolution. On the contrary, the Kosovo myth regained importance in Serbia's identity formation following the Kosovo War between 1998 and 1999, the NATO bombing and UN Security Council Resolution 1244 – which made Kosovo a de facto international protectorate. As Bieber (2002, p. 106) convincingly argues, '[the 1244 Resolution,] the expulsion of Serbs from the province coupled with the persecution of Serbs remaining *in situ* and the destruction of Serbian symbols such as churches and monasteries' all contributed to the fact that the Kosovo myth was reinterpreted to become 'what it was in the 1980s – a symbol of Serbian suffering in the province'.

This victimisation discourse was further maintained through the diverging interpretations by Serbian (nationalist) elites and the international community (the EU in particular) of Serbia's role in past conflicts and the demands for Serbia to deal with its past. Indeed, as highlighted above, Serbia's role in the wars of the 1990s has been predominantly framed within a victim narrative, while any attempt (either by Europe or some liberal civil society actors) to make Serbia take responsibility as 'architect of Yugoslav Breakup and the biggest perpetrator of wartime atrocities' (Subotić, 2011, p. 321) has been represented as yet 'another humiliation at the hands of the Europeans' and their internal collaborators (Russell-Omaljev, 2016, p. 103).[8] The unresolved nature of the Kosovo issue, then, not only keeps the narrative of Serbia's victimisation alive, but, as discussed in more detail in the empirical chapters, its central role in Serbian identity formation also contributes to a key normative conflict within Serbia–EU relations, especially following the unilateral declaration of independence by Kosovo in 2008 (see Part II).

Additionally, the unsettled nature of the Kosovo issue also increased the political significance of the Serbian Orthodox Church (Drezgić, 2010). Whereas political leaders tried to use religion to legitimise their claim to power after the democratic transition, the SPC – which was the only Serbian institution that remained in Kosovo after the 1244 Resolution – 'used nationalism for [its] own rehabilitation and reaffirmation' (Drezgić, 2010, p. 957). In a bid to strengthen its political position, the SPC embraced the retraditionalisation process of Serbia by emphasising the true Serbian traditional patriarchal values in opposition to the Serbian Other. Indeed, Russell-Omaljev (2016, p. 137) has convincingly argued that 'as a result of a particular cultural-essentialist understanding of the Self, contemporary nationalism in Serbia has become increasingly preoccupied with the defence and preservation of nationalist values', with Europe represented as a threat to Serbian identity that attempts 'to supplant the traditional values associated with the Serbian Orthodox Church with European foreign-imposed secular identity' (Russell-Omaljev, 2016, p. 6). As discussed in more detail in Chapters

3 and 4, in relation to LGBT issues, the SPC synod has argued that 'the Serbian nation is on the edge of survival, only to be pushed over by gays' (Pavasović Trošt and Slootmaeckers, 2015, p. 167). To illustrate, on the occasion of the 2014 Belgrade Pride, the SPC issued a statement stating that '[LGBT people] have a right to parade, but only at your own cost … but not at the cost of Serbia – bombed, ravaged, morally and economically crippled, impoverished, flooded, nailed to the pillar of shame' (quoted in Pavasović Trošt and Slootmaeckers, 2015, p. 167).

Finally, in the period following the democratic transition, there has been a resurgence in the extremist fringes of society of 'right-wing racism and ethnic hatred, expressed in violence against human rights activists, gay activists, Roma … and other groups who at the relevant time were labelled as "Others"' (Russell-Omaljev, 2016, p. 51). Such a resurgence represents a continuation of the hypermasculine traits of Serbian nationalism as established in the 1990s. Whereas the nationalism and wars of the 1990s provided men with a framework to develop a 'male–male world', this sense of belonging survives nationalist conflicts as long as a climate of (masculine) insecurity and uncertainty remains. With the military defeats challenging existing notions of militarised masculinities, combined with the poor economic prospects following the wars, a crisis of masculinity still lingers in Serbian society. As such, nationalist discourse maintained its ability to frame every threat to the nation as an immediate threat to masculinity (Schäuble, 2009). The (hyper)masculine traits of Serbian nationalism have remained appealing to those experiencing a crisis of masculinity (caused by, for example, the growing insecurity of employment) and provided the grounds to reassert their masculinity via 'Othering' based on, among others things, homophobia (Bracewell, 2000; Greenberg, 2006). For example, Jessica Greenberg (2006, pp. 321–322) has argued that after the fall of Milošević, masculine nationalism has been a 'resource that the people in Serbia, and in other post-socialist contexts, have drawn on in times of social and political crisis'. She further observed that the homophobic violence surrounding the 2001 Pride occurred at the 'intersection of different modes of belonging, entitlement, action and politics' (Greenberg, 2006, p. 336). Marek Mikuš (2011) makes a similar observation on the 2010 Belgrade Pride (as discussed in more detail in Chapter 4). He asserts that the homophobic violence and riots following Pride occurred at the clash of the 'two Serbias', where the 'First Serbia' represents those adhering to the old system of belonging (based on conservative and nationalist views) and the 'Other Serbia' stands for a system of belonging based on liberal democracy, cosmopolitanism and anti-nationalism. LGBT politics have thus developed into a symbol for the 'Other Serbia', which clashes with the (still dominant) system of belonging rooted in the nationalist legacies of the 1990s.[9]

Conclusion

This chapter has presented the internal identity construction processes of the EU and Serbia, which together inform the multilayered normative struggle – as conceptualised in Chapter 1 – that informs the 'Europeanisation of LGBT rights in Serbia'. For the EU, the chapter focused on identity formation processes as part of the enlargement policy, while for Serbia, the focus was on nationalist Othering processes from the 1980s onwards. The Othering mechanisms described for both the EU and Serbia can be classified along a normative/value-based axis and a security/interest-based axis, which both result in different coexisting and/or clashing identity positions (see Figure 2.1). The presentation of these different identity positions, within both entities, demonstrate fault lines on which multilayered normative tensions can/will occur as part of Serbia's EU accession process. The first fault line created by the normative/value-based axis relates to the differentiation based on different values. It is rooted in the more recent practice of using human rights which have become a so-called standard of civilisation (Donnelly, 1998), and in relation to LGBT values, it is also rooted in the current homonationalist historical moment in which nations are judged based on their LGBT-friendliness. Whereas the EU has embraced this homonationalist move and started to identify increasingly as LGBT friendly, nationalism in Serbia has come to increasingly emphasise traditional Orthodox values, seemingly rejecting Western concepts of human and LGBT rights.

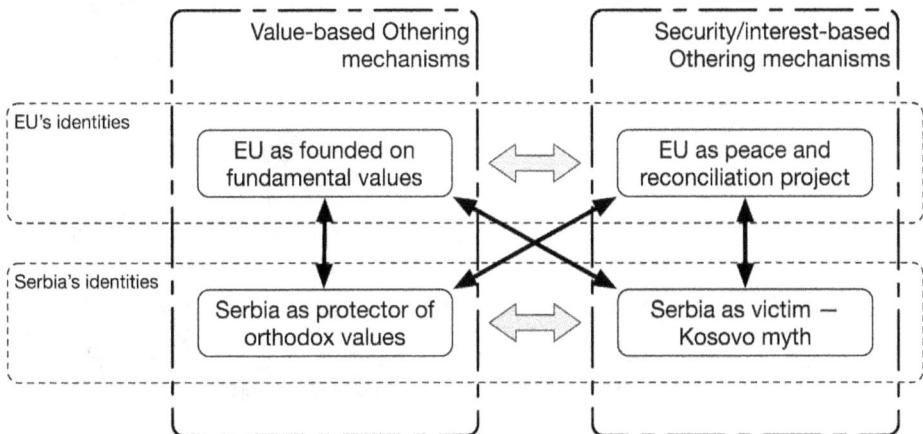

Figure 2.1 The multilayered normative structure of Serbia–EU relations
Note: Black arrows represent possible tensions within the multilayered
normative struggle. Grey arrows represent the internal relationship between
the different identities.

The second fault line is found in the security and/or interest-based axis of differentiation. Here, the EU's identity is constructed in relation to the 'past self as Other', emphasising an identity based on the notion of the EU's contribution to sustainable peace on the Continent. From this perspective, a particular driver of the EU enlargement process has been the search for regional stability through integration. For example, transitional justice (i.e. cooperation with the ICTY) and the normalisation of Serbia–Kosovo relations have been a central part of the EU's engagement with the Western Balkans. This EU identity has been in conflict with Serbia's national identity, which has been based on a reinterpretation of history from a victimhood lens. Thus, whereas the EU has been demanding that Western Balkan countries take responsibility for the wars of the 1990s, Serbia has been interpreting such demands as yet another example of Serbia being victimised by international actors. This tension has been made particularly visible by diverging positions of the EU and Serbia on the final status of Kosovo.

While these two fault lines are the most obvious, it is important to note that the distinction between the different identity positions based on either values or security/interest is analytical in nature. Indeed, the EU's identity positions, as well as Serbia's identity positions, are not necessarily mutually exclusive, but they are inherently relational in nature and can overlap, reinforce, and at times contradict each other. As such, the multilayered tensions between the EU and Serbia can occur not only within each axis of differentiation but also across axes. Which tensions occur within the EU–Serbia political integration process (as well as when and how they occur) and how they are negotiated as part of the enlargement process is discussed in more detail in the remainder of the book.

Notes

1 Some arguments in this part of the chapter have previously been published and have been reused with permission. Source: Slootmaeckers, K., 2020. Constructing European Union identity through LGBT equality promotion: Crises and shifting othering processes in the European Union enlargement. *Political Studies Review*, 18(3), pp. 346–361.
2 I use European Union to refer both to the current structure of the EU and its old, pre-Maastricht Treaty (1993) structure of the European Community.
3 Milošević was sent to Kosovo to ease the tensions between Serbs and Albanians, which had led to violence on many occasions. Milošević spoke these words in response to Serbs who had 'complained of mistreatment and beatings by the area's mostly Albanian police force' (Morus, 2007, p. 8). His statement and the media coverage it gained propelled Milošević from an unknown bureaucrat to a national hero (Edwards, 2015).

4 She argues that, as a theoretical term, 'crisis' implies a coherent system, which is restored or destroyed as an outcome of the crisis. Masculinity, as a configuration of practice within the system of gender relations, is not a system in itself and can therefore not be in crisis (one can speak of its disruption of transformation, though) (Connell, 2005).

5 Similarly, it has been argued that the Serbian Radical Party (SRS), an extreme right and nationalist opposition to the Milošević regime, also relied on militaristic notions of masculinity to mobilise its supporters (Irvine and Lilly, 2007).

6 This dynamic of masculinity can furthermore contribute to – but can never be the cause of – a violent escalation of nationalist conflicts, as it allows nationalists to tap into the 'culturally available possibility to use violence in order to achieve masculinity' (Seifert, 2009, p. 28). Nationalism and militarism provide men with the framework to develop a 'male–male world'.

7 The notions of 'First' and 'Other' Serbia refer to the two dominant identity positions within Serbia (Russell-Omaljev, 2016). The 'First Serbia' identity, which is associated with the Milošević regime and nationalism, constructs the Serbian national identity as 'rigid, motionless and static, and resistant to the idea of change' (Russell-Omaljev, 2016, p. 17), and its discourse is dominated by 'themes of tradition, religion and a highly victim-centred understanding of history, with a nationalistic orientation which frequently places emphasis on an illiberal value-system' (Russell-Omaljev, 2016, p. 20). On the other hand, the 'Other Serbia' identity emerged in the 1990s as a response to Milošević's militaristic nationalism and tends to represent 'the Serbian nation and identity as substandard, lesser and inferior to Europe, also essentialized, still backward and underdeveloped, and deprived of the opportunity for positive change' (Russell-Omaljev, 2016, p. 17). Its discourse is dominated by cosmopolitan 'themes including human rights, war crimes, the Srebrenica genocide, the Kosovo question, the siege of Sarajevo, and activism in support of Gay Pride, with an emphasis on Serbs being ... the main perpetrators in the post-Yugoslav conflicts' (Russell-Omaljev, 2016, p. 22).

8 Consider, for example, the additional political criteria for the Western Balkan region of full cooperation with the International Criminal Tribunal for the former Yugoslavia, but for Serbia also the normalisation of relations with Kosovo. The impact of these additional conditions and their interpretation from a victimhood perspective is further addressed in the empirical parts of this book.

9 To illustrate, the first train service between Belgrade and Mitrovica (a town in Kosovo with a Serbian majority), was a train decorated with the words 'Kosovo is Serbia(n)' in twenty world languages. This was considered a nationalist provocation by Kosovar authorities and was followed by military threats by the Serbian President who said he 'would be willing to send the army to defend Serbs in Kosovo, if necessary' (cited in BBC News, 2017b).

Part II

Adopting, resisting and transforming law and practices

3

Anti-discrimination policies: from the margins to differentiated politicisations

Following the adoption of the Amsterdam Treaty, the European Union has been given a clear mandate to tackle discrimination on the basis of sexual orientation. As discussed before, the ensuing adoption of the Employment Directive and the Charter of Fundamental Rights have embedded anti-discrimination principles within the *acquis communautaire*. This chapter analyses how the sexuality- and gender identity-related anti-discrimination framework developed in Serbia between 2001 and 2016 as part of the European integration process. In this period, Serbia adopted eleven laws and two strategic documents that explicitly mention the grounds of sexual orientation and/or gender identity (see Figure 3.1). The processes through which these laws and policy documents came to be, however, have been the result of complex negotiations as part of the EU integration process. Over this period, three distinct patterns in the adoption process of the legal framework can be identified, each with their own distinct configurations of relations.

The first pattern relates to the first five years after the so-called Bulldozer Revolution (5 October 2000) and the overthrow of Slobodan Milošević. This period is characterised by Serbia's initial democratisation and its rapprochement with Europe (both the EU and Council of Europe [CoE]), and limited political attention to anti-discrimination principles, let alone LGBT issues. The second (occurring between 2005 and 2009) is characterised by the politicisation of sexual orientation and gender identity in Serbian politics as part of a resurgence of nationalism, as well as the adoption of the anti-discrimination law following a pro-European political shift in 2008. The final and third pattern consists of uncontested and strategic changes and the continued expansion of the anti-discrimination framework, which seems to be part of a strategic move in which the government aims to communicate its Europeanness to the EU.

This chapter discusses these three distinct processes and patterns through the analysis of several key pieces of legislation. First is the adoption of the

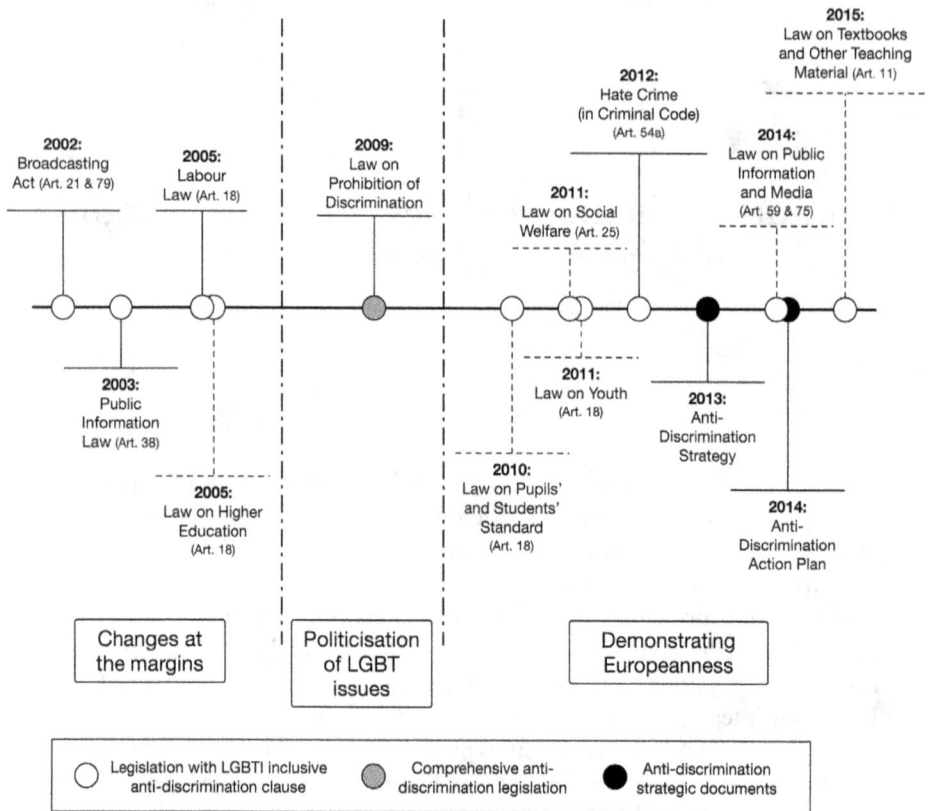

Figure 3.1 Historical overview of the adoption of Serbia's LGBT related anti-discrimination framework (2001–16)
Note: Dotted lines denote elements of the framework not discussed in the chapter.

media and labour reforms which saw the introduction of anti-discrimination clauses as part of a wider set of changes. Next, I analyse the adoption process of the anti-discrimination law in detail, with a particular focus on the contested nature of conditionalities within the Stabilisation and Association Agreement (SAA) negotiations and the visa liberalisation process. To conclude the chapter, I focus on three key legal documents adopted after the comprehensive anti-discrimination legislation: the hate crime law, and the anti-discrimination strategic documents – comprising of the anti-discrimination strategy and action plan.

Changes at the margins: LGBT rights as a political non-issue

In the immediate years following the Bulldozer Revolution the Serbian political landscape was predominantly orientated towards ending Serbia's international isolation and association and collaboration with different international organisations was high on the political agenda. At the European stage, Serbia submitted its membership application for the Council of Europe not long after the transition and took part in the EU's newly formed Stabilisation and Association process. As part of these two processes, Serbia was required to comply with human rights standards and initiate a variety of reforms (Subotić and Carey, 2014), including media law reforms (culminating in the adoption of the Broadcasting Act and Public Information Law) and labour law reforms (leading to changes in the Labour Law). These sets of laws are significant when considering Serbia's anti-discrimination framework as they are the first laws that explicitly mention sexual orientation as a protected characteristic. As shown below, how this came to be has been a combination of both Serbia's desire to (re)join the international stage, to follow what was perceived at the time to be leading European norms, and the fact homosexuality was a political non-issue.

Sexual orientation and media reform: the broadcasting act and public information law

When Serbia applied to become a member of the Council of Europe, it was required to sign and ratify all the CoE's conventions, including the Convention for Protection of Human Rights and Fundamental Freedoms (henceforth the European Convention on Human Rights, or ECHR), as well as the different protocols amending the framework of the ECHR. Additionally, the CoE's Parliamentary Assembly (in its Opinion No. 239) urged Serbia to undertake media reforms and

> to enact, in sufficient time for its implementation before the next elections the draft broadcasting law in Serbia, which has been adopted by the Serbian Government, agreed upon by the experts of the Council of Europe and was recently referred to the Serbian Parliament with urgency, and to enact, in sufficient time for its implementation before the next elections, legislation on public information in Serbia, placing particular emphasis on guarantees of independence and pluralism. (Parliamentary Assembly of the Council of Europe, 2002, p. 3)

The Broadcasting Act and the Public Information Law – both part of the wider media reforms Serbia had to undertake – stand out as the first laws to explicitely mention sexual orientation as prohibited grounds of discrimination explicitly. Article 21 of the Broadcasting Act (adopted in 2002) states that the Broadcasting Agency should ensure that broadcasters refrain from programming content that includes information 'inciting to discrimination, hatred, or violence against an individual or a group of individuals on the ground of their ... sexual orientation'. Article 79, moreover, ensures that news programmes and broadcasting more generally abide by the principles of impartiality and fairness in treating different opinions, as well as preventing any form of intolerance, including on the grounds of sexual orientation. The Public Information Law (adopted in 2003) contains what is commonly interpreted as some kind of hate speech provision in so far as it only relates to publications in the media (Christians, 2011). Article 38 of the law prohibits the dissemination of information and opinions that 'incite discrimination, hatred or violence against an individual or a group of individuals on the grounds of their race ... or their sexual orientation', regardless of whether a criminal offence has been committed by the dissemination of such publication.

While the aforementioned CoE Parliamentary Assembly Opinion No. 239 might not have specifically mentioned anti-discrimination policies nor sexual orientation – in fact, its section on human rights mainly focused on Serbia's cooperation with the ICTY, dealing with the past and the creation of adequate institutions – the direct involvement of the CoE in the drafting process of the laws is a key reason why sexual orientation was included (Marko, 2015, Interviews SRB2014_7, SRB2015_11, SRB2015_17). The international push for these reforms is particularly salient considering the precious few domestic advocacy initiatives for LGBT-inclusive anti-discriminatory policies at that time.[1] Indeed, as some activists had misjudged the political climate and tried to organise Belgrade Pride in 2001 (see Chapter 4 for more details), this Pride – known as the Massacre Pride – backfired on the movement. Rather than creating more political awareness for LGBT issues and empowering LGBT people, the bloodshed and display of (state-sponsored) homophobia traumatised the emerging LGBT movement, leading activists to turn away from politics and visibility tactics (Rhodes-Kubiak, 2015).

The absence of LGBT activists at the time raises the question: if not LGBT activists, then who introduced the explicit reference to sexual orientation in these laws? While LGBT activists themselves had temporarily retreated from politics, other civil society organisations were able to put their mark on the media laws as members of the independent working groups commissioned by the government to draft the different media laws (Stojković, 2003). Additionally, and more importantly, besides working with local NGOs these working groups actively sought support and expertise from international actors to counterbalance Serbia's inexperience in regulating the media and the lack of a regulatory culture more generally. Or as Ivan Andrić, chair of the for Culture and Information Committee, explained in a parliamentary debate: 'given the fact that we as DOS [Demokratska Opozicija Srbije (Democratic Opposition of Serbia)] MPs strive to adopt all the laws in conformity with European legislation, the Committee had a number of consultations with international organisations dealing with this area. First of all, I would like to emphasise the consultations with the Council of Europe and the OSCE.'[2]

Throughout this process, European human rights standards, whether established or emerging, were considered to be an important reference framework for the drafting of the law. As Dr Vladimir Vodinelić explains, 'in spite of the fact that Serbia was not a member of the CoE, and therefore their rules and principles were not obligatory in a formal sense for us, we behaved as if it was the case. As a result, we drafted a very good legislative basis for further reforms' (quoted in Marko, 2013, p. 34). It was this strong reference point to European norms and values that culminated in sexual orientation being explicitly mentioned in the law. Rather than complying with the minimal legal standards, Serbia engaged in a process of identity convergence. To demonstrate that it belonged within the European communities, Serbia took an expansive approach to the reforms and attempted to align the new laws with the latest (emerging) international – especially European – standards. With both the European Court of Human Rights (ECtHR) having confirmed in a 1999 ruling[3] that sexual orientation is covered by Article 14 of the European Convention on Human Rights, and it being codified in the EU's Amsterdam Treaty, legislating against discrimination based on sexual orientation was perceived to be a contemporary and European issue and an important good practice that Serbia should follow (interview SRB2015_11).

To illustrate, Žarko Korać, Deputy Prime Minister (2001–4), introduced the Broadcasting Act to the Serbian Parliament (9 July 2002) by highlighting that the law introduces Serbia into modern times:

> the Broadcasting Act is one of the systemic laws that is introducing us to modern times, regarding the technology of electronic media but also regarding the democratisation of decision-making in this area and the control of work in this area ... I must say that for the first time something that is the spirit of modern times appears in this law and is, in my opinion, the great need of our society to punish something called hate speech. This means insults, ethnic, religious and other abuses of the right to public speech through electronic media, as well as abuse of children's rights.[4]

Similarly, when introducing the Public Information Law to Parliament (15 April 2003), Korać stated that:

> By this law, for the first time in [Serbia], it is regulated what the media cannot do, things that practically were not mentioned until now, such as the abuse of minors, pornography, hate speech; some things are stated more precisely, and some are explicitly forbidden for the first time by this law. These are some of the achievements of civilisation, especially the democratic countries.[5]

As homosexuality at this time was not considered an important political issue (Interview SRB2015_50), there was little opposition to the explicit reference to sexual orientation in the laws. The few interventions during the parliamentary debates explicitly opposing the inclusion of sexual orientation in the laws all conveyed the message that homosexuality should not be regulated by law; that homosexuality is best left undiscussed. For example, one of the amendments, submitted by Vojislav Šešelj (SRS), proposed to rename Article 21 of the Broadcasting Act 'Protecting the Rights and Freedoms of Man and Citizen' instead of 'Combatting Hate Speech'.[6] Šešelj insisted that sexual orientation should be deleted from the list of grounds of discrimination, as he considered homosexuality a private matter and propagating homosexuality cannot be tolerated.[7] Homosexuality, Šešelj continued, is not a matter of immorality (as suggested by Joca Arsić [Socialist Party of Serbia, SPS] earlier in the debate), but a matter of disease.[8] Hence, he argued that lawmakers should find a formulation that is appropriate, scientific and in accordance with the principles of the legal system – i.e. homosexuality should be cured and not legislated. Similarly, on the few occasions that someone spoke out in defence of the anti-discrimination articles, sexual orientation was not their main concern. For example, Čedomir Jovanović (DS) considered the Broadcasting Act to be a step towards the harmonisation of Serbian law with international and European standards. As part of this conviction, he defended Article 21 from Šešelj's criticism by pointing out that the article prevents the media from being misused in private conflicts or political calculations.[9]

What is clear from these few parliamentary interventions in relation to the anti-discrimination clauses, and homosexuality more specifically, is that while there was some contention with regard to these elements of the law (particularly coming from right-wing political parties), they remained rather marginal to the overall debate as they are seen as only a small part of the larger (and main) discussion on the independence of the media. This 'change in the margin' combined with Serbia's keen interest in aligning itself with European standards saw the first introduction of anti-discrimination clauses explicitly referencing sexual orientation.

Harmonisation of the 2005 labour law with the EU employment directive

Whereas the media reforms were part of Serbia's political rapprochement with European institutions, the impetus for the labour reform were much more driven by the international financial institutions, such as the World Bank, the International Monetary Fund (IMF), the European Bank for Reconstruction and Development, as well as the International Labour Organization (ILO).

As part of this process and in accordance with the neoliberal imperative of these international financial institutions there was considerable pressure on Serbia to liberalise its labour regulations (Upchurch, 2006). For example, in exchange for financial support to rebuild its economy, Serbia had to promise the IMF it would conduct several economic and labour market reforms, including the adoption of the 2001 labour law. Although the new labour law was drafted to please these international institutions it remained far from aligned with international standards, especially existing ILO conventions and EU directives. To illustrate the latter, the Serbian government accepted fewer than 10 per cent of the 170 observations and recommendations made by the ILO regarding the draft law (Upchurch, 2006, p. 18). Equally, the scope of the anti-discrimination clause of the 2001 labour law was rather limited and unaligned with the standards set out in the EU's Employment Framework Directive (2000/78/EC).

When a new coalition government (formed by the DSS and G17+) took office in spring 2004, and the London Club[10] of donors agreed to partially write off of Serbia's outstanding debts (2.8 billion US dollars), there was renewed cause to revisit the previous labour laws. Indeed, as Upchurch (2006) has argued, such debt relief programmes often have their price tag – i.e. in order to receive write offs and/or new credit, countries are expected to make internal reforms in line with the agendas of international financial institutions, including reforming labour law. This being the case, the new Minister of Labour proposed a new and more balanced labour law (Arandarenko and Nojkovic, 2008). Unlike the media reforms, the involvement of social partners in the drafting of the new labour law did not contribute to an improvement in the anti-discrimination clauses in the labour law; quite the opposite. With the unions mainly focused on re-establishing social dialogue previously eroded in the 2001 labour law and improving collective bargaining regulation (Arandarenko and Nojkovic, 2008), anti-discrimination was not a priority for them. Although some unions had drawn attention to the issue of discrimination, most unions in Serbia – like their counterparts in other post-socialist countries (see e.g. Koldinská, 2009; Sloat, 2005) – were not really concerned with discrimination based on gender, and certainly not with discrimination based on sexual orientation. To further illustrate, in her research on trade unions and LGBT rights, Dioli (2012) experienced great difficulty engaging with Serbian unions on the topic of LGBT rights; one union representative explicitly told her that sexual orientation is a non-existing topic for the main Serbian unions.

If not the trade unions, then who contributed to the explicit reference to sexual orientation in the anti-discrimination article of the labour law? According to long-standing Member of Parliament Gordana Čomić (Democratic Party, DS), the anti-discrimination clause was introduced in the draft law because of pressure from the women's caucus (in which she was involved) in Parliament, and sexual orientation was introduced in Article 18 by a group of MPs (mostly from G17+) 'who, at the time, had stories of people who had addressed them sharing their trouble about being uncovered [outed] or asked about their sexual orientation [in the workplace]' (Interview SRB2015_50). Whereas there are undoubtedly elements of truth in Čomić's recollection of the drafting process – G17+ MPs, after all, submitted an amendment to Article 18 to include pregnancy in Article 18 – corroborating her story remained impossible. Instead, further interviews and an analysis of the parliamentary debates suggest that the more likely reason why sexual orientation became part of the anti-discrimination clause lies in the symbolic nature of the law in terms of Serbia's EU integration process.

Indeed, at the time of drafting the 2005 labour law, the relationship between the EU and Serbia intensified: the Serbian parliament passed an EU consensus resolution (Massari, 2005) and the EU decided to 'tie Serbia to a European track' (signalling the imminent start of the SAA negotiations, Stahl, 2013, p. 456). Putting the political integration process into the next gear also meant that the EU would start monitoring Serbia's compliance with the Copenhagen criteria more closely. The adoption of a new labour law in compliance with the EU *acquis* represented an important step for Serbia towards opening SAA negotiations. To illustrate the symbolism of the law, consider how Slobodan Lavović (Social Democratic Party, SDP), Minister of Labour, introduced the law to Parliament:

> This [bringing Serbia closer to Europe] *was the goal of the work on this law.* In fact, the entire Labour Law, all its new solutions are fully harmonised with European labour laws. We're going in that direction … The next very important issue is a comprehensive ban on discrimination on all grounds, and I use this opportunity to mention it. So, in line with European standards, the Labour Law envisages a ban on all forms of discrimination, and not only a ban but also the possible sanctioning of discriminatory behaviour and, at the same time, for the first time in our labour legislation, it imposes sanctions for sexual harassment in the workplace, which is also a completely new provision, a new approach, and I think that *it is in full compliance with European standards as well as the objectives of this government.*[11] (emphasis added)

The symbolic nature of the law to signal Serbia's European path indicates that the inclusion of sexual orientation in the anti-discrimination article was a direct result of the harmonisation process of Serbian law with the EU *acquis* and thus the employment directive which explicitly mentions sexual orientation. This observation is further corroborated by the fact that sexual orientation remained a non-issue in Serbian politics. In fact, according to the minutes of the parliamentary debates, homosexuality never featured in the debate on the law, much unlike the previous debates on the media reform laws. The lack of opposition can be explained by the fact that the law was brought into alignment with the EU employment directive that explicitly mentions sexual orientation, and thus renders the previously made arguments that homosexuality should not be legislated moot.

Taking the two reforms together, it becomes clear that during the first phase of the development of Serbia's anti-discrimination framework, sexual orientation only entered Serbian legislation as a change at the margin of larger, politically more salient reforms that would bring Serbia closer to Europe. This all during a period when sexual orientation still remained relatively low on the political radar, and one when Serbia's attitude towards Europe was one of identity convergence, eagerly aligning itself with European standards.

The politicisation of sexual orientation: adopting the comprehensive anti-discrimination law

Although anti-discrimination was not high on the political agenda in the early years of Serbia's democratic transition, this was not due to a lack of civil society initiatives to adopt a comprehensive Law on the Prohibition of Discrimination (henceforth anti-discrimination law). For example, already in 2001, the Centre for Advanced Legal Studies and the Comparative Law Institute led the efforts to draft a model anti-discrimination law that, in line with emerging international standards, included articles on sexual orientation and gender identity (Interview SRB2015_42). Nevertheless, these early pushes for a comprehensive anti-discrimination law had little to no impact due to a thinly stretched civil society and fragmented state (see Kostovicova, 2006). It was not until 2005, when both domestic and international pressure on Serbia to adopt the anti-discrimination law increased, that it became more politically salient.

Domestically, one of the biggest changes occurred when civil society started to coordinate its advocacy efforts. Indeed, following the observation that 'lobbying and advocacy related to the [anti-discrimination law] was more an exception than a rule' (Interview SRB2015_60), the Coalition Against Discrimination [Koaliciju Protiv Diskriminacije, KPD] was founded in the hope of bringing together and streamlining civil society's work on the anti-discrimination law. The KPD brought together 'several organisations that were visible and vocal to work together in order to have the law adopted and implemented in practice' (Interview SRB2015_60), combining a wide variety of civil society organisations, ranging from general human rights organisations to LGBT organisations, as well as organisations and associations representing people with disabilities and Roma. This diversity of civil society partners, each with their own experiences and expertise, allowed the KPD to professionalise the lobbying for the anti-discrimination law, drawing on legal knowledge from some NGOs while utilising the political connections of others (Interview SRB2015_40). For the re-emerging LGBT movement, being part of the KPD was 'the starting point of trust-building between LGBT organisations and other human rights organisations' (Interview SRB2015_40), and thus the first steps in building alliances across the segments of civil society dealing with human rights. Moreover, the KPD gave LGBT activists a platform to explain to other human rights activists the types of discrimination LGBT people face, which in turn contributed to a better understanding among civil society organisations of why sexual orientation and gender identity should be included in the anti-discrimination law.

Parallel to the domestic coordination of advocacy work, the international pressure on Serbia increased as well, particularly with the formal start of Serbia's European integration process through the SAA negotiations, which included fundamental rights conditionality.

Stabilisation and association agreement negotiations: resurgent nationalism

From the outset, the comprehensive anti-discrimination law was made part and parcel of SAA negotiations. Indeed, the 2005 Report on the Preparedness of Serbia and Montenegro to Negotiate a Stabilisation and Association Agreement with the European Union notes that there 'is no anti-discrimination legislation and human rights institutions, such as the Ombudsman, need to be established at all necessary levels and strengthened' (European Commission, 2005b, p. 5). The Commission staff working paper accompanying the report further elaborates

> The national legislation is also mostly in accordance with international standards, but the adoption of a comprehensive Anti-Discrimination Act is necessary as a further guarantee and protection mechanism ... Serbia and Montenegro should also encourage the adoption of comprehensive social inclusion and anti-discrimination policies and measures to improve the situation of the most vulnerable social groups. (European Commission, 2005a)

Accompanying the demand to develop a comprehensive anti-discrimination framework, the EU provided Community Assistance for Reconstruction, Development and Stabilisation (CARDS) funding for Serbia to conduct a feasibility study and draft a model law (Mijačić, 2010). Although this project did result in a new government-initiated anti-discrimination draft law, it was produced in a political moment of heightened nationalist tensions and resulted in a draft that did not include specific articles on sexual orientation or gender identity (Gay Straight Alliance, 2007).

The resurgence of nationalism in the Serbian political landscape was the result of increased contestation between Serbia and the EU with regard to the SAA conditionality on Serbia's cooperation with the ICTY (see Stahl, 2011, 2013; Subotić and Carey, 2014). Following Serbia's failure to comply with a key condition to deliver the two most wanted war criminals (Ratko Mladić and Radovan Karadzić) to the tribunal, the EU decided to suspend SAA negotiations in May 2006. In response, the Serbian Prime Minister Vojislav Koštunica strongly criticised and questioned the EU's policy towards Serbia, arguing that the 'policy of a permanent setting of conditions, that has been conducted for a while towards Serbia, is deeply wrong and so far produced exclusively negative effects' (quoted in Mahony, 2006). Consequently, the government grew ever more intolerant with EU demands and increasingly relied on nationalist rhetoric to fend off electoral challenges form the Serbian Radical Party and maintain power (see Saxon, 2006). The ruling party argued that the Serbian nation needed to be protected from undue European influence; and as a spillover from the contestation around the ICTY cooperation, any suggestion of anti-discrimination law was seen as yet another attack on Serbian values and the Serbian nation (Interview SRB2015_43). With reference to sexual orientation, the Democratic Party of Serbia (DSS) maintained that homosexuality is a private matter that should not be regulated by law. According to officials of the party, by legislating discrimination based on sexual orientation, homosexuality is brought into the public domain where it can threaten the cornerstone of the Serbian nation – i.e. the family (Interview SRB2015_43).

Within this political climate and with the prospect of snap elections due to the collapse of the government following the suspension of the SAA negotiations,[12] the government withdrew the draft anti-discrimination measures from parliamentary proceedings. Although officially withdrawn to gain expert advice from the CoE (Jerosimić, 2008), the timing of the withdrawal and the general difficult political context for the ruling party suggest this decision was also politically motivated. Indeed, considering that the DSS increasingly relied on a nationalist political platform, the law simply would not fit its upcoming electoral campaign.

Whereas the political fallout of the disagreements over the SAA conditionality on cooperation with the ICTY had pushed the government-sponsored anti-discrimination law off the agenda, the 2007 snap election provided a new potential space for the KPD to push for their version of the anti-discrimination law. To achieve this goal, the coalition not only increased its visibility in the media,[13] it also organised public events to promote their draft law. Most notably, Gay Straight Alliance (GSA), in cooperation with the Anti-Trafficking Centre, organised the first public debate on the anti-discrimination law – entitled Enhancing the Rights of the LGBT Population in Serbia through the Adoption of the Anti-discrimination Law – on 15 January 2007, a few days before the elections (Gay Straight Alliance, 2007; Interview SRB2015_6). Drawing on its political connections, GSA was able to bring together representatives of three (progressive and pro-EU) political parties – DS, Liberal Democratic Party (LDP) and G17+ – COC Netherlands Foundation, the Dutch Embassy, the KPD and representatives of LGBT and other human rights organisations to participate in the event. For the first time in the history of the anti-discrimination law, (progressive) political parties were expected to publicly present their views on the draft legislation.

Although the Democratic Party (DS) said it supported the anti-discrimination law, it remained rather vague about its support for the LGBT-specific clauses within the law (Gay Straight Alliance, 2007, p. 6). In fact, the DS point of view on the anti-discrimination law could be described as reactionary or as ignorant support of LGBT rights at best.[14] Such ambiguity was due to the fact that despite its official support for human rights, including LGBT rights, there was no consensus within the party on LGBT issues. Gordana Čomić, a high-ranking member of the DS, explains that 'there were a lot of people in the party who were not happy with the obvious improvement in supporting LGBT rights' (Interview SRB2015_50). However, as explicit homophobia is not tolerated within the party, most of the internal opposition to the issue was expressed through concerns over the notion of same-sex marriages.

As part of a slightly more supportive move, the representative of G17+ simply stated during the debate that her party 'stands for all minority rights at all levels, including sexual minorities [sic] rights', adding that even same-sex marriage would be accepted by the party (quoted in Gay Straight Alliance, 2007, p. 6). The strongest support came from the LDP. Its representative explained that

> [t]he coalition around the LDP does not stand for the rights of sexual and gender minorities and for the right to be different because there is [sic] 11% of citizens of this country whose sexual orientation differs from the majority, but because it's a part of political principles and basis of our liberal ideology that we stand for and one of the main axioms of human rights without which there are no developed and stable democracies in the 21st century (quoted in Gay Straight Alliance, 2007, p. 4)

This commitment of the LDP to human and LGBT rights resonated with its electoral campaign, in which the party expressed support for LGBT rights using slogans such as 'I want you to know you shouldn't look into other people's bedrooms' and 'We are free to love whomever we want' (quoted in Gay Straight Alliance, 2007, p. 2).

Nevertheless, the increased visibility of KPD, the political debate on the anti-discrimination law, and the electoral campaign of the LDP were to little avail, as the 2007 election was overshadowed by intense debates on the status of Kosovo and the ICTY. The elections confirmed the nationalist resurgence as it delivered a decisive victory for the Serbian Radical Party (SRS) which won 28.6 per cent of the votes. In response to this resurgence of politics akin to those that underpinned the Milošević regime, the EU changed its approach to Serbia's European integration process in the hope of keeping the European momentum going. More specifically, the EU softened its ICTY conditionality and announced in February 2007 that the SAA negotiations could resume if the Serbian government demonstrated a clear 'commitment' to full cooperation with ICTY (Stahl, 2013). Although the new Koštunica (DSS) government (with the DS) was officially European orientated (Stahl, 2011), the coalition remained deeply divided over the main issues dominating the domestic political arena: ICTY cooperation and the final status of Kosovo (Subotić and Carey, 2014). While the EU's actions to maintain EU momentum in Serbia already meant that the SAA conditionality become 'perverted' (Stahl, 2011) and single-mindedly focused on ICTY cooperation, the entire political context became even more complex when the negotiations on Kosovo's final status failed. Given such strong contestations along the lines of the EU's peace identity and Serbia's relationship with Kosovo, other normative issues, such as the anti-discrimination law, were no longer a priority. In fact, any debate on the anti-discrimination law was simply impossible.

The latter is best illustrated by the fact that despite the attempts of the opposition party LDP to restart debates on the anti-discrimination law by submitting the KPD draft law to Parliament on 8 October 2007, an actual parliamentary debate on the law never happened. In response to, and frustrated by the fact that the entire political arena was dominated by the uncertainty surrounding the final status of Kosovo and the continued EU demands on Serbia to deliver war criminals to the ICTY, Čedomir Jovanović (LDP) condemned the hypocrisy of Serbian politics:

> This is a country in which you can kill whomever you want, but you cannot love … if you are homosexual you will be beaten up … I am a bad man when I say that this should be a country in which people can love whomever they want and as much as they want, but [(Bishop) Amfilohije Radović] protects killers, blesses their deeds, and on the other hand prosecutes those who want to live their lives freely. (quoted in Gay Straight Alliance, 2007, p. 2)

When Kosovo unilaterally declared independence, the already disunited government reached breaking point and collapsed. The support of many European countries for Kosovo's independence caused Serbia's nationalist parties (headed by the DSS and SRS) to question Serbia's EU integration altogether. The progressive parties, on the other hand, remained advocating for a future of Serbia within the EU. Considering such strong political division, it should not come as a surprise that the 2008 elections became a de facto referendum on Serbia's European integration.

In an attempt to keep Serbia closely connected to the European integration process (without being seen to interfere in domestic politics), the EU took a strategic decision to sign the SAA with Serbia in the run-up to the elections, thereby reinvigorating the European integration process (Subotić, 2011). This had the desired outcome, as the coalition For a European Serbia won the elections and formed a pro-European coalition government with the SPS in July 2008. With such a decisive election result, questions about the European future of Serbia were finally settled and the political landscape shifted back to European-oriented politics. In other words, after years of identity divergence processes, Serbian politics shifted back towards identity convergence. This in turn allowed for Serbia's renewed compliance with ICTY conditionality, and provided a political climate more favourable to the adoption of the anti-discrimination law. However, for this shift to lead to actual change, significant political pressure through the visa liberalisation related conditionality was required.

Visa liberalisation process: renewed conditionality to overcome domestic opposition

Parallel with the softening of SAA conditionality and the initialling of the SAA, the EU also strengthened Serbia–EU relations by signing the visa facilitation and readmission agreements with Serbia on 18 September 2007, while also promising further visa liberalisation (European Commission, 2007). The opening of the visa liberalisation negotiations, to start in 2008, was not only meant to maintain a European momentum in Serbia but was also used by the EU to re-establish the conditionality principle so that, unlike the SAA conditionality, it would no longer be tainted by the Kosovo issue and ICTY cooperation (Kostovicova, 2014). Providing the EU with a new platform to leverage reforms through a tangible benefit, the process to obtain visa-free travel became subject to a wide array of conditions. As Trauner (2009, p. 778) argues, the EU took 'advantage of [the political saliency of] the issue [of visa-free travel] by inventing "negotiations on visa liberalization"'. The conditions for visa liberalisation were spelt out in tailor-made road maps. Specifying clear country-specific benchmarks to be met, the conditions for all Western Balkan countries covered four broad areas of cooperation, including a whole new 'block' focused on external relations and fundamental rights (Kacarska, 2012).

This introduction of fundamental rights conditionality within the visa liberalisation process provided Serbian activists with a key opportunity to advocate for the adoption of the anti-discrimination law. Anticipating the possibility for renewed conditionality accompanying the visa liberalisation process, Serbian civil society organisations, in line with the boomerang model of influence (Keck and Sikkink, 1998), petitioned the EU to include the anti-discrimination legislation in the list of conditions. For example, Goran Miletić (Civil Rights Defenders), recalled several meetings with the EU institutions where he successfully argued that the anti-discrimination legislation should be included in the conditionality for the Western Balkan countries (Interview SRB2015_17).

With the anti-discrimination law added to the list of conditions for visa liberalisation, the new (2008) pro-European government made the law one of its main priorities – despite having little interest in the merits of the law (Interview SRB2015_50). The Ministry for Labour and Social Policy was tasked with overseeing the adoption of the law jointly with the newly established Ministry of Human and Minority Rights. Hoping to adopt the law as quickly as possible, the former decided to recycle the previous government's draft of the law. Already approved by the previous government, the Ministry for Labour and Social Policy had hoped that the draft law could swiftly move to parliamentary proceedings following consent from the Ministry of Human and Minority Rights (Interview SRB2015_18). However, the government's hopes for a speedy adoption process were shattered when the State Secretary for Human and Minority Rights, Marko Karadžić, refused to rubber stamp the bill. Karadžić, who previously worked for the NGO Belgrade Centre for Human Rights, was one of the few state officials who truly wanted to engage with anti-discrimination policies (Interviews SRB2015_18, SRB2015_38). Noticing the absence of articles defining discrimination based on gender identity and sexual orientation (see above), he insisted that the bill needed to be redrafted in collaboration with civil society.

When the new and improved draft was sent to the parliament in February 2009, it was received with huge opposition from the Serbian Orthodox Church, which caused the government to withdraw the bill on the eve of the schedule parliamentary debate. Karadžić recalls what happened as follows:

> I remember that we had no problems, the law was submitted to the Parliament and the night before the parliamentary session for the proposal to be discussed and adopted, my minister invited me to his office ... and he told me, 'Your proposal is not going through ... Someone from the church called the office of the President [which then] called the government to withdraw the law

proposal.' ... [After phone calls between the government and Serbian Orthodox Church,] the Prime Minister said [to me], 'Try to make at least some changes. We have received detailed instructions coming from the Serbian Orthodox Church.' (Interview SRB2015_18)

Whereas public debate on the law had been virtually absent up to this point in time, the Church's intervention made the law 'the most important political issue in [Serbia]' (Interview SRB2015_6), pitting the progressive and EU-oriented civil society (Other Serbia) against the religious communities and nationalist groups (First Serbia) who sought to defend the Serbian nation from undue European influence.

The Serbian Orthodox Church (SPC) considered the law a Western threat to Serbian 'traditional values' (Jovanović, 2013). Together with other religious communities in Serbia, the SPC published a joint statement arguing that:

> it is not clear from the draft whether some of its stipulations *limit the right of churches and religious communities to preach traditional values in their activities, such as traditional family values and marriage* ... The fact that all the traditional churches and religious communities in Serbia expressed their concern ... is an indicator that, first of all, there are real reasons for this concern, and ... that *they all are trying to protect a common interest and values of Serbian society.* (Irinej et al., 2009, translated by interpreter and emphasis added)

Although the SPC was against the law in its entirety (Interview SRB2015_17), the actual political debate quickly directed itself to the LGBT-related provisions of the law, and two key articles: Article 18, which according to the SPC, did not provide enough protection for churches to preach their values, and Article 21, which was said to violate the religious values upon which the Serbian nation is built (Jovanović, 2013). Sexual orientation and gender identity, the religious leaders argued, was introduced in the legislation under the false pretence of EU conditionality and European integration. Profoundly disagreeing with the government's (and civil society's) reading of international pressure, the religious communities countered the EU integration argument by pointing out that other EU member states do not have sexual orientation and gender identity explicitly mentioned in their anti-discrimination laws and still are in compliance with EU *acquis*. As such, they argued, deleting sexual orientation and gender identity from the law would not endanger Serbia's European integration process.

Similar arguments were made by nationalist parties and organisations. The Democratic Party of Serbia, for example, saw the advancement of LGBT rights as part of a wider 'Western' conspiracy against Serbia. Connecting the law to the EU's role in the independence of Kosovo, the DSS accused the EU of having double standards regarding Serbia, which, they said, are aimed at slowly changing Serbian traditional values and culture. In an interview, a high-ranking official from the party explained their position on the matter as follows:

> [Regarding the anti-discrimination legislation] we [DSS] believe it all to be some type of pressure by the West and that by changing this legislation, the West actually wishes to change the already established mindset of Serbia … Serbia is not hostile towards minorities or any other special structures. When I say special, I mean the homosexual community. What really bothers Serbian society is parading and emphasising this. We think that this is all part of imposing some new values. (Interview SRB2015_43)

In response to the strong opposition to the law, the proponents highlighted that it was in line with all international standards and that adopting the law was part of Serbia's obligations as a CoE member (Interview SRB2015_17). Gathering in a grand coalition, civil society further pressured the government to adopt the current draft law using four main tactics: media pressure, protests, (one-on-one) discussions with politicians, as well as involving the international community (Milićević et al., 2009). While all these domestic tactics were key to shaping domestic narratives, it was a boomerang pattern of influence and activists' strategic alignment with European institutions and international actors that proved key for the law to pass through the parliamentary process. LGBT activists, for example, sought support from their transnational colleagues, including ILGA-Europe and the International Gay and Lesbian Human Rights Commission (now Outright International), who together pressured the government to 'maintain non-discrimination based on sexual orientation, gender identity and religion in the comprehensive anti-discrimination draft law'.[15]

At the political level, Karadžić maintained that 'the Human and Minority Rights Ministry will not allow any substantial changes to the law and will demand that the law be adopted as soon as possible' (quoted in Tanjug, 2009). Despite these strong words, he was isolated within the government, and thus needed international support to pressure the government not to change the law. As such, he extensively reported on the withdrawal of the anti-discrimination law at a visa liberalisation monitoring meeting in Brussels (Interview SRB2015_18), and called on his contacts in other international organisations to speak up and exert the necessary pressure on the Serbian government to adopt the law unaltered.

Desperate to adopt an anti-discrimination law in line with international standards and EU expectations, while realising it could not politically afford to disparage the Church's objections (Interview SRB2015_50), the government made some last-minute changes to the law by rewording Articles 18 and 21. Most specifically, Article 18 was extended to provide more protection for religious communities to preach their values, and the paragraph on gender identity was deleted from Article 21. The wording of these articles changed from:

> Article 18: Discrimination exists if steps are taken against the principles of freedom of expression of belief or conviction, or if an individual or a group is denied the right to acquire, maintain, express or alter their faith or conviction, as well as the right to privately or publicly express their convictions, in accordance with the law.

> Article 21: Gender identity and sexual orientation are a private matter and no person can be called upon to publicly declare one's gender identity and sexual orientation. Everybody shall have the right to express their gender identity and sexual orientation, whereas discriminatory measures based on expression of gender identity or sexual orientation shall be prohibited. Freedom of expression of gender identity and sexual orientation shall relate to cases of transsexual persons as well.[16]

to:

> Article 18: Discrimination shall be considered to occur in the case of conduct contrary to the principle of free expression of faith or beliefs or if an individual or a group of persons is denied the right to acquire, maintain, express and change faith or beliefs, or the right to express, be it privately or publicly, or act in accordance with his/her beliefs. The conduct of priests, that is to say, religious officials, which is in keeping with a religious doctrine, beliefs or the objectives of churches and religious communities entered in the register of religious communities, in accordance with the law regulating the freedom of religion and the status of churches and religious communities, shall not be considered to constitute discrimination.

> Article 21: Sexual orientation shall be a private matter, and no one may be called to publicly declare his/her sexual orientation. Everyone shall have the right to declare his/her sexual orientation, and discriminatory treatment on account of such a declaration shall be forbidden.[17]

When the SPC realised that it would not succeed in removing sexual orientation from the law altogether, it shifted strategy. The Church now targeted the public visibility of LGBT people and lobbied for an additional paragraph that would limit the societal impact of the law – i.e. to ensure that homosexuality would remain invisible or 'closeted' in Serbian society (B92, 2009b). However, these new demands failed to persuade the government, which used the European integration process as its core arguments. Consider, for example, the comments by Minister Čiplić on his encounters with the SPC:

> [The Church] understood [why Article 21 could not be omitted], but they stuck to their own religious standpoint, to the teachings of their holy books, that [sexual orientation] should not be displayed publicly, while we [the

government] held to our position that this was not something that should be outlawed and that it was something that had to be if we want to be in Europe, and that it's a normal thing for us to have to have this kind of law with these kinds of provisions. (Quoted in B92, 2009a)

After several weeks of intense public political debate, the revised law was sent to Parliament for adoption on 13 March 2009. The parliamentary debates, too, focused on the LGBT parts of the law and were permeated with homophobia (Interview SRB2015_6). The opposing arguments strongly echoed the Church's latest demands. Opponents of the law repeated their views that homosexuality is a disorder, unnatural, and against Serbian 'traditional values', as well as against the Serbian Orthodox tradition, and argued that the public display of homosexuality is immoral and offends the morality of the citizens of Serbia.[18]

Consequently, many of the submitted amendments to Article 21 sought to either delete the article or to reduce its societal impact. To achieve the latter, opponents suggested deleting the sentence which states that everyone has the right to express their sexual orientation, or to include a clause that would limit the freedom of expression of sexual orientation so as to ensure it would not disturb Serbia's traditional environment. The proponents of the law, on the other hand, strongly relied on a Europeanisation frame to defend it, presenting the bill as part of the visa liberalisation conditionality. By doing so, the need for the law was externalised, and its domestic benefits remained underemphasised (Interviews SRB2015_34). Indeed, positive promotion of the law remained a rather marginal feature of the debates, with almost no discussion of how it would benefit Serbian citizens, nor how the anti-discrimination principle would lead to a more tolerant society (Interviews SRB2015_21, SRB2015_34). Nevertheless, the boomerang strategies and Europeanisation arguments were successful in that the law was adopted with a small majority – made possible by the support of the opposition party LDP – on 26 March 2009, with Serbia being granted visa-free travel in December 2009.

Demonstrating Europeanness: the adoption of hate crime laws and anti-discrimination strategy

Following the adoption of the comprehensive anti-discrimination law, the battle over an LGBT-inclusive anti-discrimination framework was seemingly settled. This should not be taken to imply that LGBT rights are no longer contentious in Serbia, but rather that the existence of the general anti-discrimination law meant that all future laws with anti-discrimination clauses were barely contested, and the list of protected grounds are simply copy-pasted to ensure that the new law is compliant with the comprehensive anti-discrimination law (Interview SRB2015_24). However, given the limited interest of the government in tackling discrimination or actively improving the legal framework, two key elements stand out in the post-2009 period: the adoption of the Hate Crime Law (2012) and the anti-discrimination strategic documents in the form of a Strategy (2013) and Action Plan (2014). While the hate crime law provides additional protection for LGBT people, the strategic documents outline additional actions that the government should undertake to ensure a better and safer environment for LGBT people in Serbia.

One of the first initiatives to introduce a hate crime provision into the criminal code can be traced back to 2007 when the Lawyers' Committee for Human Rights, YUCOM, established the Coalition for Tolerance against Hate Crime (YUCOM, 2015). However, the issue really entered the political agenda in 2011 after several high-profile cases of violence in Belgrade drew attention to the issue of hate-motivated violence (Interview SRB2015_31). One of the most significant events happened in October 2011 when a woman was stabbed for wearing an LGBT-related T-shirt in Central Belgrade (Garcia, 2011), and the police, despite initially arresting the assailant, released him on the grounds that, as a minor, he could not be charged for his crimes (Barlovac, 2011). Appalled by the police's inadequate response to the attack – which was interpreted as another example of how the state condones homophobic violence – Gay Straight Alliance organised a protest in front of the government building, requesting that 'the government clearly condemn homophobic violence and hatred; a national strategy be drawn up on the issue; homophobic hate crimes be included in the penal code' (Barlovac, 2011).

Following the protest, and after having learned of existing government plans of a general criminal law reform, GSA and YUCOM jointly drafted the Initiative for Supplementing the Bill on Amendments and Addendums of the Criminal Code of the Republic of Serbia,[19] and sent it to the relevant ministries and parliamentary committees (GSA Info Centre, 2011; Interview SRB2015_31).

Although initially delayed for the 2012 elections, the incoming government (a coalition of the SPS and SNS) picked up the plans to revise the criminal code (Interviews SRB2015_31, SRB2015_53). Although it seemed unlikely that a government comprised of parties with a nationalist support base would take up a hate crime initiative, there were two key reasons that made this nevertheless happen. The first relates to Serbia being granted EU candidate status in March 2012. Following this milestone in the country's EU integration process, the government had started to send all new law proposals to the European Commission for comments and advice (Interview SRB2015_23).

With the Commission supporting YUCOM's and GSA's initiative, the path was therefore cleared for the government to introduce hate crimes into the criminal code.

While international support was important in paving the way for the reforms, to fully understand why it eventually got adopted, one must also consider the wider political context with Serbia–EU relations and increasing contestation around LGBT rights. Indeed, after Belgrade Pride had been banned for the third time (see Chapter 4), Serbia faced increased criticism from the EU on its LGBT rights record. As such, it needed something to take some of the pressure off and show the EU its devotion to combatting discrimination based on sexual orientation (Interviews SRB2015_17, SRB2015_29, SRB2015_53). Adopting the hate crime law, then, seemed to be a cost-effective way of creating goodwill on the part of the EU. Similar to what happened with the first anti-discrimination clauses, the hate crime law was part of wider reforms and as such received little political attention. The adoption costs of the law were relatively small and easily outweighed by the (perceived) benefits of adopting the law – i.e. EU goodwill and praise.

With regard to the anti-discrimination strategic documents, the government avoided dealing with the issue for many years, continuously arguing that it had 'bigger fish to fry' – to use an activist's words (Interview SRB2015_30) – such as the dialogue with Kosovo and/or the economy. However, the documents entered the political arena following a 2011 recommendation for their adoption by the newly established Commissioner for the Protection of Equality (henceforth Equality Commissioner or CPE – see Chapter 5) and the EU Progress Reports repeatedly demanding Serbia deal with discrimination, as well as constant support from the European Union delegation. Mounting pressure from a multitude of sources, both domestic and international, meant that the government started the process of drafting these strategic documents after it received financial support from the Embassy of the United Kingdom, the Embassy of the Netherlands, the OSCE Mission to Serbia and the Balkan Trust for Democracy. In fact, interviewees from some of the independent institutions informally suggested that these funds were an important motivator for the government to engage with the anti-discrimination strategy, as it both reduced the political and financial cost of tackling the issue.

The overall disinterest of the government in the strategy, nevertheless, became apparent during the actual drafting process. While different working groups were formed to tackle different vulnerable groups (Interview SRB2015_11), it was civil society leading the drafting process (Interview SRB2015_23). In fact, within the working group tasked to draft the strategy with regard to discrimination against LGBT people, the government representatives never attended the meetings (Interview SRB2015_29). While the absence of government representatives enabled activists to draft a very liberal strategy that even included references to same-sex partnerships legislation, it also illustrates the government's general lack of interest in anti-discrimination and LGBT issues in particular.

Indeed, the Serbian government exhibits a rather utilitarian approach towards LGBT rights, and only 'pretends to be an ally when it suits them' (Interview SRB2015_30), or when there is a benefit in doing so (Interviews SRB2015_23, SRB2015_27) – benefits which are often linked to Serbia's EU membership aspirations. Both activists and officials from the EU delegation to Serbia have repeatedly suggested that the government has no genuine desire to improve LGBT rights and that anything that has been done has to be seen as part of Serbia's EU ambitions (Interviews SRB2014_7, SRB2015_3, SRB2015_6, SRB2015_10, SRB2015_23, SRB2015_31, SRB2015_38). As such, the adoption of the anti-discrimination strategy represented another attempt to gain positive feedback from the EU (and the international community) on Serbia's human rights standards and to show that it was ready to open EU accession negotiations (Interviews SRB2014_7, SRB2015_3, SRB2015_10, SRB2015_31).

These expected positive remarks remained largely absent, however.[20] The 2013 Progress Report was rather cautious in reporting on the adoption of the strategy. As explained in Chapter 2, the new approach to chapters 23 and 24 required candidate countries to demonstrate a real track record of implementing change. Additionally, following the Brussels Agreement on normalising Kosovo–Serbia relations, the EU refocused pre-enlargement monitoring on fundamental rights, with LGBT rights being one of the main priorities. As such, rather than applauding the adoption of the anti-discrimination strategy, the European Commission remained cautious and demanded its effective implementation (European Commission, 2013b). The action plan for the strategy was adopted in October 2014, which was cautiously praised by the EU. The 2014 Progress Report was sceptical of the government's approach to LGBT rights and expresses the 'need for a consistent and visible political commitment to promoting a culture of respect towards the LGBTI community' (European Commission, 2014, p. 13).

Conclusion

Throughout this chapter, I have highlighted the importance of both the domestic and international context in understanding the Europeanisation of the Serbian anti-discrimination legal framework. Of the three different processes that guided the adoption of the framework, each have their particular configuration of domestic and international politics, and it has been these configurations that have been an important explanation for the observed outcomes-in-process. I have demonstrated that the balancing act between Serbia's wish to reintegrate with international society and the needs of internal nationalist politics has played a crucial and different role in the different parts of the adoption process of the anti-discrimination framework. Whereas the adoption of the first protections against discrimination on the basis of sexual orientation were part of an identity convergence process and met with little opposition as they were part of wider reforms that would lift Serbia out of war-induced international isolation, this dynamic shifted from 2005 onwards. Indeed, as the European integration process began to touch upon sensitive topics, a resurgence of nationalism occurred, and LGBT issues became politicised as part of an identity divergence process. The normative tensions around the ICTY cooperation had put the EU integration process under immense pressure and forced the EU to rely on perverted conditionality to keep Serbia on a European path. It was only once the ICTY issue was settled, and the EU could link anti-discrimination to visa liberalisation negotiations, that anti-discrimination returned to the political agenda. However, the comprehensive anti-discrimination law, which included sexual orientation and gender identity, was perceived by nationalist forces as another example of undue European influence that should be halted. The law, nevertheless, was adopted after a pro-European change in government supported by the concrete benefits offered by the EU's visa liberalisation process. However, as discussed in much more detail in Chapter 5, the law remains nothing more than partial compliance in that its implementation remains lacking.

After having lost their attempt to overturn the anti-discrimination law, the nationalist opposition shifted their attention away from legislative changes and on to Belgrade Pride, the physical visibility of LGBT people in Serbia (see Chapter 4). As such, including sexual orientation in new anti-discrimination clauses became less controversial. Nevertheless, the government seemingly remained uninterested in adopting new pieces of legislation or strategic documents that would expand the legal framework. Such changes, like the hate crime law or the national strategy and action plan against discrimination, only seemed to happen with international financial aid and at times when the government needed to demonstrate its Europeanness.

Notes

1 Progressive lawyers and NGOs such as the Centre for Advanced Legal Studies included sexual orientation in their model laws based on their comparative reviews of Serbian law with European standards (Interview SRB2012_42). However,

these initiatives did not always lead to explicit change and were subject to political bargaining at the elite level.

2 Parliamentary Debate on the Principles of the Broadcasting Bill, 9 July 2002. Transcript available from: Otvoreni Parlament, no date. *Peto vanredno zasedanje, 09.07.2002.* [Online] Available at: <https://otvoreniparlament.rs/transkript/5975> [Accessed 26 Jul. 2021] (quote translated by interpreter).

3 *Mouta v. Portugal*, Application No. 33290/96, judgment of 21 December 1999.

4 Parliamentary Debate on the Principles of the Broadcasting Bill, 9 July 2002. Transcript available: Otvoreni Parlament, no date. *Peto vanredno zasedanje, 09.07.2002.* [Online] Available at: <https://otvoreniparlament.rs/transkript/5975> [Accessed 26 Jul. 2021] (quote translated by interpreter).

5 Parliamentary Debate on the Principles of the Public Information Law, 15 April 2003. Transcript available from: Otvoreni Parlament, no date. *Peta sednica, prvog redovnog zasedanja, 15.04.2003.* [Online] Available at: <https://otvoreniparlament.rs/transkript/6018> [Accessed 26 Jul. 2021] (quote translated by interpreter).

6 See Parliamentary Debate on the Broadcasting Bill, 10 July 2002. Transcript available from Otvoreni Parlament, no date. *Peto vanredno zasedanje, 09.07.2002.* [Online] Available at: <https://otvoreniparlament.rs/transkript/5975?page=10> [Accessed 26 Jul. 2021].

7 See Parliamentary Debate on the Broadcasting Bill, 10 July 2002. Transcript available from: Otvoreni Parlament, no date. *Peto vanredno zasedanje, 09.07.2002.* [Online] Available at: <https://otvoreniparlament.rs/transkript/5975?page=11> [Accessed 26 Jul. 2021].

8 This view was in line with common medical opinions regarding homosexuality. It was only in 2008 that the Serbian Medical Society issued a statement in which it declared that homosexuality was no longer considered to be a deviation or illness (Rhodes-Kubiak, 2015).

9 See Parliamentary Debate on the Principles of the Broadcasting Bill, 9 July 2002. Transcript available from Otvoreni Parlament, no date. *Peto vanredno zasedanje, 09.07.2002.* [Online] Available at: <https://otvoreniparlament.rs/transkript/5975?page=5> [Accessed 26 Jul. 2021].

10 The London Club is an informal group of private creditors that is responsible for rescheduling countries' debt payments to commercial banks (Hudes, 1984).

11 See Parliamentary Debate on the Principles of the Labour Law. Transcript available from: Otvoreni Parlament, no date. *Prvo vanredno zasedanje, 31.01.2005.* [Online] Available at: <https://otvoreniparlament.rs/transkript/6182> [Accessed 26 Jul. 2021] (quote translated by interpreter).

12 The suspension of the SAA negotiation was one step too far for coalition partner G17+, who no longer wanted to tolerate the non-cooperative policy set out by the DSS. As such, G17+ withdrew from the government, leading to its collapse, and snap elections were set for January 2007.

13 The KPD became more publicly active, issuing an increasing number of press releases, see Koaliciju Protiv Diskriminacije, no date. Soapštenja. [Online] Available at: <www.stopdiskriminaciji.org/saopstenja> [Accessed 2 Mar. 2016, no longer available].

14 Gay Straight Alliance (2007) argued that due to the refusal of the DS to endorse KPD's draft law, the party implicitly supports the government's draft and its inadequate protections for LGBT people. GSA also drew attention to statements made by the party's leader Boris Tadić, in which he questioned the desirability of same-sex marriages. Although Tadić said he was not against homosexuals, he questioned whether same-sex marriage would be good for children's well-being (quoted in Gay Straight Alliance, 2007, p. 4).

15 Letter available from: Outright International, 2009. *Letter to Serbia.* [Online] Available at: <https://outrightinternational.org/sites/default/files/239-1.pdf> [Accessed 14 Apr. 2022].

16 Source YUCOM (2009).

17 Source: unofficial UNDP Translation of Law. See Ravnaprovnost, 2016. Anti-discrimination legislation of the Republic of Serbia. [Online] Available at: http://ravnopravnost.gov.rs/en/legislation/republic-of-serbia-legislation [Accessed 14 Apr. 2022].

18 See for example the intervention of Gordana Paunović-Milosavljevič (SRS) on: Otvoreni Parlament, no date. *Druga sednica, prvog redovnog zasedanja, 19.03.2009.* [Online] Available at: <https://otvoreniparlament.rs/transkript/658 7?tagId=60267&page=11> [Accessed 26 Jul. 2021].

19 GSA and YUCOM, 2012. *Initiative for Supplementing the Bill on Amendments and Addendums of the Criminal Code of the Republic of Serbia.* [Online] Available at: <http://en.gsa.org.rs/wp-content/uploads/2012/08/20120203-YUCOM-GSA-initiative-hate-crime-2.pdf> [Accessed 28 Jul. 2021].

20 Serbia was awarded the opening of the accession negotiations, but this decision is generally attributed to progress in the normalisation of the relations with Kosovo (i.e. the signing of the Brussels Agreement earlier in 2013).

4

Taking it to the streets: Belgrade Pride as a litmus test for Serbia's Europeanisation

Whereas the anti-discrimination legislation has clear (albeit limited) standards within the EU *acquis*, LGBT Pride parades, the focus of this chapter, are not a matter of EU law. To complicate the issue even further, as there is no European standard on organising Pride – not every EU member organises Pride and some EU members have banned Pride events in the past – the EU cannot rely on formal conditionality to demand such events from candidate countries (Interview EC2015_1). Hence, Pride cannot be considered to be a hard, yes/no, condition for Serbia in relation to its EU accession, nor a legal compliance issue. Yet Pride has morphed into an important aspect within the accession process. Indeed, as organising Pride relates to a number of different fundamental rights issues – most notably freedom of assembly and freedom of expression – as well as rule of law issues, it has become an important litmus test for candidate EU member states (Interview EC2013_3). In other words, though the EU does not formally require candidate countries to organise Pride, as this chapter will demonstrate, over time it has required them to facilitate and secure these events, if and when activists want to organise them.

As Pride events are not a matter of legal compliance and are exemplary of the politics of Europeanisation, this chapter analyses the politics underpinning the organisation process of Belgrade Pride between 2001 and 2015, focusing on the transactions between Pride organisers, the Serbian state, and opponents of LGBT visibility, and on the ways in which Serbia's EU accession process has shaped and been shaped by these transactions. Overall, the chapter demonstrates how the politics of Pride have been influenced by the tension between international standards of civilisation and domestic nationalist politics. At the same time, the chapter shows that the influence of the EU accession process on a soft issue such as Pride is subject to political prioritisation processes at both the international and domestic level.

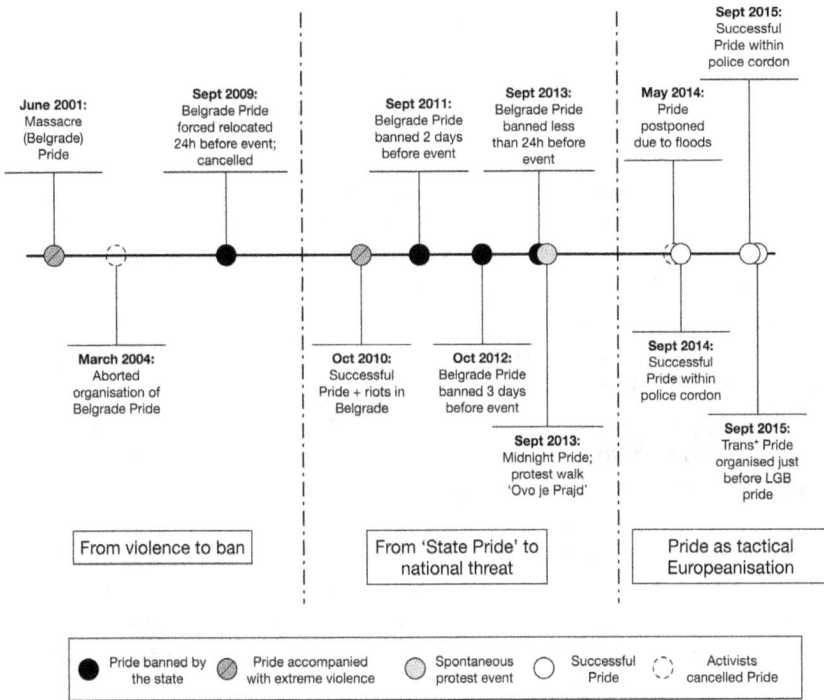

Figure 4.1 Historical overview of the organisation of Belgrade Pride
(2000–15)

The chapter discusses the history of Belgrade Pride in Serbia in a chronological manner, within three distinct periods. Figure 4.1 presents an overview of all Belgrade Pride attempts between 2001 and 2015, and the applied periodisation. The first period (2001–09), 'From violence to ban', tells the early history of Pride, which is characterised by the inexperience of both activists and the state, and the politics of intimidation. The second period (2010–13), 'From "State Pride" to national threat', focuses on the 2010 Pride, the anti-gay riots and the three years of Pride bans that followed. This phase is characterised by political manoeuvring around Pride, balancing different competing and controversial expectations within Serbia's EU accession process, as well as the securitisation of Pride. The third and last period (2014–15), 'Pride as tactical Europeanisation', is characterised by important political shifts in both European and domestic politics, through which Belgrade Pride was transformed into a state-coopted project that represented the pro-Europeanness and reform-enabling character of the ruling elite.

Belgrade Pride: from violence to ban

The Massacre Pride and its aftermath

Inspired by the democratic changes that followed the October 2000 Bulldozer Revolution, a small group of LGBT activists believed they could seize the moment to make a public statement about the political and social homophobia fostered by the nationalist politics of the 1990s (Rhodes-Kubiak, 2015). Drawing from their previous experiences of street activism – as part of their involvement in the anti-war movement (see Mladjenovic, 2001) – and international models of activism, this small group started organising the first Belgrade Pride in 2001. With limited and mostly individual resources, the activists registered their 'assembly in motion' with the police for 30 June 2001; only two days earlier the recently ousted President, Slobodan Milošević, had been extradited to the International Criminal Tribunal for the former Yugoslavia.

While the timing of the first Pride might align itself with the commemoration of the 1969 Stonewall riots, the closeness to the extradition of Milošević is indicative of a misreading of the political climate by both organisers and police: both overestimating the depth and level of the democratisation reforms and underestimating the resilience and anger of the nationalist forces in Serbia. Indeed, with the benefit of hindsight, it is clear that neither the activists nor the police expected these groups to act out their frustration and anger on anyone they deemed a provocation, including LGBT people who previously were branded traitors to the nation (see Chapter 2).

This political misjudgement, combined with the fact that both the organisers and (to some extent) the police were inexperienced in organising this type of event, meant that neither were prepared for any form of organised opposition to the Pride initiative. Reflecting on the first Pride attempt, the head of the Department for Organisation, Prevention and Community Policing (henceforth community policing department) admitted in an interview (in what I can only describe as an understatement) that cooperation between the police and organisers was not as it should have been, and that necessary security checks and safety assessments were not conducted (Interview SRB2015_41). In fact, protective measures to ensure the safety of Pride participants had been deemed unnecessary by the police, despite the many planned counter-demonstrations and the abundance of posters plastered throughout the city calling for action to '[p]revent the spreading of unchristian immorality and perverse orgies' (Djurić, 2001). Consequently, a day that was intended to mark the first public celebration of LGBT lives in Serbia became a bloody scene – the event is now referred to as the 'Massacre Pride' – leaving at least forty civilians and eight police officers injured. When activists and Pride participants gathered in *Trg Republike* [Republic Square – Belgrade's main square], they were met by a thousand-strong crowd. The opponents, who reportedly had come specifically to break up Pride and beat up participants as well as bystanders who were perceived to be gay, approached and attacked the parade while chanting slurs such as 'kill the faggots' (Simo, 2001). With only fifty police officers deployed simply to *enable* Pride (Interview SRB2015_41), the police were unable to protect Pride participants from such a violent crowd, nor were they reportedly willing to. Eyewitnesses recall how police officers were simply standing by, watching the violence, only intervening to protect themselves. Additionally, it was reported that the police contributed to the violence by making several homophobic remarks, including 'Why should we protect them?', and 'They got what they deserved' (Djurić, 2001).

In the days that followed, political discourse firmly blamed the Pride organisers for the violence, arguing that they had provoked Serbia with their 'perversity'. For example, responding to the allegations that the police did not do enough to protect Pride, Belgrade police chief Boško Buha simply said that he did not expect such violence and that '[a]s a society, we are not mature enough to accept such demonstrations of perversity' (quoted in Simo, 2001). Similarly, the Prime Minister, Zoran Đinđić, proclaimed that it was 'too early to stand this test of tolerance in a country that has been in isolation for so long, and which has had a repressive patriarchal culture' (quoted in Simo, 2001; also Interviews SRB2015_18, SRB2015_52).

Liberal civil society organisations, on the other hand, condemned the violence as well as the offhand responses by authorities. In a joint statement, they argued that the absence of a sufficient police presence highlighted the explicit lack of willingness to protect vulnerable citizens. Linking Pride to Serbia's democratisation and European integration, the organisers stated that:

> Although yesterday's escalation of violence is an obvious result of ten years of growing hatred towards everything that is different … *our new democratic government failed one of the first tests related to human rights.* Yesterday's lukewarm reaction of the police and government have shown that the attack on the 'other' is still permitted and even desirable [in Serbia] … *These events are not tolerated in civilised countries. If the intent of the authorities is to take Serbia to Europe, they are on the wrong path.* (Labris and Gayten-LGBT, 2001, translated by interpreter and emphasis added)

While this statement in many ways foreshadows the future politics of Belgrade Pride, the immediate consequences of the Massacre Pride for Serbian LGBT activism were devastating. What could have been the beginning of LGBT visibility became the absolute opposite: the bloodshed instilled a deep fear in many activists, causing them to retreat from political activism (Rhodes-Kubiak, 2015, p. 125).

As devastating as the Massacre Pride was for LGBT activism, it would be wrong to ignore the unintended effect Pride had on the workings of the police force. The violence and inability (or unwillingness) of the policy to prevent it presented them with an important signal 'that something [had to] change in [policing] procedures, as well as in the understanding and execution of certain laws and police work' (Interview SRB2015_41). In the years to follow, and as part of wider police reforms (Downes, 2004), Serbia established a new police department, the Department for Organisation, Prevention and Community Policing, which was given the explicit responsibility of liaising with the LGBT activists. And although the relationship between the police and Pride organisers remained difficult for many years, the establishment of the new department is the beginning of change to come.

Indeed, inspired by some of these changes, a small group of activists came together in October 2003 to begin organising a new Belgrade Pride event to take place in June 2004. However, after months of preparation, the organisers abandoned their plans following arson attacks on Serbian Orthodox churches in Kosovo, to which Serbian demonstrators retaliated by burning down a mosque in Belgrade (BBC News, 2004). In this context, having a Pride event was not in the interest of the government, as another violent Pride would undermine its efforts to convince the international community that the human rights of Serbian communities in Kosovo were severely endangered, while also demonstrating Serbia's record on protecting (other) minorities (Interview SRB2015_41). Under strong political pressure, the community policing department urged Pride organisers to cancel the event, arguing that the police would not be able to stop nationalist groups from attacking the Pride (Interviews SRB2015_6, SRB2015_17, SRB2015_41, SRB2015_52). Still traumatised by the 2001 Pride, activists caved and shelved their plans to organise one for 2004.

Intimidated organisers: the de facto banned 2009 Pride

It took nearly five years, a pro-European election that marked the end of the openly nationalist period, and the adoption of the general anti-discrimination law, for Pride to return to activists' political agenda. Indeed, feeling supported by the EU's pressure on Serbia to keep sexual orientation in the anti-discrimination law, activists believed the time to be ripe to work on LGBT visibility once again (Interview SRB2015_17). Two organisations – Labris and Gay Straight Alliance[1] – proclaimed 2009 to be a decisive year for the Serbian LGBT population – a year in which they could overcome their fears and become advocates of LGBT equality, rather than victims of inequality. Announcing their plans to organise Pride [Parada Ponosa], they argued that it would be based on 'basic human rights, namely the right to freedom of assembly ... a political protest, a procession in which one marginalised group in society ... becomes visible and contributes to the respect for human rights' (Dragana Vučković quoted in Beta, 2009, translated by interpreter). Moreover, drawing on the success of EU conditionality to push for the anti-discrimination law, Boris Milićević (GSA) added that the EU and other international organisations would 'closely monitor what is happening regarding the position of LGBT people in Serbia' (quoted in Beta, 2009). Indeed, the 2009 Pride was domestically and internationally perceived to be an important test of Serbia's maturity and its modernisation after the fall of Milošević, as well as the first real test of Serbia's commitment to, and the implementation of, the newly adopted anti-discrimination law (Nielsen, 2013a).

Faced with this international and EU support for Pride, the pro-EU government elected in 2008 was not in a position to (openly) oppose Belgrade Pride as it was rhetorically trapped by its pro-European electoral platform. Hence, it publicly supported the initiative, albeit reluctantly. Given that the DS-led government was struggling to maintain its grip on the state – battling strong nationalist opposition and being fearful of going against the wishes of the Church – it walked a thin line of both supporting and opposing Pride (Interviews SRB2015_18, SRB2015_50). Government officials navigated this uncomfortable position by answering media questions about Pride with references to the adoption of the anti-discrimination law, presenting Pride as a logical extension of the law (Stakić, 2011, 2015), while immediately adding that they did not 'share their [LGBT activists] beliefs or values' (Blagojević, 2011, p. 37).

Behind the scenes, however, the government was clearly not interested in organising Pride (see leaked diplomatic cable: Pederson, 2009). In fact, activists have widely reported that both the government and police engaged in a subtle, yet effective, behind-the-scenes campaign against Pride, where they played on the inexperience of the Pride organisers (consisting mainly of women following the earlier withdrawal of GSA from the organising committee) to intimidate them into cancelling it (Ejdus and Božović, 2019). One often-mentioned mechanism of intimidation is the complex administrative process of obtaining the permits to organise Pride. Committee member Mina Božović called the process a bureaucratic nightmare:

> It turned out it was a very administrative and very tricky procedure. This was one of the ways in which the government was trying to sabotage the Pride. It is a big event, so you need to get a permit to close the street, but before that, you need a permit that all the cars on the street need to be removed, but you cannot get a permit for the cars before you have one for the street. So, they were trying to bury you in those licences. (Interview SRB2015_12)

Additionally, the state used Pride participants' protection and other security issues as another pressuring tool. With the experience of the 2001 Massacre Pride in mind, as well as the strong opposition to the anti-discrimination law, the organisers hired a respected security expert, Zoran Dragišić, to conduct a preliminary safety assessment in July 2009. Although recognising the risks, Dragišić found that organising Belgrade Pride would be possible when authorities took all necessary preventive measures to reduce the risks of the event (Interviews SRB2015_12, SRB2015_41). In the immediate days after the report was released, the cooperation between the community policing department and the organisers seemed to improve, with both parties having several meetings to examine all possible scenarios and how to safeguard Pride (Interview SRB2015_41). However, it was during these meetings that the state apparatus played on the inexperience of the organisers to intimidate them. They did so by trying to shift responsibility for the security of Pride to the organisers by twisting the wording of the law to suggest that organisers were responsible for the safety of participants as well as the city as a whole (Interview SRB2015_12; see also Ejdus and Božović, 2019). Additionally, security risks were systematically exaggerated (Interview SRB2015_12). In what one activist described as a subtle form of brainwashing, the Pride committee was required to watch hours of instructional videos in which several scenarios were shown of how Pride could be attacked, including cars smashing into the parade or even a paraglider attack.[2]

Such intimidation was further strengthened by the overwhelming media visibility of the opposition to Pride (Johnson, 2012). Although the organisers tried to frame Pride in terms of human rights and as a test of the EU's principles of anti-discrimination, the media coverage predominantly portrayed the extreme right's framing of Pride as an 'anti-Serbian provocation', and/or a 'Parade of Shame' (Johnson, 2012). In addition to this discursive opposition, nationalist groups also physically threatened the Pride parade as well as the lives of LGBT people. Slogans such as 'We are waiting for you', 'Death to faggots' and 'Blood will flow across Belgrade, the parade will not take place' were abundantly visible throughout Belgrade (Johnson, 2012; Nielsen, 2013a).

The potential of the so-called 'patriotic bloc' to mobilise against Pride was evidenced during the first 'Family Walk' that took place on 12 September 2009 (Mikuš, 2015). During this event, extreme right organisations, with the support of the SPC, strongly condemned the public display of homosexuality (and thus Pride), while positioning themselves as the only group that could defend traditional Serbian and orthodox family values from vices such as homosexuality, democratisation, modernisation and market liberalisation – all processes associated with European integration (Stakić, 2015). In order to protect Serbia, they were ready to resort to extreme measures and violence. Indeed, during a live televised interview covering the Family Walk, the leader of the extremist organisation Obraz, Mladen Obradović, suggested as much:

> Everyone knows what will happen if they go ahead with that parade of shame, and the responsibility for that will be of those who organized it. They cannot expect to poke their finger in the eye of our nation and go unpunished. (quoted in Anastasijević, 2009)

Although the SPC refrained from making any official statements, its opposition was made quite clear through the statements of several prominent bishops condemning the public visibility of homosexuality. For example, Metropolitan Amfilohije Radović called the 2009 Pride parade 'a parade of shame', quoting the Serbian popular expression 'what the mad are proud of, ashames the smart' (cited in Stakić, 2011, p. 56). He further referred to Pride as 'a parade of Sodom and Gomorrah', adding that the 'tree that does not bear fruit should be cut down and thrown into fire' (cited in Bojić, 2009).

Faced with such high levels of public homophobia and following recent incidents of homophobic violence in Belgrade, the Pride committee repeatedly asked the Serbian police to make concrete plans for the protection of the event, but to little avail (Ejdus and Božović, 2019). Authorities simply suggested moving Pride to the periphery of the city (Interview SRB2015_41). Despite the personal distress caused by police intimidation and widespread violence both in the media and on the streets, activists did not consider this a viable solution, as for Pride to achieve its goals of gaining visibility and reclaiming public space it needed to happen in central Belgrade (Interview SRB2015_12). The authorities, however, did not yield, and less than twenty-four hours before the scheduled start of Pride, organisers were informed that the Ministry of the Interior had decided it could only take place if moved to the outskirts of the city. In other words, rather than explicitly banning Pride, the authorities had opted for the extralegal option of moving the event to Ušće, a promenade at the confluence of the Sava and Danube rivers (Interview SRB2015_41).

For the Pride committee the relocation represented a de facto ban, so they cancelled the event – an interpretation the constitutional court later confirmed (B92, 2011b). The organisers claimed that by banning Pride the state had capitulated to the extreme right:

> Even though the decree given by the Ministry of the Interior is written in the form of a recommendation for the change of location of the Pride March ... *it is absolutely unmistakable that the Pride March 2009 has been banned.* Despite the declarations of support given by the highest representatives of the government ... [t]here was no act to support the rhetoric. This decree is a formal admittance of the government ... that they are not able to adequately

prevent and sanction the threats coming from the clero-fascist organizations, nor are they able to ensure the constitutional rights and freedoms of the citizens who publicly announced their legal assembly ... The State failed the fundamental test, the next exam period is approaching fast. *The Republic of Serbia has capitulated*, we have not. (Belgrade Pride 2009 Organising Committee, 2009, emphasis added)

Although it was the first time a (potential) candidate member state banned an LGBT Pride event, and thus a new development for the EU in the enlargement process, it was not the first banned Pride in Europe. Indeed, after the 2004 enlargement some new member states banned LGBT Pride parades (e.g. the 2005 and 2006 Warsaw Pride), which led to the 2007 European Court of Human Rights (ECtHR) ruling that banning LGBT Pride parades violates the European Convention on Human Rights guaranteed right to freedom of assembly[3] and two European Parliament resolutions[4] on homophobia in Europe. Contrary to the EP's previous stance on the matter, the Commission's reaction to the banned 2009 Belgrade Pride was rather mild. To illustrate, the 2009 Progress Report only mentions the banned Pride as an example of where progress was yet to be made; or, put differently, the Pride ban was not seen as an example of Serbia's unwillingness to implement the anti-discrimination law, but rather as a sign of Serbia's slow progress in the protection of the freedom of assembly (European Commission, 2009, p. 15).

As expected, given its previous resolutions, some members of the European Parliament were much more vocal on the Pride ban. Michael Cashman, then President of the EP LGBT Intergroup, claimed: 'by failing to guarantee the right to a peaceful demonstration for LGBT people, Serbia has shown that it is not ready to become a member of the EU' (quoted in Wockner, 2009). But the most condemning voices came from the United States. The US Embassy saw the banned Pride as a failure of the government to pass a litmus test for Serbia's commitment to the values promoted in the newly adopted anti-discrimination law. In a leaked diplomatic cable, Tory Pederson, Chief of Mission, commented:

Despite Serbian officials' game effort to portray their role in the cancellation of the Belgrade Pride Parade as the only rational course of action in face of legitimate threats of violence, the reality is that *this decision again demonstrated the government's lack of leadership in the face of difficult issues. It was not the first time that a government which identifies itself with European values chose to take the easy way out rather than confront a real or imaginary bogeyman.* Instead of taking a decisive and courageous stance in support of freedom, the government limited itself to belated declarations of support and allowed extremist groups to dictate state policy. (Pederson, 2009, emphasis added)

Overall, both domestically and internationally, the government's failure to protect the Pride parade was seen at varying degrees, as a failure of the government to Europeanise Serbia – as a failed litmus test of Serbia's 'Europeanness'.

From 'State Pride' to national threat

Though Serbia was not severely criticised in the immediate aftermath of the ban, the fact that Pride was banned did cause the international community to notice the event as something they would continue to monitor in the future. Indeed, in future years, international pressure to support Pride started to play a more important role. As discussed in detail below, the increased international pressure on Serbia to maintain Belgrade Pride enabled the formation of political alliances that contributed to a 'successful' 2010 'State Pride' (Mikuš, 2011), while shifting priorities, both domestically and internationally, contributed to the three consecutive bans of Pride.

Forging political alliances: towards a state-oriented approach to organising Pride

The process of how the 2010 Belgrade Pride came to be started with a sense of confusion among activists when, in January 2010, the Minister for Human and Minority Rights, Svetozar Čiplić, declared that there would be a Pride event in Belgrade that year (Tanjug, 2010). This declaration raised many eyebrows and questions as, at that time, most of the 2009 organisers were unsure whether they were ready to once again face the stress and death threats associated with organising Pride (Interview SRB2015_52). While some suggest that behind-the-scenes international pressure led to the declaration, we will probably never know what sparked the state to take such a pre-emptive stance. What we can say is that it provided activists with the spark to start preparing the event. Indeed, in the days that followed, two organisations – Gay Straight Alliance (GSA) and Queeria – began preparations for the 2010 Pride (Interview SRB2015_52).

The involvement of GSA in the organisation of Pride brought new aspects to the overall process. Whereas the 2009 Pride organisers perhaps lacked political experience, GSA had plenty. Based on the founders' political knowledge and connections, GSA used its typical state-orientated modus operandi to organise the 2010 Belgrade Pride. One of the first things GSA did was try to forge political alliances to support Pride (Bogdanović, 2012; Interview SRB2015_31). GSA was able to secure political support from most political parties by playing on pro-EU parties' need to prove their commitment to Serbia's European integration and the implementation of the anti-discrimination law. Indeed, with all 'eyes of the international community and the European Union on [the Serbian] government' (Lazar Pavlović quoted in Rettman, 2010), and the Council of the European Union's decision on Serbia's application for EU membership expected in autumn 2010 (Mikuš, 2011), supporting the 2010 Belgrade Pride became an important avenue for the Serbian government and political establishment to showcase Serbia's Europeanness (Interviews SRB2015_9, SRB2015_13, SRB2015_27, SRB2015_31, SRB2015_35). The only parties where this strategy did not work – unsurprisingly, given their nationalistic politics – where the Serbian Radical Party (SRS) and its breakaway party the Serbian Progressive Party (SNS);[5] neither supported Pride nor the promotion of LGBT rights (Bogdanović, 2012).

As such, the 2010 Belgrade Pride became closely intertwined with Serbia's EU accession process from the outset (Interviews SRB2015_6 and SRB2015_31). Whereas the EU had informally been insisting that Serbia should allow Belgrade Pride, this EU pressure became more formalised when Vincent Degert, then head of the EU Delegation to Serbia, signed a petition to support the 2010 Belgrade Pride (Gay Straight Alliance, 2011). The Serbian government, similarly, linked Pride discursively to the EU integration process, by expressing support for Pride by explicitly invoking the EU's values (Gay Straight Alliance, 2011). To illustrate this, Minister of the Interior, Ivica Dačić, proclaimed: 'As a politician who advocates European values and democracy, I support the Pride Parade, and as Minister of the Interior, it is my duty to ensure the safety of its participants' (quoted in Gay Straight Alliance, 2011, p. 38).

With the newly gained political support for the 2010 Belgrade Pride initiative, there was some improvement in the cooperation between organisers and state institutions – especially the community policing department, as 'the police were now *truly* ready to provide protection to participants, and to plan extensive security measures' (Interview SRB2015_41, emphasis added). The intimidation strategies employed by the state institutions in 2009 remained largely absent in 2010, and the police drafted concrete security plans. Mina Božović, an independent activist who was part of both Pride committees, explains:

> [I]n 2010, because the government knew that they would have Pride ... it was much easier. Because before [in 2009] you would have like a dozen of meetings with them [state institutions and the police] and ... you ask 'Ok, is it [Pride] going to happen or not?', and they reply 'Oh we will see, we are waiting for some security reports.' But in 2010 there was a minimum of appointments that the government had with the committee. (Interview SRB2015_12)

To keep the momentum going and maintain pressure on the Serbian state, the GSA employed 'boomerang strategies' by keeping the EU Delegation to Serbia updated about their cooperation with the state. The delegation, in turn (informally) reminded the Serbian government of the importance of a successful, well-protected Belgrade Pride for Serbia's European integration process (Interviews SRB2015_9, SRB2015_23).

Despite GSA's elaborate strategy to 'co-organise' Pride with the state (Interviews SRB2015_13, SRB2015_19, SRB2015_20), a reason why the 2010 Pride is now referred to as the 'State Pride' (Mikuš, 2011), government officials never actually met with the organisers. The only tangible cooperation was between organisers and the police, with the latter playing a mediator role between the state, organisers and even opponents (Mikuš, 2011).

One would be mistaken, however, to read the changed political landscape and the increased rhetorical support for Pride as a signal of any real commitment by the state to allow Pride to happen. Indeed, the various forms of behind-the-scenes state resistance remained. Most notably, as the police seemingly sought to avoid a clash with the ethnonationalist and extremist civil society organisations, they did not take any actions aimed at preventing anti-Pride violence. For example, despite claiming that they were monitoring different online forums and social media to gauge the security risks for Belgrade Pride, any gathered intelligence was not actioned on. The police actively ignored the online brainstorming sessions in which nationalist groups were discussing how they could hide any type of weapon (short of guns) throughout the city to attack Pride participants once they made it through the security perimeter (Interview SRB2015_54). The most poignant example of the lack of proactive police action happened on the morning of the Pride. When walking her dog early that morning, Mina Božović noticed how Mladen Obradović, the leader of Obraz, was instructing several people on how to attack Pride (Interview SRB2015_12). Despite the fact that this happened right next to a group of police officers, nothing was done to prevent the attack from happening.

On a societal level, the 2010 Pride was again organised in a very hostile environment. Following the fact that both organisers and the state rhetorically linked Pride to the EU integration process, the opposition framed Pride as a Western (anti-Serbian) perversion (Mikuš, 2011). As Nielsen (2013a, p. 1043) argues, a significant 'part of the strategy of the opponents of the parade was to identify the opposition to the parade as a "patriotic act" and hence as linked to support for the Serbian stance on Kosovo, opposition to NATO and the EU'. The SPC further legitimised such discourses by branding Belgrade Pride a Western imposition of an issue that went against the moral fabric of Serbian society (Pavasović Trošt and Slootmaeckers, 2015). For example, on the eve of the 2010 Pride, Metropolitan Amfilohije Radović condemned it as 'violent propaganda', and the Holy Synod of Bishops described Pride as a threat to public morality (Mikuš, 2015, p. 23).

These tactics and rhetoric, in many ways, represent a continuation of those developed in 2009 – e.g. another Family Walk was organised one day before Pride (Mikuš, 2011) – with one significant difference. Unlike in 2009, where threats to the Pride were almost always explicitly linked to right-wing organisations, no such links were made explicit in 2010. Indeed, although the city of Belgrade was once again covered in posters and graffiti containing slogans like: 'Death to faggots', 'Faggots, we are waiting for you', 'Blood will pour on the streets / There won't be a gay parade' and 'Kill, slaughter, so there are no faggots' (Mikuš, 2015; Pavasović Trošt and Kovacevic, 2013), these remained mainly anonymous. In fact, following ongoing court cases against these organisations for inciting violence (see Nielsen, 2013a), all opposing (extremist) parties explicitly refrained from publicly inciting violence against Pride. In insider settings and online forums, on the other hand, extremist organisations were actively planning their (violent) response to the 2010 Belgrade Pride (Mikuš, 2015; Interview SRB2015_54).

On the eve of the 2010 Pride, the Minister of the Interior, Ivica Dačić, in a feeble attempt to prevent violence, tried to appeal to Pride opponents that it was 'very important for Serbia that such a gathering, which may not be to the liking of the majority of Serbia's citizens, goes without incidents', and that is in the interest of the entire state and police that 'they [Pride opponents] do not use violence against those who organise something based on their constitutional and legal rights' (quoted in Fonet et al., 2010). However, as I recount below, these appeals were unheard/ignored.

Belgrade is burning: the 2010 'State Pride' and anti-gay riots

On the morning of 10 October 2010, everything was set for Belgrade Pride. The area surrounding the Pride venue was hermetically sealed, and Belgrade resembled nothing less than a militarised zone (Interview SRB2015_41). In what can only be described as an extremely tense atmosphere (Mikuš, 2011), Pride participants made their way to Manjež Park to take part in the first Belgrade Pride in almost a decade.

The programme of the day started with a series of speeches, mostly by international representatives. For example, the Head of the EU Delegation to Serbia opened the event and stressed in his remarks that Pride was an important event and an indicator of society's rejection of violence, and that this day had been awaited for years (cited in Harley, 2010). These words were heard by a crowd of over a thousand, consisting mostly of international guests, the Minister for Human and Minority Rights, NGO sector professionals and some local LGBT people and their supporters. The international configuration of Belgrade Pride strengthened the already present link between the Pride parade and Serbia's European future. Indeed, Marek Mikuš (2011, p. 836), who participated in the event, described the Pride as a rather globalised European phenomenon:

> In their rather predictable and formal speeches in English, the foreign guest repeatedly referred to the EU, whose flag could be seen in the crowd, along with rainbow flags, a purple Union Jack, but no Serbian flag. Surrounded by the globalised iconography of the LGBT movement and cheesy Western pop, I could not help feeling that almost the only local thing about the Parade were the militarised, violent conditions under which it was happening. If the speakers mentioned Serbia, they mostly denoted it negatively, as a site of deviation from the European norms of respect for human rights that the Parade begins to rectify.

Meanwhile in the neighbouring street, just outside the security perimeter, hooligans from otherwise opposing football clubs and the rather fragmented 'patriotic bloc' combined forces to break through the police cordon to attack Pride, calling 'on the police to "go to Kosovo" rather than "babysit the faggots"', and chanting homophobic slurs like 'we will fuck the faggots' (Mikuš, 2011, p. 844). Unable to reach Pride participants, the 6,000 to 8,000 hooligans eventually clashed with the police in what the head of the community policing department called a coordinated and pre-planned riot: many rioters had come to Belgrade from the countryside, and attacks constantly moved from one part of the city to another – in an attempt to weaken the Pride defences – reportedly orchestrated and coordinated by individuals on scooters (Interview SRB2015_41). The violence lasted several hours, targeting those institutions typically perceived as pro-government and/or pro-EU, leading to damages to the city estimated to exceed one million euros and a total of 140 injured people – mostly police officers (Stojanović, 2010b).

The premeditated character of the riots and the lack of preventive measures perfectly illustrates the state's Janus-faced attitude towards the 2010 Pride, and their engagement with the event as a form of partial compliance. Although the authorities had demonstrated a commitment to make Pride happen, the same could be said for the riots (Nielsen, 2013a). For example, security expert Zoran Dragišić argued that because 'police did not want to get on bad terms with either the EU or the right-wing extremists', they allowed both Pride and the riots to happen (quoted in Ejdus and Božović, 2019, p. 501).

The double-faced character of the state's support for Pride was further highlighted by politicians' immediate reactions to Pride and the accompanying riots. Whereas before the event, politicians, at least rhetorically, supported

Pride, they were quick to distance themselves from it after the riots. Relying on the previously established link between Pride and EU integration, the government externalised the responsibility for Pride and the associated violence (Mikuš, 2011). For example, Minister of the Interior, Ivica Dačić, while praising the police for their work and promising punishment for the rioters, blamed the EU for forcing Belgrade Pride upon Serbia, thereby causing the riots (Nielsen, 2013a). In what could be considered the beginning of a new identity divergence process, he argued he was not the one who had decided whether Pride would happen, but that it was decided on 5 October 2000, when Serbian citizens decided to join the EU and to adopt European values (cited in Mikuš, 2011, p. 835). Dačić further added that the EU had been 'attacking him for a year because the previous [2009] Pride was cancelled' (in seebiz.eu, 2010). More explicitly, on a different occasion, Dačić publicly admitted he was against the parade in downtown Belgrade, but that he allowed it because the EU had set it as a condition for Serbia's integration: 'It was not a written condition, but they [the EU] did ask us to do it – Yes' (quoted in Kovačević and Jelovac, 2010, translated by interpreter). Similarly, the mayor of Belgrade publicly blamed the Pride organisers for provoking violence (Gould and Moe, 2015). Serbian Orthodox Church officials added further voice to these sentiments. For example, in a public statement on the events of 10 October 2010, Metropolitan Amfilohije Radović argued that the rioters only reacted to a more severe form of violence that was generated by the public manifestation of homosexuality in the streets of Belgrade (quoted in Stakić, 2011, p. 56).

Contrary to the domestic 'blaming the victim' discourses, international observers focused on the 'successfulness' of Pride. Rob Miller (2010), a journalist for the *Guardian*, declared that, despite its 'imperfections', the 2010 Pride could be considered a success compared to the 2001 Pride. Similarly, dignitaries from the Dutch and American embassies reportedly commended the 'Serbian government's support for the parade as a positive example of its embrace of Western, liberal values' (cited in Kirchick, 2010).

The EP rapporteur for Serbia, Jelko Kacin, voiced a more cynical view when he publicly declaring that the violence, as well as the lack of government initiatives to prevent it, had sent the wrong signal to Europe that could potentially hurt Serbia's bid to join the EU (Stojanović, 2010a). Yet his concerns were not shared by the other EU institutions. The EU Delegation to Serbia, for example, viewed the Pride as a success as the state managed to protect the participants from attackers – a real breakthrough in Serbia's respect for the rule of law and human rights (Interview SRB2015_23). Similarly, the European Commission did not question the lack of preventive measures. The 2010 Progress Report reads:

The Belgrade Pride parade took place in October 2010 thus representing a step forward in promoting constitutionally guaranteed fundamental rights. However, violent clashes occurred between the police and rioters protesting against the Parade ... *The response of the police was adequate and a large number of the perpetrators were arrested.* (European Commission, 2010, pp. 13–14, emphasis added)

Two months after the 2010 Belgrade Pride, the Council of the European Union decided to forward Serbia's membership application to the Commission as a reward for Serbia's compliance with EU conditionality, including maintaining Belgrade Pride (Ejdus and Božović, 2019). Thus, sending a message to Serbian politicians that securing Pride, regardless of the conditions in which it takes place, helped to improve Serbia's position in the European integration process.

Security threats and consecutive Pride bans (2011–13)

The violence associated with 2010 hugely impacted the organisation of Belgrade Pride in the years to come, not only by dividing activists' opinions on the desirability of Pride but also by intensifying the securitisation process, which led to three consecutive bans of Pride. Concluding that the 2010 Pride organisation had resulted in disaster – not only because of the riots and empty state promises, but also due to (mostly financial) disputes within the organisational committee – activists from Queeria decided to register a new organisation, Parada Ponosa – Beograd [Pride Parade – Belgrade], which would solely deal with the organisation of (future) Belgrade Prides (Interview SRB2015_52). Although intended to centralise and professionalise the organisation of Belgrade Pride, the move (unintentionally) alienated parts of the LGBT activist community and resulted in GSA withdrawing from organising the event.

With the loss of GSA as a partner, the organising committee lost its strong political connections. Though a gamechanger, the fallout of losing GSA's political network was, nevertheless, mediated by the involvement of other more mainstream human rights organisations – in particular, Civil Rights Defenders and the Youth Initiative for Human Rights (YiHR) – which brought their organisational and administrative capacity into the Pride committee. With this, Belgrade Pride started to professionalise and develop organisational memory.

That being said, the 2011 Pride organisation committee faced similar obstacles to those experienced in previous years. First, although the police did not openly oppose the Pride initiative, the cooperation between the Ministry of the Interior was once again marred by different forms of 'technical obstructions' (Interviews SRB2014_2, SRB2015_2, SRB2015_12, SRB2015_17,

SRB2015_52). Organisers again struggled to obtain the necessary permits, facing disproportionate barriers. For example, whereas other public gatherings only have to submit a minimal amount of paperwork to register (i.e. one or two documents), the Pride organisers reported that they need a folder of 'various studies, assessments and communal licenses that are rarely (if ever) demanded from any other public event' (Ejdus and Božović, 2019, p. 502; Interviews SRB2014_2, SRB2015_2). Indeed, a key Pride organiser explained that they had the impression that the police treated them as one part of a dichotomy of two opposing extremes that were provoking one another (Interview SRB2015_17). To illustrate, Pride organisers were constantly asked to reschedule in order to prevent a clash with a religious holiday or an important football match to avoid that Pride would 'provoke' violence; yet opponents were allowed to register their counter-demonstrations as soon as Pride was officially announced (Interviews SRB2015_43; SRB2015_46).

Second, the political obstacles also persisted. Perhaps unsurprisingly given the political disengagement with Pride after the 2010 anti-gay riots, the 2011 Pride could not gain substantial political support. With both presidential and parliamentary elections planned for early 2012, politicians were reluctant to declare any support for Pride publicly. Considering that the DS-led government had been battling against a strong nationalist opposition in the previous years, it could be said that the government seemed 'not brave enough' (Interview SRB2015_57) to support the unpopular Pride (Interview SRB2015_50). This was certainly the case when nationalist tensions further flared up following the deterioration of Serbia–Kosovo relations over the summer of 2011 (Interviews SRB2015_5, SRB2015_6, SRB2015_11). The impact of the Kosovo crisis on the fate of Pride – and the issue-linkage between the two – is best illustrated by statements of Ivica Dačić, then Minister of the Interior, who declared that '[i]n the situation where aggression in northern Kosovo can begin at any moment ... the gay Pride [is] the last thing we need' (quoted in Stojanović, 2011).

To add to the already volatile political climate surrounding Belgrade Pride, politicians also continued to insinuate that (the 'EU-imposed') Pride – and not extremist groups – threatened Serbia's national security (Ejdus and Božović, 2019; Nielsen, 2013a). Indeed, Dačić at one point suggested that if the EU wants Pride to happen in Serbia, they should provide the necessary police force and equipment to ensure police officers would not fall victim to the violence that is provoked by such an event (cited in Nielsen, 2013a, p. 1046). Similarly, the mayor of Belgrade, Dragan Đilas (DS), stated he would never support an event that endangers the safety of Belgrade (cited in Gligorijević, 2011), and that if he had the power to ban Pride, he would do so (B92, 2011a).

Amid this political context, the state banned the 2011 Belgrade Pride two days before it was due to take place, along with all other demonstrations planned for that weekend (Interview SRB2015_41). Despite the fact that 'security risks' were cited as the official reason for the ban, the underpinning security assessment was nothing more than a list of planned counter-demonstrations (Interviews SRB2014_3, SRB2015_42). The absence of a thorough security assessment leaves many to conclude that the ban was politically motivated (Interviews SRB2014_3, SRB2014_7, SRB2015_2, SRB2015_10, SRB2015_11, SRB2015_12, SRB2015_17, SRB2015_20, SRB2015_50, SRB2015_53). For example, discussing the ban on a talk show, the head of the Journalists' Association of Serbia concluded: 'this year [in contrast to 2010] the authorities decided [with an eye on the upcoming elections] it was more profitable to let the US Embassy and Brussels [EU] get angry, but to avoid irritating that majority [which opposes Pride]' (quoted in B92, 2011c). In fact, the head of the community policing department all but confirmed this interpretation in an interview. Although refusing to explicitly comment on the political character of the Pride bans, he strongly implied that the decision to ban Pride had been subject to political pressure:

> [The Pride ban] is a complex matter, and I would not go into the political aspects of that decision … [T]he days before the Pride ban were really intense. You cannot believe how dynamic the public discussions were, the pressures, the statements, the press, [and] political influences of course … That much I can say … However, you must bear in mind that in contemporary society all these questions [Kosovo, ICTY, EU integration and Pride] are almost inseparable … And that many questions [e.g. Kosovo] remain without a solution. And when several of those questions [Kosovo and Pride] are brought into the spotlight together it produces even greater tensions. (Interview SRB2015_41, author's interpretation in square brackets are based on earlier statements of the interviewee during the interview)

In order to reduce the fallout of the ban, and in an attempt to deflect public attention from any potential state weakness, the government framed it as a twofold victory for the state. First, as President Tadić claimed, by banning Pride the state demonstrated its *ability* to protect LGBT and Serbian citizens (quoted in BBC News, 2011). Second, Dačić claimed the Pride ban signalled that Serbia is able to withstand undue EU pressure:

> Unfortunately, we have become too submissive to pressure [referring to EU pressure on Kosovo], so now they [the EU] think that they can blackmail us for everything that occurs to them. Everyone needs to understand that parades and various prayer marches are an internal problem of Serbia … I am the Minister of Internal Affairs, not the Commissioner for Internal Affairs of the

EU. Probably, I know better than them what are the security risks for my state. (Dačić quoted in Nielsen, 2013a, p. 1046)

Despite the newly announced 'fundamentals first' approach (see Chapter 2), the EU remained remarkably silent on the issue. Contrary to the EP, which protested the ban by questioning Serbia's readiness to become an EU member (Intergroup on LGBT Rights, 2011), the Commission did not engage with the Pride ban. For example, the EC's opinion on Serbia's EU candidacy application, published only weeks after the ban, did not mention Pride at all, and contrary to MEPs' questioning of Serbia's 'Europeanness', the Commission's overall opinion was positive and Serbia was granted EU candidacy status, conditional on the normalisation of Serbia–Kosovo relations (see also Kostovicova, 2014). Thus, whereas in the previous year holding Pride seemingly helped Serbia to improve its position in the European integration process, banning Pride in 2011 did not damage that position. Indeed, the absence of comments on the Pride ban in the EC's opinion is the beginning of the EU's inconsistent approach to LBGT rights, and fundamental rights more broadly, within Serbia's EU accession process.

As I will elaborate on below, whereas the 'new approach' to EU enlargement has put fundamental rights at the foreground of the accession process (Slootmaeckers and Touquet, 2016; see also Chapter 2), the Kosovo issue has pushed it to the background on many occasions. As a European Commission official commented:

> Personally – and this is not the Commission's position – I think we [the Commission] are being soft on Serbia on some issues [including Pride] because we want them to further cooperate. We want things to go well with Kosovo … It is always a political game … so I think we are being soft on Serbia in the technical aspects because of this whole overarching political issue that is the relationship with Kosovo. (Interview EC2014_1)

Just as the anticipation of elections prevented the 2011 Pride from happening, the 2012 elections themselves played a crucial role in the organisational process of the 2012 Pride. While the change in government created some logistical challenges (Interview SRB2015_6), the biggest impact of the election related to its outcome. The surprise victory of Tomislav Nikolić and his Serbian Progressive Party (SNS) in the presidential and parliamentary elections caused a significant power reshuffle in the Serbian political landscape (Obradović-Wochnik and Wochnik, 2014), which in turn had profound implications for the organisation of Pride, for several reasons.

At the international level, the European Union and western diplomats were – to put it mildly – nervous about the election outcome and the newly formed coalition government led by Ivica Dačić (SPS) as PM and Aleksandar Vučić (SNS) as deputy PM (Pond, 2013). Wary of the nationalist and authoritarian background of both SPS and SNS, many EU officials treated the new government suspiciously, increasing pressure on the government to demonstrate – if not prove – their recent pro-EU transformation (Bieber, 2015). With Serbia's accession negotiations being conditional on the normalisation of its relationship with Kosovo and a substantial reduction in anti-EU and nationalist parliamentary opposition, the government saw an opportunity in the ongoing Serbia–Kosovo dialogue to convince the EU of their newfound pro-Europeanness (Bieber, 2015). As such, a hierarchy of tasks emerged where the Serbia–Kosovo dialogue came to dominate EU–Serbia relations, pushing fundamental rights issues again to the background.

Whereas the pro-European transformation (or adaptation, see Vachudova, 2008, 2014) was noticeable in the parties' softened stance on the 'Kosovo issue' (Economides and Ker-Lindsay, 2015), the nationalist background of both continued to inform the political opposition to Pride. For example, in line with his previous comments on the 2011 Pride, Prime Minister and Minister of the Interior Ivica Dačić explicitly rejected EU pressure for holding Belgrade Pride – and thus also the Europeanisation discourse used by activists behind the scenes (interview SRB2015_2):

> Spare me already the stories about human rights. What human rights? It's about the safety of the people! There are countries where there are no gay parades, and they are still members of the EU. Is it possible that this is still the main topic, that we are still dealing with the gay parade as a major problem, as the ticket to the EU, which is ridiculous. (Dačić quoted in Todorović, 2013, p. 23)

With its attention diverted to the Serbia–Kosovo dialogue, the EU did not seem to take issue with such statements. In fact, MEP Jelko Kacin, EP rapporteur for Serbia, implicitly endorsed this view by publicly stating that the 'Pride Parade is not a condition for getting a date [for the beginning of the EU accession talks]. It is not', adding that having Pride, nevertheless, would help Serbia on its path to the EU (quoted in B92, 2012a, added text in original). Such messaging from the EU further reinforced the notion that successful Prides might help Serbia, but banned Prides would not hinder the accession process.

Faced with a political climate marked by strong opposition to Pride, ambiguous messages from the EU, and the need to consolidate the recent electoral victory, as well as the first meeting between Dačić and Kosovo's PM, Hashim Thaçi, only weeks away, the government decided to ban Pride two days before the scheduled event, once again for security reasons.

While Pride organisers considered the ban another capitulation by the state to extreme right groups, PM Dačić again defended the ban as another victory for the state:

It is very important for the credibility of Serbia to show the strength of the state. And this does not amount to any kind of capitulation before some who think they can use their paramilitary or any other threats to endanger the holding of public gatherings – it means that it has been assessed that, at this time, serious violations of public peace and order could occur, which would seriously jeopardise interests of the citizens and the state as a whole. (Dačić quoted in B92, 2012b)

Although most international observers and the European Parliament's LGBT Intergroup strongly condemned the second consecutive ban of Belgrade Pride (see e.g. Council of Europe, 2012; Intergroup on LGBT Rights, 2012), the reaction from the European Commission remained noticeably soft. In an official statement, the Commissioner for Enlargement, Stefan Füle, aligned himself with the Serbian government's analysis that security risks posed by extremists' threats were the main reason why Pride could not go ahead, not the lack of political support. He 'strongly condemn[ed] the intimidation and threats from extremist organisations in Serbia directed against the organisers of the Parade and regret[ted] that those threats have been assessed serious enough to justify a ban on security grounds' (Füle, 2012). By making such statements, Füle de facto absolved the state from any wrongdoing in terms of its position on LGBTI rights – as if the reason Pride could not go ahead had nothing to do with sexuality and sexual politics. One of the potential reasons why the Pride ban could be presented in such way – instead of condemning Serbia for reinforcing homophobia – is that the Serbian government was working on new hate crime legislation (see Chapter 3), which explicitly referred to sexual orientation.

Although the question of whether the EU wilfully ignored the homophobic politics underpinning a Pride ban is a matter for speculation and circumstantial evidence, what is certain is that the EU had set clear priorities within Serbia's accession process where regional stability was more important than the protection and safeguarding of fundamental rights and values. To illustrate, when Füle visited Belgrade a week later, he did not discuss Pride with the Serbian authorities. Füle's spokesperson explained this by simply indicating that there were more important issues to be discussed (cited in Korica, 2012) – i.e. the Serbia–Kosovo dialogue. In other words, despite the EU's rhetoric that LGBT rights are at the heart of so-called European values, when confronted with geopolitical issues, the EU swiftly prioritises the latter.

The hierarchy of tasks expected from Serbia became even clearer when the EU's rhetoric on Pride parades changed after a landmark deal between Serbia and Kosovo was reached. The EU-brokered Brussels Agreement resembled (at least for the EU) a pacification of the tensions between both entities (Interviews EC2014_1, EC2015_1). With the risk of regional instability significantly reduced, the EU was able to refocus its attention on fundamental values, and thus LGBT rights (Interview EC2014_1). Although the EU had informally been suggesting to Serbian state authorities that they should allow Pride in previous years (Interview SRB2015_9), the EU took a more resolute stance in 2013. For example, in May 2013, the European Commission, for the first time in a formal bilateral format, publicly requested that the Serbian government would show 'determination and under[take] activities that would make the Pride Parade possible' (Ejdus and Božović, 2019, p. 503).

With this change in political pressure, as well as the improving relationships between LGBT activists and the community policing department (Interview SRB2015_17), everything started pointing towards an increased likelihood that Belgrade Pride would take place in 2013 – especially considering that, in the early summer of 2013, Serbia was sending favourable signals about Pride. Consider, for example, how, in June 2013, the Serbian government and President Nikolić assured the visiting United Nations High Commissioner for Human Rights, Navi Pillay, that Belgrade Pride would happen that autumn (UN News Service, 2013). Similarly, activists, at the time, were informed that the initial security assessment of Pride was positive (Interview SRB2015_17) and had much more productive interactions with the police.

However, in the weeks leading up to the 2013 Belgrade Pride, whatever political support there had been for it started to rapidly deteriorate. To illustrate, PM Ivica Dačić, commented on Pride during a televised interview: 'I am in favour of everybody's constitutional right to express their diversity, but it is my right not to go there ... What am I supposed to do now, become gay, so that everything's pro-European' (quoted in B92, 2013). In what can be interpreted as an attempt to soften the impact of this statement, Dačić added that holding Pride would be 'good for Serbia because the European Union asked for it, [but it would be] a great pity if the violence that happened during the parade held in 2010 were to repeat' (quoted in B92, 2013). With these remarks, Dačić aligned himself with the nationalist discourse that Pride was a foreign (by the EU) imposed event; one that did not resonate with Serbian values. From that point onwards, political rhetoric deteriorated, to the point that days before the scheduled Pride, Dačić's opposition entered the domain of hate speech,[6] when he proclaimed that 'homosexuals have the same rights as other citizens *but don't tell me it is normal when it is not* ... If that exists in the EU countries, it doesn't mean that we have to support it' (in Ejdus and Božović, 2019, p. 505, emphasis added).

To fully understand the sudden loss of support for Pride and the discursive shift, one has to consider the political tensions and power struggles within the government. Although Dačić became Prime Minister after the 2012 elections, it was Aleksandar Vučić, First Deputy Prime Minister, who had taken over the reins as leader of the government in all but name (Fagan and Sircar, 2015). Dačić's comments thus represent a pragmatic and calculated move in which he aligned himself with the real power distribution within the government, presenting himself as a neutral figure, both for and against Pride (Interview SRB2015_6, see also Nielsen, 2013b). Although reportedly pragmatically favouring holding Pride, Dačić was waiting for Aleksandar Vučić to decide (Ejdus and Božović, 2019; Nielsen, 2013b). Indeed, the day before Pride, Vučić took control: the Bureau for the Coordination of Security Services, over which Vučić presides, met to discuss the security situation of Pride and to decide whether the 2013 Belgrade Pride would go ahead. Despite the fact that such a decision is not within its competences (Ejdus and Božović, 2019), the Bureau issued, less than 15 hours before Pride was scheduled, a ban of all public gatherings on Saturday 28 September, again citing security reasons.

Again, the security assessment was minimal – nothing more than a four-page document simply listing (irrelevant) Facebook threats and implausible suggestions, including 'uncovered' plans to attack Pride using jars of wasps and acid (Marjanović, 2013). The absence of any credible risk assessment leads to the conclusion that the decision to ban Pride was again politically motivated (Interviews SRB2014_2, SRB2014_3, SRB2015_10, SRB2015_41, SRB2015_57). With the domestically difficult-to-sell Brussels Agreement signed in April earlier that year, and with internal tensions within the government – and thus early elections becoming extremely likely – supporting Pride was simply not in the government's interests (Interviews SRB2014_2, SRB2015_6, SRB2015_54, SRB2015_57). For example, Boris Milićević, an activist who joined the SPS party board, explained Dačić's homophobic comments as follows:

> Dačić is the sort of politician who always sends clear political messages. He is the politician when he chooses the direction, he is sending a strong and clear message. So, it was obvious in 2013, when you have to basically make an agreement [the Brussels Agreement] with Thaçi [Kosovo's PM], who is one of the most hated people in Serbia, amongst Serbs, it was obvious that you cannot have a Pride, so he will send a clear message that you cannot have a Pride. So, he did that. (Interview SRB2015_6)

Contrary to Milićević, who saw Dačić's statements as a reflection of the current political climate, the Pride organisers considered the statements a political rhetorical move to please his supporters while still allowing Pride to happen (Interview SRB2015_57). They came to this conclusion because the evening prior to Pride (and its ban) the streets of Belgrade were patrolled by thousands of police officers (all in riot gear), and the Pride venue (Manjež Park) was completely sealed off to the public (Interviews SRB2014_2, SRB2015_12). As these measures had not been taken in previous years, activists did not expect the Bureau for the Coordination of Security Services to ban Pride. Neither did the police, as Pride organiser Marko Ilić recalls:

> Last year [in 2013] there was so much police gathering and surrounding ... Manjež Park, and there was so much police in the city that it was clear that they are capable of holding Pride. I was in Manjež [Park], and I was surrounded by 2,500 policemen [and] I even got reassurance from police officers who were there at the time. They said: 'Yes, we even have lunch packages, the Pride will definitely happen.' (Interview SRB2014_2)

Taken by surprise and frustrated by another Pride ban, activists took to the street in protest – now commonly known as the 'Midnight Pride' – to show Pride was here to stay. Under the banner 'Ovo je Prajd' [This is Pride], an estimated 250 people gathered at the government building and walked to the square in front of the Serbian parliament, several hundred metres ahead (Balkanist, 2013). This protest march was immediately protected by the police forces already present in the city and happened without any incidents.[7]

While international observers' reaction to the ban was very similar to previous years, a noticeable shift in the EU Commission's reaction on the ban occurred. For the first time, the 2013 Progress Report was much more direct and critical in its analysis of the Pride ban:

> [A] Pride parade that was to be held on 28 September in Belgrade was again banned, for the third year in a row, on security grounds. *This raises a number of concerns regarding the lack of sufficient political support for the protection of the rights of LGBTI population*, the lack of implementation of the constitutionally guaranteed rights of freedom of expression and assembly as well as the authorities' capacity to handle threats from radical groups. (European Commission, 2013b, pp. 45–46, emphasis added)

Whereas this explicit reference to the lack of political will might reflect a more coordinated approach to LGBT rights in the accession process (Interview EC2014_1, see also Chapter 2), the EU did not follow through on recent explicit prioritisation of LGBT rights within the fundamental rights conditionality with concrete actions. Indeed, whereas back in June 2013 the EU decided to open the EU accession negotiations with Serbia, but withheld a starting date, in December 2013 the EU rewarded Serbia for its progress in reforming and efforts in improving its relations with Kosovo by setting a date for the start of the negotiations (Deutsche Welle, 2013). Once again, Serbia got away with 'things [a third Pride ban] because [Serbia's] conditionality has been linked to Kosovo and not to the Copenhagen criteria' (MEP Marije Cornelissen quoted in Ejdus and Božović, 2019, p. 505, also interviews EC2014_1, EC2015_1, SRB2015_9, SRB2015_26).

Pride as tactical Europeanisation

The Serbian state's handling and framing of their decision to ban the 2013 Pride was twofold. On the one hand, the Pride ban was, like in previous years, framed as a victory for the state as it prevented new riots (InSerbia, 2013a). On the other hand, state officials announced the next year's Pride parade. More specifically, President Nikolić (SNS) declared: 'We [Serbia] should begin preparations for the next year's parade today' (quoted in Balkan Insight, 2013). This (sudden) support for Pride was not the result of a change of heart, but rather due to a fear that a future Pride ban would negatively impact Serbia's EU accession process. Implicitly blaming the Pride organisers for the ban, the President argued that due to the lack of involvement of all relevant stakeholders in the organisation of Pride, 'We now have a situation where a less significant event [the banning of the Pride march] may jeopardise [Serbia's] European trip' (quoted in Balkan Insight, 2013). In what some might perceive as a response to the President's call, but really was just a continuation of the Midnight Pride protest, activists announced that next year's Pride was planned for 31 May 2014 (InSerbia, 2013b).

Contrary to previous years, the 2014 Pride received much more political support. With the EU explicitly criticising the lack of political will to maintain Pride, and Serbia on the verge of opening the accession negotiations, the Serbian government had come to realise that maintaining Belgrade Pride in 2014 would be considered an important litmus test for Serbia's readiness for opening chapters (Interviews SRB2014_2, SRB2015_9, SRB2015_36, SRB2015_59), especially chapter 23 on fundamental rights, which would be a cornerstone of the process (Interviews EC2014_1, EC2015_1). Against this background, Pride organisations faced significantly fewer obstacles in their communication and cooperation with the state (Interview SRB2014_2), with activists gaining easy access to the government and relevant ministries, especially after the 2014 snap elections (Interviews SRB2014_2, SRB2015_2, SRB2015_17, SRB2015_52).

The March 2014 election resulted in a landslide victory for the SNS. The Progressive Party of Serbia received 48 per cent of the popular vote and gained an absolute majority in the parliament (Sky News, 2014). The new coalition government was led by Aleksandar Vučić (SNS) as PM and Ivica Dačić (SPS) as First Deputy PM and Minister of Foreign Affairs. Two more government reshuffles are worth mentioning: Nebojša Stefanović (SNS) who replaced Dačić as Minister of the Interior and Jadranka Joksimović (SNS), who was appointed as Minister without Portfolio in Charge of European Integration (hereafter Minister of European Integration).

This reconfiguration of the political landscape had an important impact on the organisation of Belgrade Pride. First, now that internal tensions within the government were put aside as Vučić had become the centre of power, the government no longer needed to worry about any upcoming elections, thereby reducing the political costs of allowing Pride to happen. Second, as the SNS won the elections on a strong pro-EU platform and EU negotiations had officially begun, it had become politically dangerous for Vučić to do anything that would jeopardise Serbia's relations with the EU. In fact, banning any future Pride became an unnecessary risk to Serbia's progress in the EU accession process for two reasons: 1) the EU had officially made LGBT rights a priority in its monitoring of chapter 23 on fundamental rights (see Chapter 2; see also Slootmaeckers, 2020; Slootmaeckers and Touquet, 2016), and 2) the Commission now considered Pride parades to represent a litmus test of Serbia's progress in fundamental rights and the rule of law (Interviews EC2013_3, EC2014_1, EC2015_1). Indeed, as two junior diplomats of the Ministry of Foreign Affairs explained in an interview, the EU had informally made clear that securing Pride was now seen as a condition for Serbia's advancement in the European integration process (Interview SRB2015_9). In other words, from 2014 onwards, Belgrade Pride had become politicised in the international arena as an important (homonationalist) symbol of Europeanness. Consequently, the diplomats continued to claim that the 'EU had forced Serbia's hand to have Pride' thereby disregarding the strong opinion in government that the political reality was not opportune to have Pride (Interview SRB2015_9).

Realising that '[Pride] was important for [Serbia's] EU accession process' (Interview SRB2015_59), the newly appointed Minister of European Integration, Jadranka Joksimović, became a vocal advocate of Belgrade Pride. Leaving no stone unturned, she decided 'to lend her full support to the organisation of Belgrade Pride 2014 to show that fundamental human rights are universally respected in Serbia' (Interview SRB2015_59), and became the focal point in activist-government relations. By doing so, she engaged herself to 'resolve the current stalemate' surrounding Pride, especially to put an end to the previous 'government's unwillingness' to deal with the security issues of Pride (Interview SRB2015_59). The officials from the Foreign Ministry commented on this appointment as a symbolic statement in which Serbia demonstrated its commitment to EU accession by dealing with LGBT issues (Interview SRB2015_9).

With this new supportive political climate, everything was set for Pride to happen in May 2014. However, when floods hit Serbia in May, activists decided to postpone it (InSerbia, 2014a), and to invest their time and resources in organising humanitarian actions (Interview SRB12014_2). As such, Pride was rescheduled for 28 September 2014, with preparations to continue in close cooperation with the state.

Two weeks before the rescheduled Pride, questions about the security of LGBT people and Pride participants resurfaced as a German LGBT activist, who was in Belgrade to attend an LGBT activist conference, was brutally attacked (Deutsche Welle, 2014). Although the conference was unrelated to Pride, the attack inspired European officials to speak out in favour of the upcoming Pride parade. For example, the German Federal Government Commissioner for Human Rights Policy, Christoph Straesser, told Prime Minister Vučić that a safe and successful Pride would have tremendous significance for Serbia (Ristić, 2014b). Vučić responded to these appeals by stressing that the state would do everything to ensure the protection of human rights. He said in an interview: 'We take every remark very seriously, but we also showed that the state is seriously opposing and fighting against xenophobia and homophobia. You will be able to see in the forthcoming weeks how successful we are on the issue' (quoted in Petrović, 2014, translated by interpreter).

The ambiguity of this statement on whether Pride would happen is curious given that the government had already decided that Pride would be allowed to take place. Indeed, a key Pride organiser, with a good political network, explained that, already several weeks before Pride was scheduled, he was informed by people close to PM Vučić that he did not need to worry: the government had decided that Pride would happen as another military parade was being organised as part of Putin's visit to Serbia to appease nationalist forces (Interview SRB2015_17).

Despite this early informal decision to allow Pride to go ahead, political statements remained ambiguous and vague, therefore leaving the possibility of a Pride ban wide open (Rosić Ilić, 2015). Instrumentalising this uncertainty about the fate of Pride, Vučić organised a press conference two days before Pride was scheduled. In a clever use of words, he managed to argue in favour of holding Pride, without alienating nationalist opposition to it:

> I respect the constitutional obligations of the state and it is my obligation to guarantee safety and security to all citizens. It is my democratic right to choose not to take part in the Pride Parade and I do not have the slightest intention of attending it ... I cannot take a leisurely walk on Sunday, I have other business than walking, and I would not attend the Parade even if I had nothing better to do. That is my choice. It is my choice to decide whether to go out with my children on Sunday or pay a working visit to Tekija. This is my choice. (quoted in B92, 2014b)

The statement is quite informative as to how Pride became a tool of tactical Europeanisation, differently instrumentalised for the international and domestic arena. Whereas Ivica Dačić in the previous years linked Pride to the EU, Vučić did not explicitly externalise the responsibility for Pride. On the contrary, Vučić framed it in such a way that a successful Pride would be regarded as his victory. For Vučić, the 2014 Pride was an opportunity to bolster his (inter)national image as a pro-EU force, able to reform the country, while at the same time reconfirming (his support for) traditional Serbian values in two ways: first, by making it clear he would never attend a Pride event, and more so by stressing that he did not care for the politics behind Pride, he reconfirmed his dismay for the event; second, by stating that he would rather spend the day with his family – would he not have had more important things to do? – Vučić reaffirmed his support for Serbian 'traditional values' (Rosić Ilić, 2015). To top it all off, by highlighting the security feature of Pride and – more importantly – his capacity to respect Serbia's constitution, Vučić was further able to strengthen his electoral popularity, which is strongly rooted in his image as the key figure controlling safety and security.

Notwithstanding Vučić's intervention, Pride never received a formal go-ahead. The deadline for banning Pride lapsed without a formal announcement, as the Bureau for the Coordination of Security Services, despite meeting the night before Pride, never issued their security assessment. Under the assumption that no news means good news, Belgrade Pride happened for the first time since 2010. Protected by an estimated 7,000 police officers, a group of about a thousand LGBT people, human rights activists, international activists and diplomats, and friends and allies of the LGBT population in Serbia took to the streets. Joined by the Mayor of Belgrade, the Minister of European Integration and the Minister of Culture, the Pride parade marched from the government building to the square in front the Serbian parliament (Balkan Insight, 2014a). Despite the fact that Belgrade looked like it was under siege – with the presence of armoured vehicles and riot police dominating the city – the 2014 Pride was widely considered a 'successful and peaceful' event. Indeed, although there were protests against Pride, riots like those in 2010 did not happen.

The absence of violence in 2014 remains remarkable and has raised many (still unanswered) questions about the relationship between the state and these extremist groups. Whereas, in May 2014, the right-wing political party Dveri warned the government that allowing Belgrade Pride would lead to 'war on the streets of Serbia' (Balkan Insight, 2014b), their protests in September remained peaceful. Similarly, the far-right movement, 1389, previously associated with the 2010 riots, explicitly called on its sympathisers to refrain from violence against Pride (InSerbia, 2014b). One explanation for the absence of violence could be that the political climate in Serbia has changed. As these right-wing organisations have been trying to access

mainstream politics – most of them became a political party and stood for
the elections (Mikuš, 2015) – it is plausible that the use of violence and
scaremongering is no longer an appropriate tactic for these organisations.
An alternative explanation, however, highlights the changed relationship
between the ruling elite and these extremist groups. To illustrate, Rory
Archer (2014) has rather convincingly suggested that the absence of violence
has probably more to do 'with murky networks of power and cooperation
between Vučić's government and Serbia's many far right groups' – networks
which could be traced back to the 1990s (see also Nielsen, 2013a). With a
military parade planned for Putin's visit only a few weeks after the 2014
Pride, it has also been argued that some deal had been struck between the
government and the extremist groups (Interview SRB2015_17), where the
military parade was organised to reclaim 'Pride' as a paradigm of nationalism
and hegemonic masculinity (Igrutinović, 2015). Although it is impossible
to prove such a deal, the fact that Vučić explicitly thanked the opponents
of Pride for refraining from violence (B92, 2014a) – and thus their understanding of the (difficult) position of Serbia – seems to point in this direction,
at least partially.

This first 'peaceful' Belgrade Pride was well received by international
observers, who credited the Serbian government for creating the conditions
to maintain Pride without incidents (Ristić, 2014a). Whereas EU officials
in their immediate reaction called the peaceful Belgrade Pride 'a milestone
in the modern history of democratic Serbia' (quoted in Ristić, 2014a), the
formal analysis, presented in the 2014 Progress Report, was a bit more
sceptical. Contrary to 2010, the Commission did not consider Pride proof
of progress, but rather argued that it was but one step in the improvement
of fundamental rights in Serbia. As such – and in line with the discursive
shift of the 2013 Progress Report – the Commission commended Pride,
while simultaneously calling for increased political support for the promotion
of fundamental rights:

> The holding of the Pride parade in Belgrade on 28 September without major
> incident marked a substantial step towards the effective exercise in Serbia of
> human rights in general and LGBTI ... rights in particular. Notwithstanding the
> government's good preparatory work for this event, enhanced political support
> for the promotion of fundamental freedoms is needed. There is also a need
> for a consistent and visible political commitment to promoting a culture of
> respect towards the LGBTI community. (European Commission, 2014, p. 13)

The 2014 Pride and the absence of violence created an important precedent
that informed much of the organisational process of the 2015 Pride. With
both the political climate in Serbia and the EU's scrutiny of Belgrade Pride
remaining the same, a ban of the 2015 Pride would damage Vučić's carefully

crafted image of the pro-EU reformer. As such, the organisational process of the 2015 Belgrade Pride followed a similar process as the previous year – i.e. cooperation between the government and Pride organisers remained constructive (led by the Minister of European Integration, Jadranka Joksimović) and the official framing of Pride continued to focus on the security aspects (with Vučić as the provider and protector of citizens' safety and security).

Nevertheless, a few differences can be observed. First, Pride organisers faced fewer administrative obstacles. Although they still require more documents than any other public gathering and obtaining all permits remains a difficult and labour-intensive process, improved communication between the different city administration departments facilitated the work of the Pride organisers (Interview SRB2015_2). A second and probably more important difference is that a second Pride event was scheduled for 20 September 2015. To highlight the specific problems faced by trans* people – who have been rather invisible in Serbian LGBT activism (Interview SRB2015_7) – a group of activists announced they would organise a Trans* Pride alongside Belgrade Pride. Although it could be argued that a second LGBT-related event would increase the security threats associated with Pride, this was not the case. As the Trans* Pride was an 'immobile gathering', within the same security zone as Belgrade Pride, and would end before Belgrade Pride started, both events were treated as one big event in terms of the security analysis. After a positive risk assessment, both events were protected by 6,500 police officers and happened without any major incident. And indeed, since then Pride has gone ahead each year without noteworthy incidents.

Conclusion

Throughout this chapter, I have demonstrated that the organisation of Belgrade Pride has predominantly been a product of particular configurations of domestic and international politics, in which the context of Serbia's EU accession process has played an important role with diverging effects. Indeed, the three different periods discussed in this chapter present a story of engagement and disengagement of various political actors throughout the fifteen-year history of Belgrade Pride, clearly demonstrating the need for a relational and transnational approach to understanding Europeanisation processes. Most importantly, throughout the chapter I have drawn attention to the fact that one can only fully understand the political processes at one (e.g. domestic) scale by taking into account the other political landscapes (e.g. international scale) in which Belgrade Pride takes place.

During the first phase of Pride history, the strong presence of nationalist politics, state intimidation as well as a weakened LGBT movement had tempered activists' interest in organising Pride. With little to no domestic initiatives, Pride did not feature on the international community's agenda. It was only after the election of the pro-EU government in 2008, and the adoption of the anti-discrimination law in 2009, that activists considered the time ripe for organising Belgrade Pride. However, they overestimated the pro-EU character of the government as the strong nationalist opposition prevented it from allowing the event to go ahead, despite it being rhetorically trapped into supporting Pride. Hence, the 2009 Pride was 'banned' by the government, which in turn introduced Pride as a topic on the international agenda.

Throughout the chapter, I have shown that this increased international attention, especially as a part of the EU accession process, played an important role in the government's engagement and disengagement with Pride in the second phase. Indeed, the organisation of Belgrade Pride in this period was heavily influenced by shifting priorities within Serbia's EU accession process as well as a relatively unstable political climate. In 2010, the government decided to support – not to say co-organise – Belgrade Pride as a move to demonstrate its pro-EU credentials, but used the extreme violence that followed the 2010 Pride as an excuse to ban Pride for the next three years on security grounds and thus 'postpone' dealing with it, while dealing with other more important and sensitive issues, most notably Kosovo and elections. The latter was made possible by the EU's favouring of geopolitical identities over normative ones when multiple struggles occurred at once. Prioritising regional stability over fundamental rights (see hierarchy of tasks), the EU rewarded Serbia for its efforts in normalising its relationship with Kosovo, though ignoring fundamental rights issues, including Pride. The third phase of the history of Belgrade Pride saw the return of the event after Vučić came to power. With the Kosovo issue more or less 'resolved', and the EU refocusing on fundamental rights, Vučić used Pride to bolster his image of the 'reformer'. Maintaining Pride became Vučić's victory, domestically demonstrating his power and dominance in Serbian politics, as well as a way to demonstrate Serbia's commitment to European integration on the international scene.

Overall, the history of Pride in Serbia is one where EU pressure and conditionality has contributed to both the successes of and bans on Belgrade Pride. When faced with competing normative tensions, the EU engaged in 'priority of tasks' processes to first secure regional stability to then (re)direct its attention to human rights issues.

Although, over time, Pride has become an annual feature in Belgrade, the question remains what the costs have been to get to this stage in terms of the political nature of the event and LGBT politics more widely. While this chapter has already illuminated ways in which the Serbian government has used Pride as part of tactical Europeanisation processes since 2014 in an attempt to both accept yet resist the event, the impact of the organisational processes and politics on the queer politics of Pride will be discussed in more details in Chapter 6.

Notes

1 Gay Straight Alliance withdrew from the organising committee early on in the process following internal disagreements between organisations.
2 Informal conversation with Pride organiser, May 2015. The work of Ejdus and Božović (2019) also highlights the extreme securitisation of Pride as a way of scaring the organisers into cancelling.
3 See *Bączkowski and Others v Poland* (application no. 1543/06).
4 See European Parliament resolution of 18 January 2006 on homophobia in Europe (P6_TA(2006)0018) and European Parliament resolution of 26 April 2007 on homophobia in Europe (P6_TA(2007)0167).
5 Tomislav Nikolić and Aleksandar Vučić split from the SRS in 2008 to form the SNS in order to pursue their pro-European agenda. With a more moderate and pro-EU agenda, the SNS displayed what Vachudova (2008, 2014) has described as an 'adaptation model' towards the EU. With this model Vachudova (2014, p. 128) argues that former 'authoritarian and anti-EU parties make themselves EU-compatible, realizing that this is the only way to get back into the electoral game'.
6 The Commissioner for Equality concluded that these comments did indeed amount to hate speech, and ordered Dačić to apologise to the LGBT community, by meeting with the representatives of Labris.
7 No incidents occurred, largely due to the extremists' responses to the 2013 Pride ban. Interpreting the ban as another victory of theirs – arguing that 'banning the Pride is the first step in defending family values' – extremist activists withdrew their protests (Balkan Inside, 2013). Only hours before, right-wing supporters had blocked traffic in Belgrade – without plans to go anywhere until the Pride was banned – and when the ban was issued these activists began to disperse. Their retreat created the possibility for LGBT activists to claim the streets for their protest hours later.

Part III

Looking beyond policy towards
lived experiences

5

The attitudinal panopticon and the limited implementation of the anti-discrimination framework

Discussing diversity work, Sara Ahmed (2017) reminds us that when institutions are obliged by law to introduce diversity and equality policies, they may appoint diversity workers in order to comply with law and external conditions, but that these appointments can be just about appearances. To give someone a diversity mandate 'might be how an institution appears willing to be transformed' (Ahmed, 2017, p. 94). Although Ahmed was referring to equality work in universities, the same principles can apply to states, as they too are institutions obliged to engage with equality policies through external forces. Indeed, as discussed in Chapter 3, the adoption process of the anti-discrimination framework in Serbia was in large part the result of conditionalities of some sort where the government adopted new legislation because it was told to. In this chapter,[1] I turn to the implementation of this legislative framework, which has been described by observers as generally lacking – as the mandates given by law to change the country were simply about being seen to be willing to change. For example, while the European Parliament resolution on Serbia's 2015 Progress Report welcomes 'the fact that Serbia has an adequate legal and institutional framework for protecting human rights and fundamental freedoms', it also expressed concerns about 'the remaining shortcomings in its implementation, particularly with regard to preventing discrimination against vulnerable groups, including … LGBTI people' (European Parliament, 2016: article 18).

The Europeanisation literature, by now, has well established that when government adopt legislation due to external pressure (i.e. conditionality), this legislation tends to remain weakly implemented (Czernielewska et al., 2004; Graff, 2006; Haughton, 2011; Huszka, 2017; O'Dwyer, 2012; Rechel, 2008; Schimmelfennig and Sedelmeier, 2005b). In addition to the flaws of the conditionality principle itself, several other explanations for limited implementation have been identified within the EU enlargement process itself. These include a dearth of expertise on the issue within EU institutions, lack of standards, and heterogeneity in the protection of minorities rights among member states giving candidate countries leeway to manoeuvre politically on the issue (Rechel, 2008). Similarly, the inconsistent application of conditionality and superficial monitoring of minority issues also contributed to the limited implementation of the newly introduced policies (Nancheva, 2007; Rechel, 2008).

With the domestic turn in Europeanisation literature, the domestic institutional setting has also been shown to be another important explanation for limited implementation. Falkner and Treib (2008), for example, argued that the limited implementation of equality policies is due to weak local enforcement mechanisms of the new adopted rules. They highlighted how the new equality norms are 'empty letters', unable to be implemented due to the malfunctioning of the judiciary system as well as due to the fact that equality bodies are lacking the capacity and/or visibility to fully function. Others have also pointed out that EU enlargement is an elite-driven process which fails to produce societal readjustment (Galbreath, 2003). That being the case, it is suggested that implementation gaps are also a result of a lack of 'normative resonance' (Brosig, 2010).

Although the link between domestic societal structures, and particularly the need for normative resonance, have been commented on within the Europeanisation literature (see e.g. Grosse, 2010; Malová and Dolný, 2008; Mendelski, 2015, 2016), they have not been sufficiently analysed. This omission is in large part due to the legislative and institutional bias within the literature, as well as its subscription to what Scheingold (2004) calls the 'Myth of Rights'. This Myth of Rights directly links legal change, rights, and remedies to social change, perpetuating an underlying assumption that formal compliance and the adoption of new rules and institutions will in time lead to social change. However, as I have argued elsewhere (Slootmaeckers, 2022), this assumption is problematic for two reasons: 1) these newly established institutions can be used to legitimise illiberal policies and de-democratisation processes (Bermeo, 2016), and 2) fundamental rights cannot be reduced to laws and institutions as they are inherently embedded in the cultural and social fabric of societies (Slootmaeckers and O'Dwyer, 2018). In order to overcome this issue, this chapter seeks to extend the Europeanisation analysis of limited implementation beyond the political and institutional barriers, to also include an analysis of how the lack of societal transformation itself prevents implementation of legislation.

To discuss the implementation of Serbia's anti-discrimination framework, I will analyse the establishment of the new equality body, the Commissioner for the Protection of Equality (CPE) and its workings, as well as the judicial system's handling of anti-discrimination and hate crime cases. Empirically, the analysis is complicated by the lack of statistical data which is caused by the absence of a centralised and standardised system for collecting, recording and analysing data in cases of discrimination that could provide evidence on how widespread discrimination is, as well as on how well the law has been implemented (Commissioner for the Protection of Equality, 2016). To overcome this lack of in-depth statistical and case-specific data, I rely on data obtained through the semi-structured interviews conducted with a wide array of actors, including but not limited to (LGBT) activists, legal aid providers, legal scholars, the former Commissioner for the Protection of Equality (CPE), and representatives of the Judicial Academy, Organization for Security and Co-operation in Europe (OSCE) office in Serbia, the Ministry of Justice, the Serbian equality bodies, and the community policing department. The data from the interviews is triangulated with and expanded by document analysis of the (annual) reports produced by the CPE and civil society organisations, as well as a review and secondary analysis of existing resources.

The Commissioner for the Protection of Equality

The first step to implementing the 2009 anti-discrimination law was to 'establish the Commissioner for the Protection of Equality ... as an independent state organ' (Art. 1) within sixty days after the relevant articles of the law entered into force (Art. 61). The procedure to elect the new equality body is quite simple: first, each parliamentary group is allowed to propose a candidate to the Committee for Constitutional Affairs which then selects one candidate to be considered for the role. The Parliament, in turn, elects the CPE by a simple majority for a period of five years. To qualify for the CPE position, candidates need to have 1) a law degree, 2) at least ten years' legal experience in the field of human rights, and 3) display high moral and professional qualities (Art. 28).

Despite a simple and clear procedure, the opposition Liberal Democratic Party (LDP) was the only parliamentary group to submit its candidate, Goran Miletić, before the set deadline. With extensive experience in the field of human rights, the support of the Coalition Against Discrimination (KPD) and over two hundred human rights NGOs, Miletić presented a very good CPE candidate. The ruling Democratic Party (DS), however, did not agree, and proposed its own candidate, Milutin Đuričić, a week after the deadline. While the late nomination of Đuričić was interpreted by civil society as the government's lack of commitment to the anti-discrimination legislation (Gay Straight Alliance, 2011; Petrović, 2011), it was Đuričić himself who was deemed a controversial choice for the role, and became heavily contested by human rights NGOs. Civil society organisations in particular, led by the Coalition Against Discrimination, questioned whether Đuričić had the required high moral and professional qualities based on his involvement with 1990's nationalist propaganda that openly supported the Milošević regime (Petrović, 2011). Following the public campaign against his candidacy, Đuričić decided to withdraw from the race for CPE, citing the (unnecessary) politicisation of his candidacy and by extension the CPE institution (Blić, 2010). Although this left Goran Miletić as the only viable candidate for the CPE position, he did enjoy the necessary political support to be elected (Milanović Hrašovec, 2010). In fact, the ruling party tried to disqualify him by arguing that Miletić did not have the necessary legal experience in human rights and interpreted the 'ten years' legal experience' requirement in a very narrow way – adding an extralegal criterion: the need to have ten years' experience of arguing human rights cases in court. Unable to elect a candidate, the committee declared the search unsuccessful and reopened the procedure.

The second search process incited an episode of political homophobia in response to the resubmission of Goran Miletić as CPE candidate by the LDP. In a newspaper interview, Svetozar Čiplić, Minister for Human and Minority Rights, stated that the government would never support Miletić as CPE (cited in Beta and Večernje Novosti, 2010). He claimed that by not supporting him, the government was ensuring the impartiality of the CPE institution. In fact, referring to Miletić's sexuality and his involvement in the organisation of Belgrade Pride, Čiplić argued that the CPE must defend the interests of all minority groups, and not only of those to which the CPE belongs – i.e. LGBT people. The homophobic undertones of such a statement became more explicit in an informal, behind-the-scenes political campaign in which it was claimed that Goran Miletić would push for Pride parades all over Serbia (Interview SRB2015_17). Despite this strong opposition to Miletić, the government only presented its nominee – Nevena Petrušić, Dean of the Law Faculty of the University of Niš – several weeks after the deadline (Petrović, 2011). Although the Coalition Against Discrimination remained sceptical about Petrušić's qualities for CPE, she enjoyed the support of about a hundred other civil society organisations. As such, Petrušić, as a government-preferred candidate with civil society support, represented a compromise solution for the impasse of the first election round and was appointed by the Parliament on 5 May 2010 (Petrović, 2011).

After being elected CPE, Nevena Petrušić experienced further political barriers in her work to set up the institutions as she experienced unexplained delays in the adoption of the secondary legislation required for the institution to start operating (Petrović, 2011). Additionally, coming from 'an academic environment ... [without political] personal contacts to use' (Interview SRB2015_47), Petrušić struggled to secure the necessary resources and adequate office space in particular (Petrušić, 2011, 2012). Being forced to work from small and temporary office spaces significantly limited 'the development of the Office of the Commissioner to its full capacity, which can be [of] negative effect to the efficiency of the work and tasks given to the Commissioner' (Petrušić, 2012, p. 16). The 256 sq. m. apartment – where the CPE resided until late 2016 – only provided the physical space for twenty-three employees out of the sixty-plus employees budgeted for.

While the lack of human resources are a limiting factor for the functioning of the CPE, especially considering the increasing workload of the institution, Nevena Petrušić was able to overcome some of these barriers by relying on international support for the institution. Indeed, EU-funded projects aided the CPE institution by providing both material and intellectual resources (Petrušić, 2014). These projects, Petrušić argued, were 'very important for the institution because first the capacities of the [CPE] were raised. There were many trainings … and of course study visits to other similar institutions in the region' (Interview SRB2015_47). Additionally, the CPE became a member of Equinet, the European Network of Equality Bodies, which organises, among other activities, information exchange and training seminars for staff members of European equality bodies. Additional training sessions were organised to increase the knowledge of staff members in cooperation with, and often funded by, international organisations active in Serbia (Petrušić, 2012). Finally, the CPE collaborated with local NGOs in a two-way exchange: the CPE educated the civil society organisation in the anti-discrimination legislation and how to report issues, and NGOs provided the CPE with expertise in the situation of specific groups vulnerable to discrimination (Interviews SRB2015_1, SRB2015_47).

With such international support, the CPE was able to deliver quality service and process over 4,300 cases in the first CPE mandate (2010–15). The professionalisation of the CPE office is not only demonstrated by the yearly increase of cases processed by the institution (see Figure 5.1), but also by the changing nature of the cases on which the CPE works. For example, while at first the institution predominantly worked by processing the complaints it received, the CPE became more proactive in later years by issuing an increasing number of recommendations on how to improve equality in Serbia.

Although the majority of the work of the CPE (still) consists of processing complaints, the Commissioner can also file lawsuits for protection against discrimination (strategic litigation), file misdemeanour charges, inform the public about the most common, typical and severe cases of discrimination (warnings), and recommend to public administration and other state bodies measures to improve equality and protection against discrimination (Petrušić, 2011). Of these actions, strategic litigation is seen as one of the CPE's more

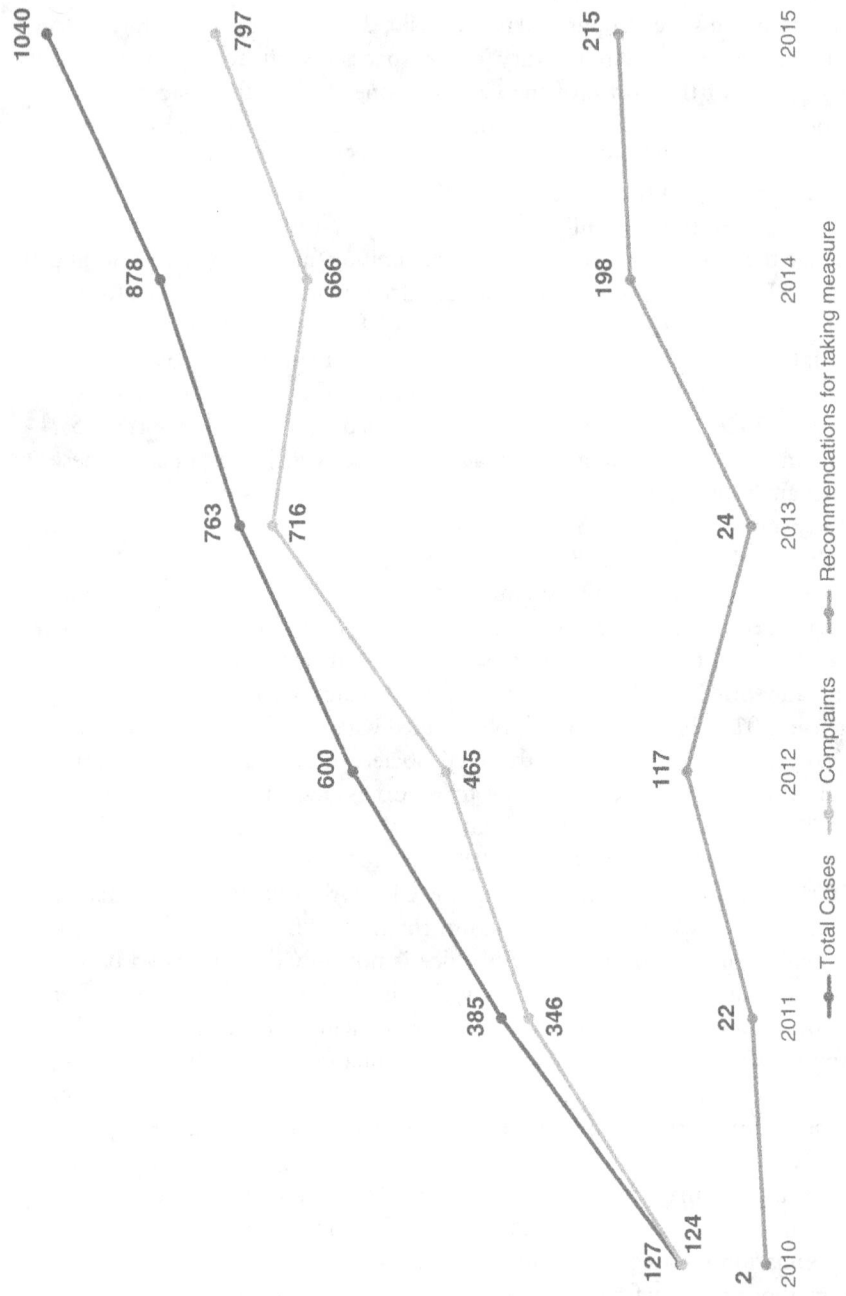

Figure 5.1 Annual overview of cases processed by the CPE (2010–15)

Source: Compiled by author based on annual reports of the CPE and personal communications with CPE officials.

Legend: Total Cases — Complaints — Recommendations for taking measure

Year	Total Cases	Complaints	Recommendations for taking measure
2010	127	124	2
2011	385	346	22
2012	600	465	117
2013	763	716	24
2014	878	666	198
2015	1040	797	215

powerful practices to improve implementation of the anti-discrimination framework. Indeed, Petrušić, in an email interview, describes it as an important part of the CPE's 'advocacy strategy', and has the aim to contribute 'to the correct interpretation and correct application of the anti-discrimination provisions, to influence the development of court practice … to support the rule of law and to contribute towards better access to justice' (Interview SRB2016_1).

According to the anti-discrimination law, the CPE can initiate a lawsuit as part of its own duty in cases of discrimination against an individual after receiving consent from the victim or without the consent of victims for those cases that involve discrimination against a group of individuals connected by the same ground (Interview SRB2016_1). Strategic litigation is a particularly valuable mechanism for those 'cases of common and widespread discrimination, especially those that are publicly tolerated and approved and provoke discrimination of members of social groups that are vulnerable and marginalised' (Interview SRB2016_1).

When querying why instances of homophobic hate speech by politicians, including the case of PM Dačić who called homosexuals abnormal on national television in the lead-up to the 2013 Belgrade Pride (see Chapter 4), have not been selected as a strategic litigation case, Petrušić repeatedly explained that the limited capacity of the CPE has been the main reason for the under usage of strategic litigation. She did not want to comment, however, on why discrimination against LGBT people, at the time, had not been selected as a strategic litigation case (Interviews SRB2015_47, SRB2016_1). Nevertheless, a high-ranked employee of the institution provided additional insights when they explained that the CPE approach to their work was one of avoiding political conflicts. The employee clarified that the CPE wants to establish itself 'as an independent body, an ally, as someone who is working on the same thing. [Because] if you [the CPE] are in conflict and you are on the opposite side, then you cannot really achieve much' (Interview SRB2015_1). Selecting cases of hate speech by politicians for strategic litigation, then, could be seen as a conflictual strategy, especially taking into account that some politicians (e.g. Dragan Marković [Palma]) already refused to comply with the Commissioner's recommendations (Interviews SRB2015_1, SRB2015_47).

Apart from the strain on the institutional capacity, partly caused by the evergrowing caseload and understaffing (see Figure 5.1), the CPE reported several other barriers to her work. First, she noted that the increased visibility of the CPE led to (indirect) political pressure on the institution. To illustrate, in an interview conducted after the end of her mandate, Petrušić revealed that she had been blackmailed into hiring some individuals 'close to the authorities', which was aimed at compromising the independence of the

CPE (Interview SRB2015_47). She said that when she went to report 'the assistant who was blackmailing [her] ... the prosecutor told [Petrušić] that they did not have the authority to prosecute [the assistant], but that [she could] sue them privately' (Interview SRB2015_47). When explaining to the prosecutor that she had never experienced attacks or blackmailing as a professor at the University of Niš, and that the state should investigate each such attack, Petrušić reported that the prosecutor began to threaten her:

> He [the prosecutor] threatened me. He demanded that I hire the person, and said 'If that does not happen' – so he was issuing threats – and when I asked 'What will happen if I do not do that?', he said 'Well, there will be an awful media campaign and you will resign after this campaign.' (Interview SRB2015_47)

Media campaigns aimed to undermine the authority of independent institutions are not an uncommon political tool in Serbia to silence opposition (Aleksić, 2015). In the case of the CPE, in 2012 the tabloid *Kurir* launched a smear campaign in which it was claimed that Petrušić discriminated against a Roma woman by not extending her contract (Georgievski, 2013). Similarly, the Protector of Citizens (the Ombudsman), Saša Janković, has been subject to many such media campaigns. For example, one such campaign occurred in 2015 after Janković argued in his annual report that Serbia's record on human rights was unsatisfactory (see Andrić, 2015; InSerbia, 2015). With headlines like *The darkest secret of Sasa Janković – he doesn't want you to know this* and *Janković – Gun without permission and friend involved in Arkan's murder*, it was suggested that Janković was involved in a murder in the 1990s (see Janjić, 2015). Evaluating these incidents and reflecting on her time as CPE, Petrušić concludes that:

> what actually can be said is that the role of independent institutions is still not understood ... In general, I have the impression that the whole story about human rights is essentially not understood by our politicians. So, I have the impression they are really doing that [human rights protection] because of someone over there [the EU], and not because our society needs it. (Interview SRB2015_47)

The undermining of the CPE's authority also speaks to another limitation to the potential impact of the CPE on Serbia's political and societal landscape: the limited enforceability of the Commissioner's opinions and recommendations. Although a perpetrator, by law, has to comply with the recommendation on ways to eliminate a violation of rights, the CPE has no mechanism available to enforce compliance; it can only issue a warning when they fail to comply and rely on its 'authority and standing in society' to 'pressure' compliance. In terms of the latter, the Commissioner is authorised to inform the public about the lack of compliance if the recommendation is not complied with after an additional thirty days following the warning. However, without the ability to take punitive measures, naming and shaming is the only mechanism at the institution's disposal to ensure compliance (Interview SRB2015_1). Although recommendations in individual cases are generally acted upon, a substantial portion of recommendations remain ignored. Even though a certain degree of non-compliance is to be expected, the fact that the list of non-compliers includes state institutions and government ministries (see Petrušić, 2012) suggests that the CPE's authority remains contested, including by state actors.

Similarly, Petrušić experienced resistance to her 'general recommendations, which are included in [the CPE's] report', and noted that 'asking the state to take measures – not ad hoc measures, but long-running measures – that will solve certain [discrimination problems], remained difficult' (Interview SRB2015_47). Indeed, many of the recommendations made in the annual reports are repeated year after year with seemingly no action taken, despite Parliament's consideration and approval of these reports. For example, the recommendation to take measures to integrate materials on equality in school curricula and to eradicate discriminatory elements from syllabuses has been referred to on a yearly basis. Other repeated (and seemingly ignored) recommendations include the need to establish a 'unique and centralised system of collecting, registering and analysing data about discrimination cases' (Petrušić, 2012, p. 104; see also 2014, p. 104) and to work on the effective and continual education and 'training of judges, public prosecutors, police officers and public servants in the area of [the] anti-discrimination law' (Petrušić, 2014, p. 131).

The CPE also reported that the lack of understanding of the concept of discrimination in both the population and the judiciary system, and the fact that victims are reluctant to report instances of discrimination or hate crimes, are important barriers to the implementation of anti-discrimination legislation, as discussed below (Interviews SRB2015_1, SRB2015_47, SRB2016_1).

The judicial route and its barriers to implementation

While the CPE was established to improve access to justice for victims of discrimination through the creation of a complaint procedure that is 'not excessively formal and [that] is based on ensuring necessary urgency in the procedure ... [and is] free of charge regardless of the outcome' (Petrušić, 2011, p. 20), it does not seek to replace the existing judicial routes to justice. However, within the judicial route to seeking justice, there is a consensus among a wide variety of interviewees – including legal scholars, independent institutions, and activists – that a lack of systematic training of judges and other functions in the judiciary is a key implementation barrier. The lack of this systematic training has led observers to conclude that the rulings in discrimination and hate crime cases remain sensitive to individual judges' (mis)understandings of the law and/or their sensitivities to the issue (Stjelja et al., 2014).

In a review of the judicial practice on discrimination cases, the CPE found that judges 'do not recognise the case of discrimination as such' (Interview SRB2015_1), and that court decisions in cases of discrimination, among other things, fail to take into consideration the reversed burden of proof. According to the anti-discrimination law, when a plaintiff can demonstrate that the defendant might have committed an act of discrimination – i.e. they have been able to make the case that it is possible that they were treated differently based on a personal characteristic by the defendant – the burden of proof shifts to the defendant who needs to prove that the differential treatment was justified. However, the 'court proceedings [on the investigated anti-discrimination cases] were conducted by the [general] rules of the Law on Civil Procedure, failing to appreciate the moment when the burden of proof should be shifted from the plaintiff to the defendant' (Petrušić, 2013, p. 12). Indeed, courts have interpreted the reversed burden of proof in such a way that plaintiffs are still expected to actively prove discrimination (Antonijević et al., 2014). Such interpretation leaves victims at a disadvantage as discrimination is often difficult to prove, particularly when indirect and/ or covert.

Additionally, judges are often unclear when and how they should apply the anti-discrimination legislation (Interview SRB2015_11). For example, the fact that discrimination is covered by multiple laws has been pointed out as an important reason why judges find it difficult to reconcile and determine the appropriate law for cases (Decker et al., 2014). In many cases, other better-known laws have been used rather than the unfamiliar anti-discrimination law (Interview SRB2015_11). In fact, a 2014 study has revealed that the number of anti-discrimination cases brought to court is extremely low (Antonijević et al., 2014). Between 2010 and 2013, only 184 procedures seeking protection from discrimination were initiated in the whole of Serbia, with 103 of these cases still ongoing in 2014, and in only 10 cases was discrimination established, albeit sometimes only via the Court of Appeal. The backlog in cases, despite the fact that anti-discrimination cases are classified as urgent cases, also indicates that the implementation of the anti-discrimination legislation is also subject to general problems of the efficiency of the Serbian judiciary (Interview SRB2016_3).

Not only is there a limited (and sometimes flawed) application of the law, it also seems that people working in the judiciary and public administration, including the police, do not fully understand the legal concept of discrimination (Petrušić, 2014, p. 31). The case against Dragan Marković (Palma) for his homophobic comments about the 2011 Pride (for details, see Mićić, 2014) provides a good example of the inconsistent application of the anti-discrimination law and the lack of understanding of the underlying principles of the law. While the first instance judgment found Palma guilty of severe discrimination, the same judge reversed their decision during the retrial ordered by the Court of Appeal after it had squashed the initial verdict on technical grounds. In the first verdict, they reasoned that

> in this particular case, Marković [Palma] presented a personal characteristic of sexual orientation as an illness and something not normal and he did this in the media, thus committing the aggravated case of discrimination, as well as that according to Article 13 of the Anti-Discrimination Law, it was determined as a severe form of discrimination and inciting of inequality, hatred and intolerance based on sexual orientation, which is a serious form of discrimination especially if it is done through the mass media, and in this particular case personal priority, or sexual orientation, by the defendant (Marković) is shown as an illness as something abnormal through the mass media, which makes it an aggregated case of discrimination. (quoted in Mićić, 2014, p. 50)

In the retrial, the judge ruled that the complaints by GSA were unfounded, reasoning that although Palma's statement does contain characteristics of discriminatory behaviour, it is 'not to the extent to which it is required to be given an official statement by the court in order to determine it as an actor of discrimination' (quoted in Mićić, 2014, p. 51). Moreover, based on the fact that the CPE had issued an opinion and recommendation against Palma for hate speech – a recommendation Palma refused to comply with – the judge argued that Palma has already been sanctioned enough by the CPE and that the 'court should not be a government body which will establish whether there was a discriminatory behaviour every time one of the social categories listed in the Anti-discrimination Law finds itself offended or discriminated against according to its own value system', adding that Palma expressed a view that was 'in accordance with the program of his party, and that it was his own judgement and the court cannot judge over value judgement', and if the court were to accept the lawsuit Palma 'would be prevented from having his private opinion and freedom of speech, therefore, any establishing of his statements as discriminatory was in complete contradiction with the purpose to which the Anti-discrimination Law is enacted' (quoted in Mićić, 2014, pp. 51–52). Although the Court of Appeal later overturned this verdict (Gay Straight Alliance, 2014), the reasoning itself shows how misunderstood the law is by judges.

A similar pattern is observed among the police force. A 2015 survey conducted by the Police Academy revealed that half the police force was unable to identify discrimination (reported in Commissioner for the Protection of Equality, 2016, pp. 45–46), leaving police officers unable to respond appropriately to victims of discrimination (Interview SRB2016_4). To explain this, a professor at the Academy of Criminalistics and Police Studies (henceforth also Police Academy) drew attention to the lack of attention to human rights and discrimination in the curriculum (Interview SRB2016_4). More importantly however, he questioned the broader training and hiring practices of the police force. Whereas the Ministry of the Interior hires between 1,500 and 1,700 police officers on an annual basis, the Police Academy only enrols 350 students a year, of which only half reach graduation (Interview SRB2016_4). This discrepancy in numbers, as well as the fact that there is no legal requirement for the Ministry of the Interior to hire Police Academy graduates, means that a majority of the police force does not receive comprehensive training on human rights issues, including discrimination.

This being the case, it should not come as a surprise that how someone is treated when reporting discrimination or a hate crime still 'depends on the personal attitudes of the person [to whom discrimination and/or violence is reported]' (Interview SRB2015_20). More often than not, police officers still respond to LGBT victims with a lack of understanding and sometimes even prejudice and/or homophobia (Interview SRB2015_13, SRB2015_20). In the least extreme cases of misunderstandings by police officers, the hate-based motives of violence against LGBT people are simply not registered as such, and the incident is instead classified as a mere street fight (Interview SRB2015_13). A more extreme illustration is the inappropriate police response to a hate crime against a trans man in Vlasotince, a town in south-east Serbia. In October 2016, the NGO Egal reported that a trans man was physically attacked by a group of men, already known by authorities for harassing the man for over a year without legal repercussions (personal communication via email). When the police arrived at the scene, the officers' behaviour was described as unprofessional as they reportedly did nothing to apprehend the attackers, but instead laughed at the victim while seemingly dismissing the incident.

It is worth noting that the observation that police forces and the judiciary have not been educated enough on the anti-discrimination law should not be taken for an absolute lack of training initiatives, but rather that there is no streamlined process for the training of police officers, judges and lawyers (Interviews SRB2016_3, SRB2016_4). Whereas a systematisation of training is yet to occur, efforts have been made to improve the understanding of the anti-discrimination law within the judicial system. In the years following the adoption of the anti-discrimination strategy and action plan, further initiatives have been taken to improve sensitivity to discrimination and hate crimes among the police force. For example, in 2014, Labris – with the support of the Dutch Embassy – reached an agreement with the Ministry of the Interior to run training sessions with the police force focusing on how to work with victims of homophobic hate crimes (Todorović, 2015). In addition to police training, the Ministry of the Interior appointed eight liaison officers for the LGBT population, including one at the national level (Interview SRB2015_41; see also ILGA-Europe, 2016). Other initiatives aimed at improving court practices and judicial training. For example, the CPE and the Judicial Academy began to organise a Moot Court to provide (future) lawyers and judges with experience of cases of discrimination based on sexual orientation (Interview SRB2015_47; see also Todorović, 2015). Furthermore, after inconsistent verdicts in the Court of Appeal, the Judicial Academy organised a series of round tables to discuss the different rulings and come to an agreement on how to harmonise the case law (Interview SRB2016_3). And in 2015, the OSCE Mission to Serbia, in cooperation with the Judicial Training Academy, launched an initiative to develop curricula on anti-discrimination legislation that will become part of the permanent training of future judges (OSCE, 2015).

The attitudinal panopticon and the failed promise of institutional change

While the above analysed barriers relating to the lack of political will and limited institutional capacities to implement the laws – barriers already frequently covered in the Europeanisation literature – they are insufficient for understanding the lack of implementation, and another barrier is to be found in society more widely. One of these societal barriers is that there is a limited understanding of the concept of discrimination, and the anti-discrimination law, within Serbian society more broadly. Although a 2013 survey revealed that the majority (80 per cent) of the Serbian population agreed with the statement that denying someone a right simply because of a personal characteristic is unjustifiable, a substantial portion (16 per cent) declared that they think discrimination is justified in certain circumstances (CeSID, 2013).[2] More importantly, however, despite their basic understanding of what discrimination means, people do not always seem to be able to recognise it when it occurs or when they discriminate (Interviews SRB2015_6, SRB2015_13, SRB2015_20, SRB2015_25, SRB2015_40, SRB2015_42, SRB2015_47, SRB2015_54). This lack of recognition of discrimination can anecdotally be illustrated by a moment in the courtroom where a father – who was sued for physically assaulting his gay son – reasoned that the attack was justified because of his son's sexuality.

While a lack of understanding is prevalent among perpetrators, an analysis of the complaints received by the CPE between 2010 and 2015 also demonstrated that many complainants do not fully grasp the concept of discrimination. For example, an average of 26.02 per cent of the complaints did not mention a ground of discrimination (see Figure 5.2). Following this observation, it is not surprising that a third of the cases received by the CPE (on average 36.39 per cent) were dismissed because it was immediately clear that no discrimination had occurred, either because no personal characteristic was mentioned or because there was no probable link between the personal characteristic and the act which was claimed to be discriminatory. Similarly, only a small proportion of complaints (on average 8.66 per cent) led to the finding that discrimination had indeed occurred. Although these statistics support the observation that people do not fully grasp the concept of discrimination, one must remain cautious when drawing this conclusion solely based on the small number of successful claims since the limited success could also be attributed to the fact that proving discrimination can be difficult. However, taking all the different statistics together, a lack of understanding among complainants becomes apparent.

In addition to the lack of understanding of the concept of discrimination, the general population in Serbia remains rather uninformed about the mechanism of the anti-discrimination law. Whereas, according to a 2013 poll, 71 per cent of respondents are aware of the existence of the anti-discrimination law, 80 per cent of these people believe that sanctions against discrimination are only applied selectively (CeSID, 2013). Moreover, of those who indicated they had experienced discrimination, 67.5 per cent said they would not report it, with almost half of them (44 per cent) citing not knowing who to report discrimination to as their main reason for not reporting, and almost a third (29 per cent) highlighting a lack of confidence in institutions. The lack of knowledge and trust in institutions means that discrimination remains generally under-reported, which inherently limits the impact of the CPE, and the anti-discrimination law more generally, in Serbian society.

While some of the above barriers could be overcome by stronger and more visible institutions, as suggested by Falkner and Treib (2008), the persistent under-reporting of discrimination by victims remains a key barrier that cannot be reduced to weak institutions. Although under-reporting occurs for all forms of discrimination, it is said to be especially the case in LGBT-related cases (Interviews SRB2012_1, SRB2012_2, SRB2015_1, SRB2015_2, SRB2015_6, SRB2015_19, SRB2015_29, SRB2015_34, SRB2015_42, SRB2015_47). According to a recent European Union Agency for Fundamental Rights (FRA) (2020) survey, only 9 per cent of LGBT people who experienced discrimination reported it. The low percentage of reported cases is a serious

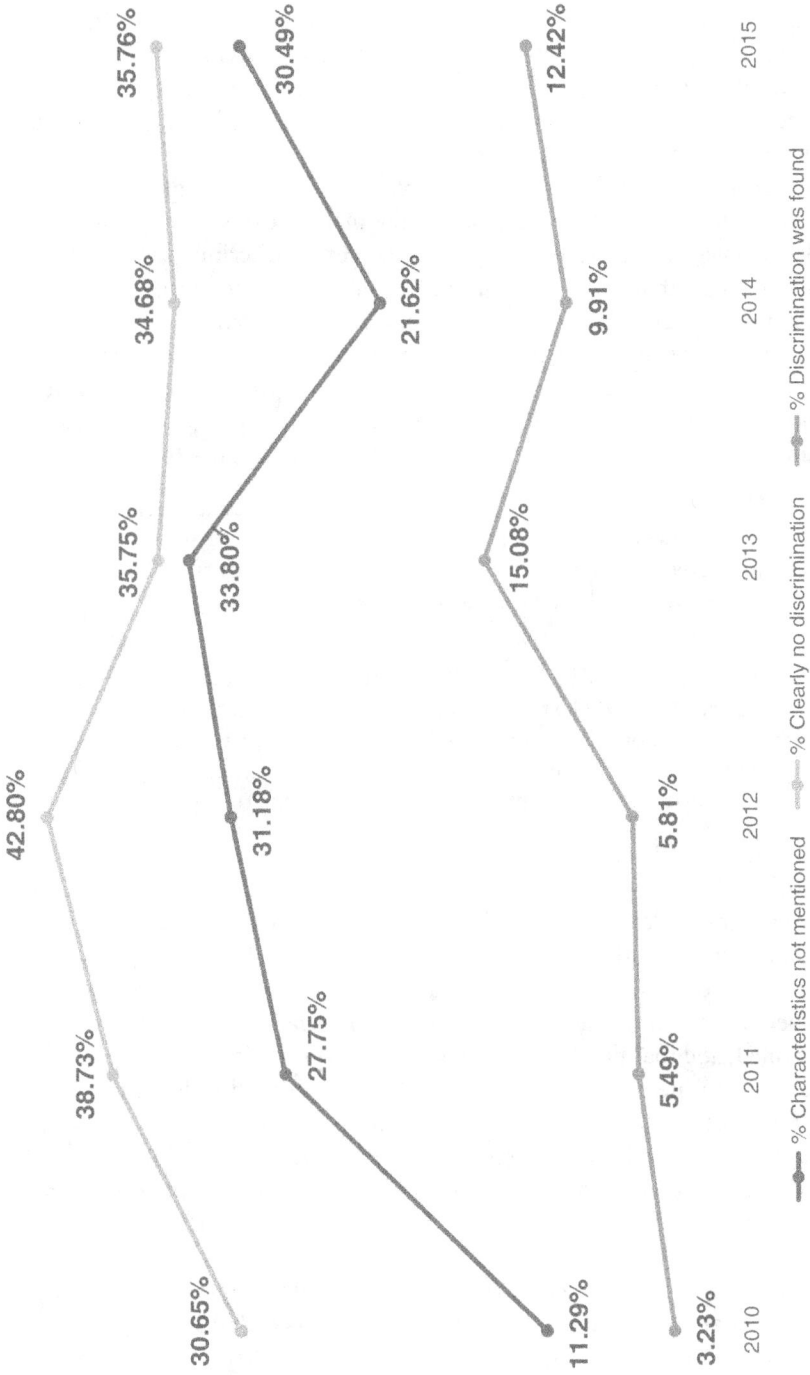

Figure 5.2 Annual overview of dismissed cases and positive outcome of proceedings (percentages of total cases submitted 2010–15)

Source: Compiled by the author based on CPE annual reports.

Legend: % Characteristics not mentioned · % Clearly no discrimination · % Discrimination was found

Year	% Characteristics not mentioned	% Clearly no discrimination	% Discrimination was found
2010	30.65%	11.29%	3.23%
2011	38.73%	27.75%	5.49%
2012	42.80%	31.18%	5.81%
2013	35.75%	33.80%	15.08%
2014	34.68%	21.62%	9.91%
2015	35.76%	30.49%	12.42%

barrier considering that, 'laws can remain just on paper for a long time if there is nobody to use them', and 'the conditions for LGBT people to use the Law on the Prohibition of Discrimination are still not met' (SRB2015_19). In other words, in order to understand the implementation gap, we need to understand the causes of under-reporting.

The weakness of the institutions, as explained above, are a partial explanation for under-reporting. Indeed, one of the main reasons why non-activist LGBT people do not want to report instances of discrimination or hate crimes is a fear that doing so would result in further victimisation and/or humiliation, or that their complaint would not be taken seriously by the police (Interviews SRB2015_25, SRB2015_34, SRB2015_38, SRB2015_54). This fear builds on the victims' experiences with unprofessional behaviour of under-educated police officers, as illustrated by following anecdotal evidence of people who did report discrimination and/or hate crimes to the police:

> It once happened to me. I was getting some kind of threats, and I went to the police, even though they were really fine, they [did not take me seriously and] said: 'Just forget about it, don't worry about it, do not let it bother you.' (Interview SRB2015_54, authors additions based on previous statements in the interview)

> When I reached out to the police, I thought that they would protect me. However, they behaved like the ones who attacked and threatened me. Trying to intimidate me, one of the police officers asked me 'Do you know who I am when I'm not wearing this uniform?! I'm dressed in black and I'm wearing boots.' (Anonymous respondent quoted in Stjelja et al., 2014, p. 39)

The weakness of institutions and the limited training of relevant authorities, although important, is not a sufficient explanation for under-reporting discrimination. Solely focusing on the weakness of institutions assumes that the law and its institutions will lead to social change if they are strong enough. Yet such a linear point of view reproduces the Myth of Rights and does not consider that the implementation of laws and social culture are inherently intertwined, and that the law can change society when it is implemented well, but also that it needs societal change to be implemented well (Scheingold, 2004). In other words, we need to consider how the hegemonic value system of society also constitutes a barrier to the implementation of the law.

To understand why the lack of social change itself is a barrier to the implementation of the law, I draw on my theory of the attitudinal panopticon (Slootmaeckers, 2022). The attitudinal panopticon is a concept that captures visibility regimes created by societal attitudes and the disciplining power emanating from them, and enables us to conceptualise how the lack of normative resonance leads to an implementation gap (Slootmaeckers, 2022). In short, the theory states that the attitudinal panopticon acts as a barrier to the implementation of anti-discrimination policies by making it socially costly to visibly differ from the norm, which in turns prevents people from engaging with their rights. Seeking justice through fundamental rights mechanisms requires those who are different to stand up, speak out and become visible as an act of resistance to the dominant discriminatory culture. However, when the attitudinal panopticon is strong enough – i.e. discriminatory attitudes are held by a majority of the people – such acts may lead to increased visibility and potentially new forms of discrimination and thus prevent people from using the law. As Sara Ahmed (2017, p. 141) explains, 'to expose a problem is to pose a problem', and posing a problem is to invite the disciplinary processes to engage you in order to maintain the status quo. Writing about sexual harassment, but referring to bullying and discrimination in more general terms, she explains that these processes work

> by increasing the costs of fighting against something, making it easier to accept something than to struggle against something, even if that acceptance is itself the site of your own diminishment; how you end up taking up less and less space. It is because we perceive this wall [attitudinal panopticon] that we end up having to modify our perception (perhaps this is what it means to get 'used to it'). You might feel you cannot afford to become alienated from those around you; not only might you lose access to material resources … but you might lose friends, connections that matter. (Ahmed, 2017, p. 141)

Indeed, a fear of the social repercussions of reporting discrimination and hate crimes has frequently been mentioned by interviewees as an explanation for under-reporting. To understand why this is the case, let us consider the Serbian cultural and attitudinal landscape, in terms of views on discrimination and homophobia, and how this impacts LGBT people. Surveys have repeatedly shown that a large proportion of the Serbian population consider homosexuality a disease and think homosexuals should keep their identity and actions within 'four walls' – i.e. homosexuality should remain invisible (CeSID, 2013; Gay Straight Alliance, 2010; National Democratic Institute, 2015). Similarly, opinion polls have consistently demonstrated that there is a considerable social distance between citizens and LGBT people in Serbia (CeSID, 2013; European Union Agency for Fundamental Rights, 2020). Surrounded by such an environment, LGBT people internalise homophobia and self-regulate their actions to avoid homophobic abuse (Kuhar and Švab, 2008; Stojčić and Petrović, 2016). In Serbia, becoming aware of one's sexuality is often 'followed by insecurity, the feeling of guilt, loneliness, fear or rejection by family and friends and the feeling that let them down, as well as fear for one's safety' (Stojčić and Petrović, 2016, p. 166). Coming out, then, represents a daunting act, with rejection and ostracisation from friends and family, or the risk of being fired from their job being perceived to be the most likely consequences (Interviews SRB2015_1, SRB2015_38).

Against this background, reporting hate crimes and/or discrimination is perceived by LGBT people as dangerous and as something better avoided as the process inevitably requires LGBT people to come out. Indeed, the first instance where victims of discrimination and/or hate crime have to publicly declare their sexuality is the moment when they report the incident – i.e. they need to publicly declare that they have been discriminated against or attacked because of their sexual orientation. In other words, reporting discrimination or instances of harassment inevitably means coming out. Although initial declarations occur in a confidential setting, as soon as the victim makes an official statement, officers have the obligation to submit that statement to the prosecutor, leading it to enter the public domain (Interview SRB2014_7, SRB2015_17, SRB2015_19). From that moment onwards, the case can be reported in the media, which risks further 'outing' the victim. But even if the media does not get involved, the danger of being 'outed' – and the associated repercussions – remains real as the victim will receive an invitation to the court to their home address, which is often the parental home, which sparks parents to raise difficult questions about the reasons for the invitation – questions that many victims would rather avoid.

To illustrate, a lesbian from Subotica stated that she probably would not report hate crimes or discrimination, despite the law (interview SRB2015_54). Because she is not out, she fears her parents might discover her sexuality if she presses charges. Another even more telling illustration is the case of a gay man who was blackmailed because of his sexuality. An activist, who provided support in the case, narrates how the victim refused to pursue a court case out of fear of being outed:

> For example, during one of my last cases, I was taking a guy to the police station. The issue was blackmailing – the worst part was that he was blackmailed by LGBT people, and that is very common, people who have nothing to lose, who are either out or live alone, know that a gay person or lesbian would not report blackmail. They then ask for money if they have some compromising material – a photo or something else. He [the victim] had already given 200 euros a few times, and when they asked for 500 euros he did not have the money and turned to me. ... I suggested to him that we go to the police together. I went there with him, introduced myself, and they [the police] pointed me straight away to an inspector in charge of these issues – actually the civil-operative [liaison] officer. [The officer explained in a friendly way to the victim that] blackmail is a severe criminal offence and that everything said at that time would remain within these four walls, but from the moment he gives a statement and when they arrest the suspects, they [the police], *ex officio*, have to submit the case to the prosecutor, and then the case goes to the

registry office of the court, the investigating judge, the lawyers of the accused, their family and perhaps the media too. The guy said: 'No, I do not want to report. I would rather give money than have my family finding out. I am giving money in order for my family not to find out.' (Interview SRB2015_19)

While this anecdotal evidence already provides support for the theory of the attitudinal panopticon, further evidence of the disciplining nature of persistent societal discriminatory attitudes can be found in the preliminary results of the recent FRA survey (European Union Agency for Fundamental Rights, 2020). As I have demonstrated elsewhere (Slootmaeckers, 2022), this survey revealed that both the feeling that reporting the discrimination would not lead to any change, and the unwillingness to out oneself in the process, are among the top three cited reasons for not reporting discrimination. This further confirms the notion of the attitudinal panopticon theory, where victims avoid reporting their experiences as it is associated with more risk than benefits.

I want to conclude the analysis with a final observation on how the problem of under-reporting is further amplified by the institutional setting discussed earlier, as well as a general disconnect between activists and LGBT people in Serbia (Interview SRB2014_6, SRB2014_7, SRB2015_10, SRB2015_13, SRB2015_14, SRB2015_19, SRB2015_23, SRB2015_30, SRB2015_39, SRB2015_51, SRB2015_53). Although it is beyond the scope of this book to examine this dynamic to the fullest, one must understand that this disconnect is largely due to the project-based professionalised nature of LGBT activism in Serbia. As most LGBT organisations are dependent on foreign donors, they are often heavily influenced by donors' agendas, which rarely include funds for 'community'-oriented projects (interviews SRB20145_14, SRB2015_19, SRB2015_39). Indeed, over the years, LGBT activists in Serbia have reported that their work has predominantly focused on advocacy initiatives and Belgrade Pride, both activities that strongly rely on cooperation with the state. Consequently, LGBT NGOs have been critiqued for not 'having done enough regarding the empowerment of LGBT people to report [discrimination and or hate crimes]' as community work, although not absent, has shifted to the background (Interview SRB2015_19). The increased focus on Belgrade Pride and its violent imagery, in particular, has contributed to the increased gap between the activist community and LGBT people in Serbia, and thus also to the problem of under-reporting. As discussed in more detail in Chapter 6, the political position of Belgrade Pride in Serbia's EU accession process has put LGBT people at greater risk of violence during the Pride parade period (Interview SRB2014_6). Moreover, the persistent securitisation of Pride has, as some observers comment, sent a message to the LGBT people that they are not safe in Serbia and that the state is not (always) willing to protect them (Interview SRB2015_3, SRB2015_6). Surrounded by such negative messages about their sexuality, it is reasonable to assume that this strengthens the attitudinal panopticon which in turn reduces the willingness to report instances of discrimination and hate crime.

Conclusion

In line with previous research findings that reforms driven by external incentives are often nothing more than 'Potemkin Europeanisation' or formal compliance (Davydova, 2012; O'Dwyer, 2012; Schimmelfennig and Sedelmeier, 2005b), this chapter has demonstrated that the implementation of the anti-discrimination framework is hindered by three different types of barriers: political, institutional and societal barriers. For example, the difficult process of establishing the CPE as well as the (indirect) political pressure aimed at undermining the independence of independent institutions, suggest that the political elite remains at best sceptical about anti-discrimination policies. Institutionally, the CPE is a young and developing institution with 'teething problems' (Falkner and Treib, 2008, p. 305), without the capacity and enforceability to perform its job to the fullest. Additionally, a continuing lack of understanding of the concept of discrimination and the anti-discrimination law, both in the judiciary system and society as a whole, acts as a constraint on the establishment of the case law needed to harmonise the court practices in the area of anti-discrimination. At the societal level, the implementation of the anti-discrimination law also seems to be hindered by the lack of people who are prepared to use the law, as discrimination cases remain under-reported.

This latter observation is important as it demonstrates that, while important, EU practices, and domestic institutional and political barriers, remain insufficient explanations to fully grasp why fundamental rights legislation remains weakly implemented. To fully grasp why laws are not sufficient to create social change, we must examine the societal context in which laws are adopted. Using the theory of the attitudinal panopticon (Slootmaeckers, 2022), I have demonstrated that persistent societal attitudes create visibility regimes that govern people who are different from the norm to self-regulate their actions and stop them from challenging the status quo by reporting injustices. The lack of social change becomes a disciplining environment in which people whose rights have been violated are prevented from seeking justice out of fear of further and more severe violations of their rights.

These findings raise important questions with regard to the Europeanisation literature's implicit assumption that (formal) compliance with EU rules and adoption of institutions eventually leads to social change. The rather narrow understanding of the EU's impact on domestic politics, by orienting itself towards changes in public policy, not in values and attitudes, is shown to obscure how the lack of social change itself become a barrier to the proper functioning of the laws. Thus, by demonstrating the importance of societal factors for our understanding of why norm promotion does not lead to the hoped-for outcomes, the chapter points to a major flaw in the EU enlargement strategy. In particular, I demonstrated that the EU's current focus on the adoption of policies and the creation of institutions (which often remain quite weak) is not sufficient for the promotion of fundamental values abroad. Rather than directing its energy to the so-called socialisation of elites, the EU should actively involve the public in its enlargement process to engage in actions and policies that enable social transformations and cultural shifts. Without doing so, the social environment may become a barrier for the envisioned reforms. Secondly, the EU should also become aware of the political process that underpins the enlargement process. Doing so would enable it to move beyond using fundamental rights as a means to demark differences (Slootmaeckers, 2020), and to engage with its own fundamental rights regime more intensely. Such a more honest fundamental rights policy requires the EU to first define more clearly what it considers to be its values and norms (beyond their institutional incarnations), but also help to overcome current unaccountability of member states in regard to norm violations. Hence, to overcome the problems identified in this chapter and the book more widely, the EU needs to develop a policy that engages more deeply with the content of the EU's normative regime, rather than its form, both within and outside its borders.

Notes

1 Parts of this chapter have been previously published and are reused with permission of Oxford University Press: Slootmaeckers, K. 2022. Unpacking normative resonance: The attitudinal panopticon and the implementation gap of LGBT rights in Serbia. *Social Politics: International Studies in Gender, State & Society*, 29(1), pp. 1–23.
2 Although 16 per cent seems like a small proportion of society at first glance, a more detailed analysis of the survey design suggest that this question might be biased by socially desirable answers. This is mainly due to normative and value-laden question working and an unbalanced answer set (Slootmaeckers, 2022).

6

The emergence of the Ghost Pride and the transnational dislocation of LGBT politics

In Chapter 4, I demonstrated how Belgrade Pride has become deeply imbedded in Serbia's European integration process and evolved into a litmus test for Europeanisation. In this chapter, I explore and seek to better understand how this process has shaped Pride as an activist tool for the promotion of LGBT visibility and engendering progressive change.[1] Although it has been recognised that Belgrade Pride, as part of Serbia's EU accession process, forced the topic of LGBT issues into the public debate and forced the state authorities to recognise the presence of LGBT lives (at least to some extent), it has also been noted by many interviewees that these achievements might have been partly hollowed out by a problematic transfer of Pride as a (Western-originated) activist tool to Serbia, as well as Pride's turbulent organisational history.

Before delving into the politics of Belgrade Pride in more detail, however, I want to take the time to reflect on the history of Pride, its role within LGBT activist practice and its international context – i.e. its role in 'Western' LGBT history as well as its globalisation and transfer to other parts of the world. Although the political, cultural and social context of the 'Western' Prides are not comparable to those in Eastern Europe or Serbia, one must recognise that Pride is a local, vernacularised version of a globalised event (Thoreson, 2014). In other words, while every Pride has its own local origin, particularities and politics, the idea of Pride within LGBT activism is globalised so that we cannot understand local incarnations without its wider context and history. This reference to Pride's history, however, should not be mistaken for a sequential account of LGBT history, nor that Serbian activist must and will follow the Western pattern of fighting for their rights. On the contrary, agreeing with Kulpa and Mizielińska's (2011) critique that the 'East' needs its own complex understanding of time, the Western history of Pride is used here as a 'heuristic tool to help organise … findings. It can be amended and does not imply that specific groups necessarily go through every stage. It is also involved in the construction of both a memory and mythology of lesbian and gay activism, which are still alive in many parts of the worlds and hence need to be studied' (Paternotte and Tremblay, 2015, p. 7).

At the risk of oversimplifying, the practice of organising Pride parades is said to have its origin in the 1969 Stonewall riots, which marked a qualitative change in the way the movement approached its activism. In the wake of the riots, the gay liberation philosophy gained significant traction in the movement as it moved away from 'gay shame' to 'gay pride', seeking to build a (grassroots) movement which would be ready to become visible in society (Armstrong and Crage, 2006; Carter, 2004; Duberman, 1993). As part of this, activists organised to commemorate the Stonewall riots at a national level by organising protests, marches and parades in different cities (Carter, 2004). By showing that it is through the 'strength of mass solidarity in a movement that individuals [become] empowered to come out' (Weeks, 2015, p. 50), these first demonstrations created a 'collective effervescence by visually and experientially counteracting the view that homosexuality is private and shameful' (Armstrong and Crage, 2006, p. 472). They thus showed the potential of a collective display of solidarity to construct powerful identities as well as to develop a 'strong affirmation of the ideal of community – a sense of belonging that [does] not obliterate the individual self but made a positive sense of self achievable', which in turn enables political agency (Weeks, 2015, p. 50).

In the following decades, the idea of Pride travelled across the globe (albeit initially in the 'West') to become one of the most powerful and visible initiatives of the LGBT movement. Although modular in nature, taking on different shapes and forms across the world, the notion/practice of Pride is said to be aimed at a configuration of four aims: 1) community building by providing a sense of collective identity, 2) increasing visibility via collective coming out, used to demand (legal and/or societal) changes, 3) forcing the state to recognise LGBT people, and/or 4) the transgression of heterosexual public spaces (Ammaturo, 2015a; Armstrong and Crage, 2006; Browne, 2007; Duggan, 2010; Renkin, 2013; Stella, 2013; Woodcock, 2004).

That being said, it would be short-sighted to assume that all Prides have the same political goals and formations or that these have been the same over time. Simply looking to the history of Pride already demonstrates how much its nature and political character changed over time and space. For example, following the transformation of the radical gay liberation movement into a more moderate LGBT rights movement in much of the western world, many of the Pride parades changed as well – evolving into mass events, festival-like tourist attractions, often mediatised through sensationalised and sexualised imagery. Moreover, as they became institutionalised and, in some instances, commercialised, Pride marches' relationship with politics – although never absent – has become more ambiguous (Ammaturo, 2015a), often abandoning radical claims for change. With the rise of homonationalism, and the integration of LGBT politics in international relations, in some contexts, Pride has been instrumentalised by state institutions for their (homonationalist) goals. Ammaturo (2015a, p. 28) eloquently argued that, as LGBT people have 'become the symbols of the nation's tolerance and openness, contrasted with other countries' presumed backwardness', Pride participants – despite their intention to protest the political status quo – may 'end up contributing to the creation of a positive image of the same institutional apparatus that they seek to critique' (Ammaturo, 2015a, p. 28).

While it is not my aim to compare Serbia's Pride to the Western experience and practice of Pride, having an understanding of the history of Pride, as discussed above, remains important as, although qualitatively different from Western Prides, Pride in Serbia cannot be understood outside the political context and history of Pride more generally. This is certainly the case as the notion of Pride remains deeply embedded in the history of 'Western' Prides, as well as their current imagery. And it is true in Central, Eastern, and Southeastern European countries, which after the collapse of communism adopted a 'Western style of political and social engagement, without much questioning of its historical particularism and suitability for their context' (Mizielińska and Kulpa, 2011, p. 14). Civil society organisations in these countries developed with strong support from foreign (often Western) donors, who provided not only financial assistance, but also moulded activist agendas (Butterfield, 2016). As such, the transfer of 'Western' modes of activism introduced discourses of visibility, coming out and collective identity in 'Eastern' LGBT activism (Dioli, 2009; Lambevski, 2009; Woodcock, 2009), including the idea that Pride is an 'essential' strategy to increase LGBT visibility.

However, the globalisation of Pride as an activist tool did not happen without difficulties. Indeed, the transfer of Pride has been fraught with complications due to the fact that by bringing the practice to different contexts it becomes partially decoupled from its Western history without fully undoing the linkage with the globalised imagery of the Western mass events. To illustrate, whereas Western LGBT (i.e. gay liberation) organisations flourished as a 'reaction of a *structurally disadvantaged* population facing an extremely homophobic legal system' as well as systematic police harassment (Bilić, 2016d, p. 207, original emphasis), the current wave of LGBT organisa-tions in Central and Eastern Europe are part of an NGO-ised civil society consisting of a largely professionalised version of activism (Butterfield, 2016; Woodcock, 2009). Hence, whereas Western Pride parades were organised by, for, and with a grassroots movement which was ready to 'come out' – both individually and collectively – and participate in identity politics, Pride events in the 'East' seem decoupled from such a grassroots base.

This geotemporal dislocation of Pride parades in other parts of the world is not always recognised by NGO-ised and donor-driven activists, as there is a strong assumption among international actors that the visibility politics of Pride have a universal effectiveness, easily transferable or even exportable across cultural and geographical divides (Stella, 2012). Such views of Pride leave little room to consider its Western history and the globalised (sexualised) imagery of Prides, which inherently surround and confound Pride attempts outside the Western geotemporality, and how this shaped Pride's politics. For example, with the readily available images of 'Western' Prides, one can ask whose visibility does Pride in other places create: that of the local LGBT people or a 'global (yet Western) gay'? For example, in the context of Russia, Stella (2007, 2012, 2013) observed that when Pride is organised by a small number of LGBT activists with international support, but without the involvement of the 'grassroots community', it may end up rendering the community it wants to empower invisible, while at the same time reinforcing the locally held assumption that homosexuality is a Western import.

In addition to the implications of the potential geotemporal dislocation of imported activist tools, the politics of Pride are also shaped by the way in which LGBT rights are used to measure the modernness of nations, with Pride often serving as a litmus test for progress. As shown in Chapter 4, this has often led to a backlash as Prides are positioned as 'security threats' that 'might incite violence from religious and extremist groups and result in a general backlash against gay people' (Stella, 2012, p. 153). This often leads to militarised Pride events reliant on heavy security measures to protect participants. These circumstances, however, raise questions about the messages sent by such Pride events and their ability to create a collective identity and feelings of belonging. Indeed, Mercer (cited in Rhodes-Kubiak, 2015, p. 76) already highlighted that the 'heavy security often needed to protect … Pride parades in post-Communist Europe is counterproductive in the messages it sends to the wider society … reinforcing the association between LGBT activities, danger, and insecurity in the public consciousness'.

Taking into account the above history and complexity of the transnational politics of Pride events, this chapter seeks to unpack how the international politics of Pride have shaped Belgrade Pride. It pays particular attention to the unintended consequences of the 'Europeanisation' of Pride. It examines how European 'pink testing' (Rahman, 2014) using Pride affects the domestic politics of Pride by reinscribing the international character of a practice that was previously vernacularised. In doing so, the chapter highlights the potential negative impact of using Pride as a litmus test in the context of violence and heavy security measures, particularly when it remains discon-nected from its grassroots. In such a context, it is shown that rather than producing a collective identity – providing space for LGBT people to come out – Pride can then push people deeper into the closet, thereby destabilising the political potential of an imagined LGBT community. Moreover, while greater visibility often – in almost any context – leads to increased opposition (Ayoub, 2016; Stein, 2012), the disconnect between the local 'community' and Pride, combined with the strong linkage with international images of Pride, can lead to the appropriation of these visibility attempts by opponents of LGBT rights in their own (nationalist) politics.

Belgrade Pride as a community building tool?

From the first attempt to organise the Belgrade Pride parade in 2001, Pride in Serbia has been geotemporally dislocated and, as Bilić (2016d, p. 207) rather convincingly argues:

> Much of the controversy (and overt violence) accompanying Pride organisation shows that this manifestation was belatedly transferred as a commodified political instrument in the context of (visual) globalisation in which the images of the Western Pride … are easily available, consequently undermining the idea that such a protest in Serbia 'authentically' stems from local grievances.

Indeed, while the aim of the first Pride attempt in 2001 was to take a stand against the political and societal homophobia fostered by the nationalist politics of the 1990s (Interview SRB2015_10), it remains questionable whether it was able to do so. Organised by a small (and arguably elite) group of activists, the 2001 Pride enjoyed little support of a grassroots 'community', and seemed rather detached from Serbian LGBT people and their grievances. To illustrate, one long-term activist noted that the 2001 Pride was not known by the 'community', nor other friendly civil society organisations. They highlighted that 'the information about the first Pride was not public; it circulated among relatively few people' (Interview SRB2015_45). Hence, while the 2001 Pride has been interpreted by some as the symbolic coming out of LGBT issues in Serbia (see Rhodes-Kubiak, 2015, p. 124), the type of LGBT issues that actually became visible might have been less localised than organisers had hoped for (Bilić, 2016d).

Indeed, despite the fact that activists only cautiously invoked Europe as a reference point, opponents relied strongly on the international aspect and actively drew attention to the readily available sexualised imagery of Western Prides to take a stance against, what they called, the 'spreading of unchristian immorality and perverse orgies' (cited in Djurić, 2001). For example, one extremist opponent stated in a televised interview: 'This is not Berlin or Paris. This is Serbia. This kind of things does not happen here ... these faggots, homosexuals and all that is going on against the Serbian people' (quoted in Bilić, 2016a, p. 121). As such, it seems Pride was unable to create visibility of local LGBT people and their problems, and instead increased the visibility of what it sought to challenge: the image of a 'globalised gay identity' (Bilić, 2016a) – what opponents labelled 'homosexualism' – i.e. LGBT visibility and Belgrade Pride was part of a Western attempt to destroy Serbian values (Interviews SRB2015_43, SRB2015_45, SRB2015_46).

Similarly, in 2009, Belgrade Pride was caught in a similar dynamic of internationalisation and local decoupling. First, whereas most media coverage on LGBT issues remained rather non-local after the 2001 Pride (interview SRB2014_7), the controversy associated with the adoption of the anti-discrimination law further cemented LGBT rights as an international issue. As discussed in Chapter 3 in more detail, both sides of the debate used a European argument to gain political support for or against the law: while LGBT rights advocates heavily relied on EU (visa liberalisation) conditionality, opponents framed the law as a (Western) attack on Serbian values. Drawing on the relative 'success' of the European framing in the lobbying for the anti-discrimination law, both domestic and international actors tried to link Belgrade Pride to the anti-discrimination law – as a first real test of the law. And through this linkage with the anti-discrimination law, Pride could not escape its internationalisation whereby it inherently became linked to the European integration process. Whether intended or not, Pride had become part and parcel of Serbia's path to the EU – often linking Pride with Serbia's Europeanness. Recall, for example, the remarks of Michael Cashman, who had proclaimed that the 2009 Pride ban had shown that Serbia 'is not ready to become a member of the EU' (quoted in Wockner, 2009). Similarly, in 2010, Western embassies considered the 'successful' Belgrade Pride an 'example of [Serbia's] embrace of Western, liberal values' (cited in Kirchick, 2010). And as previously demonstrated in Chapter 4, the initial 'Europeanness' of Belgrade Pride was only further reinforced by the international framing and imagery of the 2010 Pride. The externalisation of Pride by prominent politicians, as well as the 'litmus test-isation' of Pride by the EU in response to Pride bans (Slootmaeckers, 2017), further delocalised the visibility of Pride (Bilić, 2016a; Mikuš, 2011), as did the representation of Pride in the media.

Although the early Pride attempts put LGBT issues on the media's radar (Interview SRB2015_6), local LGBT lived experiences have not become more visible. In fact, the media reporting on Belgrade Pride has contributed to the invisibility of local LGBT lives in two ways. First, whereas most articles on LGBT issues are published during the period leading up to and immediately following Belgrade Pride (Todorović, 2013), coverage throughout the year focuses predominantly on foreign LGBT news (Interview SRB2014_7), which further contributes to the visibility of a globalised gay identity. Second, the reporting on the Belgrade Pride parade focuses almost exclusively on the state response to security issues surrounding the event, thereby 'effectively stifling all other discussion around the ... discrimination faced by members of LGBT communities and what can be done to counter it' (Igrutinović, 2015, p. 63) – thus rendering local LGBT lives invisible (Interview SRB2012_1).

The internationalisation and linkage of Pride with a 'globalised gay identity', together with the lack of creating meaningful visibility of LGBT people's lived experiences, in the period analysed, meant that Belgrade Pride also lost its potential to engender an LGBT community in Serbia, as it has not (yet) been able to display a sense of mass solidarity that empowers others to come out (see Weeks, 2015). If one considers the images of successful Belgrade Pride parades – which showed riots, or extreme military presence, much like a city under siege – it should come as no surprise that the 'magical emotional impact' (Armstrong and Crage, 2006, p. 472) that LGBT Prides are said to have had elsewhere, might not occur. To illustrate, in 2009 Belgrade was covered in graffiti threatening Pride and homosexuals more generally. Whereas these threats remained present during the 2010 Pride, the violence and riots following that event demonstrated how real the threats were. Although such incidents did not happen in the Prides following 2014, the high level of securitisation – Pride only made possible through the deployment of 7,000 police officers in riot gear and armoured vehicles – reinforced the idea that LGBT people are not safe in Serbia unless protected by extraordinary security measures. Media pictures of the 2014 and 2015 Pride also show how Belgrade Pride took place in a 'security bubble', invisible to passers-by and impossible to join, raising questions as to whether it was able to generate a 'magical' moment of mass solidarity.

More generally, some have argued that the increased framing of Belgrade Pride as a litmus test for Serbia's Europeanness by both domestic and international actors has put LGBT people at greater risk of violence during the Pride parade period. According to the community policing department, there is a yearly spike in hate crimes against LGBT people in the period leading up to and following Pride (Interview SRB2015_41). While it must be recognised that increased visibility is often associated with increased opposition (Ayoub, 2016), the administrative difficulties and complex relationships with the state left activists with little resources to organise Pride in a way that would provide any sense of community and/or support.

The lack of meaningful visibility of lived LGBT experiences, the persistent securitisation of Pride combined with the discursive and visual linkage with violence, has been identified as the main reason for the growing disconnect between activists and the people they claim to represent (Stojčić, 2014; see also Interviews SRB20145_14, SRB2015_19, SRB2015_39). In fact, most participants of the 2010, 2014 and 2015 Prides were predominantly international delegates, from international institutions and international human and LGBT rights civil society, domestic civil society, political representatives and straight allies (Interview SRB2015_12, and author's fieldnotes). Aleksandar Prica eloquently explains the disconnect between Pride and the local LGBT 'community':

> Generally, LGBT persons have much more problems during the Pride and during the time when Pride is being organised than during the entire year ... When the Pride is cancelled, a message is sent to the LGBT people that the state cannot protect them. LGBT people ... simply don't want Pride. (Interview SRB2015_19)

A study by the Centre for Queer Studies in Belgrade further confirms Prica's observation (Stojaković, 2014). Of the 416 LGBT people interviewed, only 29 per cent supported Belgrade Pride; 26 per cent did not, and 7 per cent had no opinion. The remaining 38 per cent, while supporting the idea of Pride, did not agree with the way it is organised (Stojčić, 2014). Although these figures already provide a strong indication that LGBT people do not support the (contemporary version of) Belgrade Pride, the detachment of activists and LGBT people becomes even more prominent when one considers the differences in activists' and non-activists' replies to the question of whether they would attend the next Pride: 46 per cent of activists and 11 per cent of non-activists would take part in Pride, while 16 and 53 per cent, respectively, would not participate (Stojčić, 2014). Such attitudes towards Pride, the study highlights, are predominantly shaped by fears about safety. Of the surveyed LGBT respondents, 36 per cent think that Pride 'brings more damage than benefits', and similarly, 42 per cent agreed with the statement that the 'Pride parade contributes to the increase of fear and hatred towards LGBT people' (Stojčić, 2014, p. 147).

The Europeanisation of Belgrade Pride into a litmus test cannot be ignored when considering these safety concerns, as the LGBTI rights issues within the Europeanisation process have engendered strong and violent nationalist opposition (see Chapter 4). Reflecting on this reality, the Belgrade-based NGO Gay Lesbian Info Centre (GLIC, 2013) issued a statement in 2013 arguing that the EU's involvement in Pride has resulted in more harm than good for the Serbian LGBT population:

> Gay Lesbian Info Centre demands that the LGBT population [be] no longer used to condition Serbia's accession to the European Union, because such a practice not only does not yield any results, but actually contributes to the increase of homophobia and animosity against the LGBT population in Serbia

> ... We believe that it is inappropriate to expose the LGBT population even
> more to the negative emotions of Serbian citizens and that is exactly what [EP
> rapporteur for Serbia] Jelko Kacin's statements do. Because of such statements,
> the LGBT population is singled out as a culprit for the fact that Serbia is not
> entering the European Union ... [I]f the EU does not help us to improve the
> status of LGBT people in Serbia, at least it should not make our job more
> difficult. The LGBT population in Serbia is frustrated by the fact that it is
> constantly positioned between the right-wings and the left-wings, between the
> European Union and Serbia, between human rights activists and hooligans
> and that it is the only one to end up harmed in this 'game'. This population
> is particularly frustrated by the fact that those who are declaratively in favour
> of LGBT rights do not at all consider what their actions do to the LGBT
> community itself. (translated in Bilić, 2016a, p. 139)

Up to this point I have demonstrated how LGBT people have withdrawn
from Belgrade, but the reverse process can also be observed. Indeed, the
internationalisation and Europeanisation of Belgrade Pride has forced activists
away from engaging with LGBT people when organising the event. Whereas
it could be said that Belgrade Pride has always had an elitist character – or
as Boban Stojanović, a key Pride organiser, admits: '[Pride] does not come
from the need of the community. It comes from some exclusive knowledge
of individuals' (Interview SRB2015_52) – this only intensified as the organisation of Pride became fraught with uncertainty and bans. In order to make
Pride happen, Pride organisers reportedly spend over ninety per cent of
their time in communication with state representatives and the international
community, with little resources left to engage LGBT people (Interviews
SRB2014_6, SRB2015_51). By doing so, the already weak link with LGBT
people in Serbia was further severed as 'only the activist circles [seem to]
know the point of Pride. LGBT people do not [know] because nobody is
practically working with them on that issue, to explain what is Pride and
why Pride matters' (Interview SRB2015_19). Indeed, Boban Stojanović
concurs:

> Our idea was to have the community more involved, but with the banning
> [of Pride] it was not a priority. The Pride bans brought something new: to
> have Pride as a form, as an event. [With the bans in] 2011, 2012, and 2013
> – partially, because we had Midnight Pride – there was not much space for
> community work ... You can have a campaign in which you explain what
> you want, why [Pride] is important, etc., but in those several years, it was
> almost impossible ... because there is this other, bigger discussion: Pride, yes
> or no? Pride, safe or not? Pride, ban or not? (Interview SRB2015_52)

Although non-Pride organising activists recognise these political conditions, they nevertheless seem to hold organisers partly responsible for the
disconnect with the LGBT population, especially highlighting their poor

communication with the 'community' and activist scene. Or as one activist eloquently describes:

> They [Pride organisers] need to talk to the community more. They need a link with the community ... [they] need to have some point where people can connect with, and that is the problem with Pride. If [good communication] is there, it will happen, but I have no idea what is happening. As part of the community, as an activist and part of the community, I have no idea what is happening [in the Pride week and with the parade]. (Interview SRB2015_40)

Additionally, the discursive shift towards a (human) rights-based framing of Pride has added to this disconnect by changing the role of Pride within wider activism (Interviews SRB2014_2, SRB2015_2, SRB2015_4, SRB2015_10, SRB2015_12, SRB2015_16, SRB2015_17, SRB2015_54). Whereas the 2009 Pride was framed as 'a political protest, a procession in which one marginalised group in society ... becomes visible and contributes to the respect for human rights' (Dragana Vučković quoted in Beta, 2009, translated by interpreter), the cancellation/ban of the 2009 Pride firmly positioned Belgrade Pride within the human rights discourse (interview SRB2015_12). Faced with the impossibility of organising Belgrade Pride, organisers indicated that, from 2010 onwards, they were increasingly pushed to frame Pride as the expression of LGBT people's (constitutional and human right to) freedom of assembly (Interview SRB2015_2). The international approach to Pride only strengthened that shift. As discussed in Chapter 4, the international community responded to the Pride bans by reminding Serbia primarily of its responsibility to guarantee the exercise of freedom of assembly. Indeed, for the EU, Pride is a 'question of freedom of expression, [and] freedom of assembly' (Interview EC2013_2). In fact, as there is no EU standard on Pride parades (i.e. not all member states have Pride events), the only way in which the EU can pressure Serbia to maintain the Pride parade is by emphasising freedom of assembly (Interviews EC2013_2, EC2013_3, SRB2015_23, SRB2015_26, EC2015_1). With activists often considering Europeanisation arguments the only successful approach to the Serbian government, Pride organisers were further pushed to align themselves with the international human rights frames and made, as many activists attest, Pride a goal in itself, rather than a tool (Interviews SRB2014_2, SRB2015_2, SRB2015_4, SRB2015_12, SRB2015_16, SRB2015_17, SRB2015_54).

Moreover, this human rights framework remained rather unchallenged as activists have highlighted that while 'successful' Prides are applauded by the EU, few actors seemed to ask more critical questions about the quality of Pride and how it contributes to improving the lived experiences of local LGBT people (Interview SRB2015_4, SRB2015_10). In fact, some activists have argued that the almost exclusive focus of the EU on Pride has seemingly given the impression that LGBT lives are reducible to this one event (Interview SRB2015_10). In her critical blog post, queer activist Lazara Marinković (2015, original emphasis) highlights the problems of the international overemphasising of the successfulness of Pride:

> Without going deep into the problematic of the Belgrade Pride March itself, of the organizer's ... complete detachment from the LGBT community and the everyday reality of LGBT people in Serbia, we can conclude that Belgrade Pride March 2014 didn't bring *any* positive social change at all ... Further more [sic], Serbia's example of Belgrade Pride parade was used in the OSCE/ODIHR conference on freedom of assembly as an example of good practice, disregarding the overall status of the LGBT people and freedom of assembly in Serbia, which [are] both deteriorating.

A tool for whom? Belgrade Pride co-opted by the state

The detachment from the people Pride claims to represent as well as its 'litmus test-isation' (Slootmaeckers, 2017) – as a symbol of Serbia's European-ness – raise an important question about the ownership of Pride, as an interviewee suggests:

> What I really dislike about the policy coming from the European Union is that the [progress] reports are praising the events which are not actually a step forward ... Of course, in every single place around the world the first couple of Prides were problematic, but the message that has to be communicated after the Pride, I believe, has to be different from the one that we have. First of all, we do not have one. The messages sent after the 2010 Pride and even the last one were: 'The state and politicians are not against us [LGBT people], because the EU pressures [Serbia] for these "faggots" to get together', and then 'it is a huge step because we had [Pride]', but *the question one should ask is: 'Who had it [Pride]?* A few NGO activists, the EU ambassadors and 5,000 policemen, in order to write a good report so that the EU can tell that there is good progress in Serbia?' ... So, I do not know what we want out of these gay Prides. (Interview SRB2015_18, emphasis added)

This question of 'whose Pride?' is indeed a critical issue to consider when discussing its 'implementation'.[2] If Pride is not for and/or by LGBT people, then for whom and by whom is Pride organised? Answering these questions allows us to reflect on whether or not Belgrade Pride (as they occurred between 2010 and 2015) forced the Serbian state to recognise LGBT citizens.

Although it is undeniable that the organisation of Pride in Serbia has forced (some) state institutions – especially the police – to recognise LGBT people as citizens (Interviews SRB2015_11; see also Chapter 4), the same cannot necessarily be said about the Serbian government. Increasing EU pressure on Serbia to maintain Pride may have 'forced the government's hand' to deal with the issue (Interview SRB2015_9), but inconsistent pressure (see Chapter 4), combined with the earlier described 'hollowing out' of Pride as an activist tool, allowed state institutions to deal with Pride in their own way. There is a strong consensus among activists – Pride organisers and non-organisers alike – that politicians have used the activists' disconnect with the 'community' and the internationalisation of the event to transform Pride into their own political tool (Interviews SRB2014_7, SRB2015_17, SRB2015_19, SRB2015_29, SRB2015_30, SRB2015_38, SRB2015_40, SRB2015_51, SRB2015_52, SRB2015_54).

The first signs of such political co-optation of Pride already became evident during the organisation process of the 2010 'State' Pride (Mikuš, 2011). Knowing that a 'successful' 2010 Pride would demonstrate Serbia's commitment to the EU integration project, the state became actively involved in organising Pride (see Chapter 4). Although Pride organisers took advantage of this situation to have Pride, others feared that this political alliance would come at a steep price. As one long-term feminist activist noted in a discussion on the 2010 Pride:

> It seems to me that the Socialist Party of Serbia and the Serbian Progressive Party are planning to hijack our forms, render them meaningless, empty them from their political content … and then simply throw them away … the sole purpose of all of this is meeting 'the standards' [European Union conditions] … this has nothing to do with our needs, but it is something which is asked from them … they are asked for Kosovo and they are asked for this (Pride). (cited in Bilić, 2016a, p. 135)

In the following years, this fear seemed to be well-founded as the state-condoned violence – the riots[3] – accompanying Pride provided politicians with the perfect excuse to withdraw their public support for the LGBT equality cause, and Pride in particular. As previously discussed, politicians were quick to blame the LGBT activists' provocative Pride and EU pressure for the destruction of Belgrade. Moreover, as the international community – especially the EU – strategically decided to focus on the success of Pride and congratulated the state for maintaining the event, a message was sent to politicians that Pride could be used as part of their tactical Europeanisation, as an instance of 'pragmatic pink-washing in the interest of a formal fulfilment of the requirements and the criteria of the EU' (Knežević cited in Bilić, 2016a, p. 135). Such a message resonates well with previous practices of the two former nationalist and authoritarian parties (SPS and SNS) who already seem to have used LGBT rights to demonstrate their new EU-compatible politics (see Vachudova, 2014). For example, in 2009 the SNS tried to show its pro-EU attitude by declaring they would have made the

2009 Pride possible (Kurepa, 2010). Similarly, SPS elected former LGBT activist Boris Milićević (co-founder of GSA and an openly gay man) as a member of the Board of the Socialist Party of Serbia in December 2010 (B92 and Tanjug, 2010). However, in the years to follow, Milićević was given little room to influence the party's LGBT politics or to prevent its leader, Dačić, from making homophobic remarks (see Chapter 4). In fact, the only time Milićević was able to influence party politics was when he was made adviser to the Minister of European Integration, Branko Ružić (SPS), in the period just after the third consecutive Pride ban (between September 2013 and April 2014, Interview SRB2015_55).

The riot further provided the government with the arguments to push LGBT issues off the political agenda. Indeed, as discussed in Chapter 4, in a period of political instability – in which organising Pride would be too costly – the state used security reasons as a pretext to ban Pride, 'postponing' dealing with Pride until the (new) government sufficiently consolidated power (Interview SRB2015_59). Preventing criticism of pursuing an anti-LGBT agenda by adopting hate crime legislation (see Chapter 3), the banning of Pride provided the state with ample benefits and little costs. Perunović (2015) convincingly argued that the Pride bans were an opportunity for the Serbian government to exercise its sovereignty through a 'state of exception' – a (partial/total) suspension of juridical order itself where the sovereign position itself is neither internal nor external to the judicial order. In doing so, the state is able to reinforce its power position in Serbia 'under the guise of its protective role (paradoxically impotent and omnipotent at the same time)' (Perunović, 2015, p. 82) – impotent in its inability to protect Belgrade Pride from threats, and omnipotent through the claim that, by banning Pride, the Serbian government is protecting all of its citizens (but not LGBT citizens).

By banning Belgrade Pride, as well as by focusing on its security aspects, the government further pushed it into the human rights frame, thereby (unintentionally) depoliticising Pride as an activist tool. Such depoliticisation is perfectly illustrated by Vučić's characterisation of Pride as a 'leisurely walk' in 2014 (see Chapter 4). Thus, the Pride bans contributed to a transfer of ownership of Pride: from LGBT activists to the state.[4] As such, it can be argued that, in the period examined, 'Pride is [no longer] organised by civil society organisations, but by politicians' (Interview SRB2015_19). Or as two activists critically observe:

> Pride as Pride is insignificant; it is not important. But it is a tool for political parties for their political fights. Because on the issue of Pride, you will have fights between so-called left and right; anti-EU and pro-EU: against Russia and for Russia parties … You will have a clash of many people that are not LGBT on the issue of Pride, and we [LGBT people] are collateral damage …

It is interesting that pro and against, all those cases do not value the LGBT issue because they [politicians] are fighting their fights, they are not thinking about us. (Interview SRB2014_7)

[As such, Pride] is just a matter of PR. The government wants to appear as having European-oriented values, which I have to say is crap because it is not genuine and not sincere and that is why [Pride] happened last year [2014] ... It is a tool for politicians. And what I am mad about is that those organisations with the explanation that it is better to have something rather than nothing, they are excepting it. (Interview SRB2015_30)

When Pride returned to Belgrade in 2014, it was arguably again the government, and PM Vučić in particular, who stood to gain most (Interview SRB2015_17). Playing on the organisers' focus on the right to freedom of assembly, Vučić used Pride as a homonationalist move, a tool within the process of tactical Europeanisation, to bolster his (inter)national image as a reforming pro-EU force, and to highlight his capacity to enforce Serbia's constitution. For example, the highly militarised imagery of Pride helped Vučić – as personification of the state – to demonstrate that 'the [state/ Vučić's government] is incontestable in its protective role and [that] its [political] *will* is not to be contested anymore' (Perunović, 2015, p. 82). Moreover, by militarising Pride, Vučić transformed the 'State Pride' into a 'Ghost Pride' (Interview SRB2015_57) – i.e. a state-tolerated manifestation of Pride which remains invisible to the wider public.

To repurpose Brown's (2006, pp. 98–99) words, this manifestation of the Ghost Pride reflects a tolerance that 'is secured through our averted glance, by a kind of visual privatisation that is a ghostly repetition of the actual privatisation of sexuality required if homosexuals are to be tolerated at all'. Indeed, the security perimeter – officially created to protect Pride participants – has the secondary function of a 'transparent closet' (Kuhar, 2011) that keeps LGBT people's visibility invisible and outside the public sphere.[5] Apart from this physical appearance, the 'transparent closet' also exists discursively. As the public debates on Pride predominantly focus on the security aspects of the event and on whether Pride would take place, there is no discursive visibility of LGBT lived experiences and grievances. In other words, by highlighting the security aspect of Pride, the state (unintentionally) reduced LGBT visibility to the minimum – i.e. a ritualistic (or so-called 'leisurely') walk through the city void of politics. One of the Pride organisers explained how she experienced this impact on the Pride event as she felt that the state and the police were

demonstrating their power much more than they are protecting us ... Like they are exactly isolating us and protecting us in the same way, because I feel that sometimes [with Pride and other street actions] they [the police] always come, so many of them and you are like 'Is this really necessary?' You are surrounded by police, no one can pass you, and you do not have any kind of contact with the population, there is you, the circle of police and the rest of the world. (Interview SRB2015_39)

Although it is undeniable that the state has appropriated Pride as its own homonationalist tool while 'closeting' the visibility aspect of Pride, it cannot go unnoticed that Pride organisers are also complicit in the change, albeit unintentionally. Indeed, non-Pride organising LGBT activists and former activists have argued that because Pride developed as a goal in itself, disconnected from the 'community', organisers' representation of Pride has also contributed to this 'closeting' of LGBT people. For example, it has been pointed out that organisers are 'always explaining and elaborating very strongly that nobody should worry, that Pride is not going to be as it is in San Francisco, that nobody is going to be naked as if that is something that should not happen' (Interview SRB2015_30), in an attempt to make Pride less publicly contested as well as to reduce the connection with the international gay identity. By doing so, the argument goes, organisers are 'trying to prepare everybody that it is going to be a *very composed and controlled Pride* where gay people are just going to walk', and thus reducing the possibility of LGBT people expressing their lived experiences (Interview SRB2015_30, emphasis added), removing any radical claim for transformation from Pride.

Similarly, in 2013 Pride organisers decided to ignore the homophobic comments of then Prime Minister Dačić, as they assumed these comments were made to please his (nationalist) support base, though still allowing Pride. Talking about the 2013 Pride ban, a former Pride organiser questions whether they did not make too many compromises in order to make Pride happen:

> I was ashamed because, in that moment, I thought we compromised a lot for the Pride to happen. We did not react so forcefully when Ivica Dačić made homophobic statements because we did not want to make a big fuss because if he allows Pride, then it is OK, and we expected Pride to happen … It was a difficult pill to swallow, but I was like, 'OK, if we have Pride, then it was worth it.' We were all aware of the compromise, we were all disgusted with everything that was happening, but you wanted to try not the attack him. We also thought that that was part of his rhetoric, so he will allow Pride since he is trying to keep the constituency covered from all angles. (Interview SRB2015_57)

A final observation relates to the fact that Pride happens in an empty city surrounded by several thousand security personnel, barely visible to the general public, which has affected Pride's potential to transgress/queer public space. Although Belgrade Pride certainly does transgress the heterosexual public space,[6] the securitisation of the event has moved it to a temporarily privatised public space (the sealed-off city), thereby confining transgression of the heterosexual public space to the temporality and spatiality of the security bubble. Indeed, as Pride participants remain vulnerable to the heightened homophobic tension created by the event, and thus violent attacks, Pride organisers (understandably) advise participants to remove all Pride-related symbols from their bodies when leaving the premises (Fieldnotes, 20 September 2015). As such, any evidence of Pride taking place disappears immediately after the event finishes, only to return with next year's Pride. And although organisers say they are aware of this problem, they are constantly put in an impossible situation where they have to choose between their politics and the potential to endanger Pride. To illustrate, consider Predrag Azdejković's critical observations about the Pride organisers and the activist community more widely:

> It is interesting that we do not have the balls to be anti-government. If we are anti-government, next year we will not have Pride because we have Pride only when the government says so … We do not need Pride to build a better govern-ment and better relations between the EU and the government. If we cannot be critical, and we are censoring ourselves only so that the government can say 'you can have Pride', I don't see the point. It is better not to have Pride or to create that false image of Serbia being a tolerant country. No, we are not. Why are we [as activists] playing that game? (Interview SRB2015_51)

Conclusion

Although the original intention of Pride, as an activist tool, was to raise visibility for the LGBT lived experience and to build a (political) community, one cannot assume that Pride is universally effective in creating such outcomes. This is particularly the case, as Pride does not operate within a vacuum and is increasingly intertwined with international and transnational politics. Analysing the impact of Europeanisation processed on the meaning of Pride, the chapter aligned itself with Ammaturo's (2017) claim that linking LGBT rights to the appealing idea of Europe can be a harmful action. In my analysis, I have sought to question the presumed universal effectiveness of Pride of Pride as a visibility-raising strategy, and critically interrogate the EU's practice of using Pride parades as a litmus test for Europeanness in the enlargement process and its political consequences.

Based on my study of Belgrade Pride, I would contend that embedding Prides in wider international (civilisational) politics – which are part and parcel of the Europeanisation process – has serious political implications.

Indeed, the findings clearly demonstrate the EU's homocolonialist practice of what Rahman (2014, p. 281) calls 'pink testing', combined with the domestic resistance to this, has had a harmful impact on local LGBT people and politics. Whereas using Pride as a litmus test for Europeanness has led to a politicisation of the issue on the international level, forcing the Serbian state to engage with the event, it also allowed for the transformation of Pride's national politics. Over the years, Belgrade Pride has been co-opted by the state to demonstrate Europeanness towards the EU, while the militarisation of the event created a 'Ghost Pride' – a state-tolerated manifestation of Pride – which takes place in a militarised 'transparent closet' that keeps LGBT people's visibility strategies invisible and outside the public sphere, reinforcing traditional and nationalist conceptions of Serbian society.

Moreover, the intertwining of international and domestic politics surrounding Belgrade Pride meant that Pride organisers came to occupy a rather impossible position, caught between national and European politics, with limited room to escape the homocolonialist implications of the EU's pink testing. This being the case, Serbian Pride organisers opted to align themselves with the attractive idea of Europeanness in order to allow Pride to go ahead. Indeed, with the aim of overcoming the bans, but also of increasing the saliency of the issue, they framed Pride as an expression of the universal human right of freedom of assembly, linking it discursively to the European integration process. Although the internationalisation of Pride helped to make the event possible from 2014 onwards, this strategy also backfired as it led to the domestic depoliticisation of Pride. Increasingly decoupled from its local constituency, without sufficient support from its grassroots and strongly reliant on apolitical human rights discourses, Pride became a form of activism, an outcome rather than a tool to achieve change, and devoid of LGBT politics. This political reality also presents real challenges for activists to reclaim Pride as their own tool in subsequent years.

The presented findings also have important implications for the Europeanisation of LGBT rights literature. Like Bilić (2016a; 2016b), I seek to provide a more critical understanding of how Europeanisation and transnational LGBT politics shape LGBT politics in the region. Yet I believe to fully understand how the Europeanisation of Belgrade Pride has contributed to the local disconnect of Pride with the 'community', and the absence of a political agenda, we cannot just draw attention to the EU's imperial-like LGBT rights conditionality, but must also consider the limitations in opportunities for local LGBT activisms produced by the transnational character of LGBT politics more broadly. With regard to the latter, I have argued that through the particular usage of LGBT rights within the transnational context, and the interaction between domestic and international politics, that the meaning of the LGBT equality norms, and Pride in particular, has been reinterpreted. In other words, it was a complex feedback loop of domestic and international LGBT politics that produced critical challenges for activisms which, in turn, limited the politicality of Belgrade Pride. For as long as activists are caught in the liminal position between the EU and the national (within the East–West dynamic), developing a locally grounded version of Pride might prove to be difficult, but not necessarily impossible.

Notes

1 A shorter version of this analysis has previously been published and is reused with permission: Slootmaeckers, K. 2017. The litmus test of Pride: Analysing the emergence of the Belgrade 'Ghost' Pride in the context of EU accession. *East European Politics*, 33(4), pp. 517–535.

2 In his recent work, Bilić (2016d) also engaged with this question. Taking a sociological angle, Bilić raises important questions about whether the Pride organisation adequately represents LGBT people and their grievances. He highlights how the Pride parade is not able to consider the class and gender diversity within the LGBT population. While such argument reinforces the disconnect between Pride and the LGBT population I discussed earlier, here I reflect on the question 'Whose Pride?' in accordance to Mikuš' (2011) work, who has argued that the 2010 Belgrade Pride was a 'State Pride'.

3 The riots can be described as state condoned as police efforts to prevent them were rather limited. In the name of police impartiality, opponents of Pride were given ample opportunities to protest against the event and organise the riots.

4 This transfer of ownership is further aided by the increasing conflict between LGBT organisations about the usefulness of Pride, and what some perceive as the hegemonisation of Pride by the current organisers, who not only have become disconnected from LGBT people, but also from the activist community (anonymised interviews).

5 Also consider the military parade in 2014, which further closeted the visibility of LGBT people by reclaiming Pride as a militarised masculine event (Igrutinović, 2015).

6 The fact that Belgrade Pride does queer Serbia's heterosexual public space becomes clear when one considers the prayer marches that are organised only hours after the event, as these marches are explicitly meant to cleanse the city of the 'sins' promoted by the Pride (see e.g. Igrutinović et al., 2015; Mikuš, 2015).

Conclusion

> He made his government write new laws to alter some of the cruellest injustices that affected him ... These were the values he won that enlivened hope even where sluggish progress made no substantial changes in the quality or quantity of his daily bread ... The fight is far from over, because it is neither won, as some assert, nor lost, as the calamity-ridden declare. – Martin Luther King, Jr (*Where Do We Go from Here*, 2010 [1968], pp. 16–17)

We are often made to think of 'progress' as if it is something easily grasped or observed through changes in laws or the development of institutions or the absence of open conflict. But what does that mean? When is progress made? And if it has happened, for whom and why? These questions sit at the core of my research on the Europeanisation of LGBT politics in Serbia. While I do not underestimate the importance of legal change, I have sought to look beyond these institutions to ask what they mean for the wider struggle for social justice. As the Martin Luther King Jr quote above suggests: while laws can be made to change, the fight for equality and social justice is never won nor lost, but ever ongoing. Reflecting on LGBT activism and queer activism, Cathy Cohen (1997) powerfully argued for a transformative and queer politics that is continually challenging and critical, a ceaseless interrogation of power even after 'progress' or hard battles are won and change is achieved.

Vigilance and non-complacency about, as well as the critique and interrogation of, systemic changes, are needed to improve the lives of the most vulnerable and marginalised people in society: a task that rests with all of us, as we must not rest on our laurels and assume that fights are permanently won. Indeed, as diversity work now seems to be common, the mandates given to tackle inclusion are often not more than that: a mandate and a signal of vague engagement with the content of the said diversity work. Sara Ahmed (2017) reminds us that when institutions are legally obliged to introduce diversity and equality policies, they may appoint diversity workers in order to comply with the law and external conditions, but these appointments can often be more about keeping up appearances. To bestow someone with a diversity mandate 'might be how an institution appears willing to be transformed' (Ahmed, 2017, p. 94). More specifically, talking about the adoption of diversity strategies and race equality documents in the higher education sector, she reminds us of what these documents can do:

> *A document that documented the racism of the university became usable as a measure of good performance.* Here having a 'good' race equality policy got quickly translated into being good at race equality. Such a translation works to conceal the very inequalities that the document was written to reveal. The document becomes a fetish object, something that 'has' value, by being cut off from the process of documentation. In other words, its very existence is taken as evidence that the institutional world documented by the document (racism, inequality, injustice) has been overcome. (Ahmed, 2007, p. 597)

What is true for these higher education diversity documents also holds for how we look at countries and their approaches to LGBT rights and legislation. For example, every year in May, ILGA-Europe publishes its Rainbow Index to map the state of LGBT equality within Europe, measured predominantly by the legal framework in existence in each country. This produces a ranking of countries by their LGBT-friendliness – much in line with the homonationalist moment where a country's modernity is measured through its LGBT-friendliness. Yet, as Ammaturo and Slootmaeckers (2020) highlight, these rankings and associated maps create a political narrative of progress that does not always relate to, or capture, LGBT lived experiences. This disjuncture produces what they call queer utopias and dystopias. Indeed, the overbearing focus on legislative frameworks, they argue, 'displaces lived experiences of LGBTQI+ people in Europe'. That is to say, in countries with lower levels of legal protection, the image of the eternal victimhood of LGBT people is perpetuated, which does not always resonate with people's daily experiences. For some countries with more LGBT-friendly legislation, on the other hand, the focus on legal developments underestimate that access to justice (i.e. access to legal counsel, litigation, etc.) often remains difficult for many LGBT people.

Next to these questions about what progress really means and what role is played by institutions, we must continue to critically engage with the symbolic place LGBT rights have been playing within international politics. Indeed, we have been experiencing a globalisation of LGBT rights that is characterised by 'a significant acceleration and intensification of international struggles by LGBT movements' (Kollman and Waites, 2009, p. 1). With these gains and the proliferation of sexuality politics within the international realm, LGBT rights have come to be used as an important signifier for what it means to be a modern nation. The monitoring of these rights has turned out to be a powerful pressuring tool in the hands of international advocacy groups – a topic of direct political contestation, both within and among countries – but also a tool for politicians to manage their own country's international reputation (Bracke, 2012). In other words, LGBT rights have developed in what English school scholars (e.g. Bowden, 2014; Bull, 1977) would label a 'standard of civilisation' (Delatolla, 2020) – i.e. the international legitimacy of a country and/or its nationhood are evaluated based on its treatment of its LGBT population. That is to say, states can advance their so-called exceptionalism or modernity by demonstrating their tolerance of homosexuality and contrasting it to 'homophobic Others'.

Although there is no opting out from this homonationalism (Puar, 2013b), it can be resisted and/or resignified. Indeed, whereas some countries and entities (including the UN, the United States and the EU) have increasingly embraced this historical moment by using LGBT rights as a symbol for what it means to be modern, Western, or even European (Ammaturo, 2015b; Ayoub and Paternotte, 2014b), others have resisted this development by emphasising an alternative value system based on so-called traditional values (Paternotte and Kuhar, 2017) and engage in a counter-hegemonic project of what Cooper-Cunningham (2021) has labelled 'heteronormative inter-nationalism'. Some have argued that this process has contributed to international norm polarisation (Altman and Symons, 2016) where countries either align themselves with one or the other extreme. Yet it remains unclear what happens when countries are caught in the crossfire.

Is the promotion of and the resistance to LGBT equality caught within an either/or logic in which countries can only belong to either side of the dichotomy? Or is it possible for a country to simultaneously strive to belong to an international community that champions LGBT rights *and* to resist LGBT equality norms? In other words, what happens to LGBT rights and politics when they are embroiled in wider transnational politics and normative struggles that are embedded within political integration processes such as the EU enlargement process?

With all these questions in mind, this book investigated the promotion of and resistance to LGBT equality as part of Serbia's EU accession process. Despite the fact that LGBT rights have acquired important symbolic value in EU politics and discourse – e.g. Pride parades can now serve to illustrate a candidate country's endorsement of European norms – such emphasis remains in stark contrast to limited EU competences and EU's *acquis* in this field and is thereby subject to potential contestation. Against this background, I aimed to disentangle the symbolism of LGBT rights in the EU enlargement process by focusing on the promotion of and resistance to LGBT rights within it. By considering the international context of homonationalism, my research moves away from a classical approach to Europeanisation in which the impact of the EU on a third country is examined.

As Ammaturo (2015b) and Slootmaeckers (2020) have argued, the EU's promotion of LGBT equality in itself constitutes a 'pink agenda' which is aimed at building and/or reconfirming Europe's human rights exceptionalism at the expense of homophobic Others. Yet linking LGBT rights to the appealing idea of Europeanness is 'far from … a harmless operation' and has potentially 'huge political and social implications' (Ammaturo, 2017, p. 93). Taking the EU's pro-LGBT self-representation for granted in a scholarly analysis of EU enlargement, then, would not only ignore these international usages of LGBT rights, but would also contribute to a problematic reification of an East–West divide (Kulpa and Mizielińska, 2011; Kuus, 2004, 2005, 2007), in which the 'East' is always presented as forever catching up with Western Europe.

To avoid such an uncritical approach to EU enlargement, this book highlights the political nature of the process by making the negotiation of LGBT equality norms and policies in Serbia's EU accession process the object of analysis. With the aim of studying the *politics of Europeanisation*, I argued that the EU enlargement process should not be understood as a unidirectional (top-down) process in which the EU 'transplants' its rules and norms to candidate countries, but instead should be considered a political process in which the combination and imbrication of domestic and international politics produces certain outcomes. To do so, I redefined Europeanisation as a process of *negotiated transformation* in which EU policies and norms are (re)defined, contested, translated and transformed with both sides making compromises to further the political integration. In other words, both the EU and candidate countries are not only involved in formal negotiations that comprise the EU enlargement process, but in their relationship are also continuously negotiating – and thus defining and redefining – the meaning of those values and norms that the EU claims to be its founding values. Thus, the values and norms that the EU claims to be at its core are themselves a process, always under contestation and being challenged and (re)defined. So, rather than considering the so-called normative power of Europe – which too often takes EU norms for granted – we must actively consider how these norms are constituted through the EU enlargement process, but equally how their content is being negotiated and transformed as part of that process, both within the EU and candidate member states.

In order to analyse this process in a way that remains sensitive to all these considerations, Chapter 1 developed a relational and transnational conceptualisation of Europeanisation in which different hegemonic struggles and normative tensions come together in a multilayered normative struggle with its own tensions and politics (see also Chapter 2 for an overview of these normative struggles). I further argued that such a complex transnational process can only be fully understood through a longitudinal and multiscalar analysis in which policies and norms are not studied in isolation, but through their interaction with other issues.

In doing so, and by employing a relational and transnational conceptualisation of the Europeanisation process, the book has demonstrated that what the canonical Europeanisation literature describes as policy outcomes cannot be considered to be fixed endpoints of the process. Indeed, the empirical evidence presented throughout Part II has clearly shown that these policy outcomes themselves are part of a process, that they are in constant flux, marking both the end and beginning of subprocesses. Based on these observations, I argue that it is better to speak of *outcomes-in-process*, to recognise that although these outcomes-in-process are a result of a certain (sub)process, they, in turn, contribute to a reconfiguration of relations within the field, determining the actions taken within the next phase of the process. The history of LGBT politics within Serbia's EU accession process clearly reveals how EU enlargement is a process of *negotiated transitions*, in which so-called policy outcomes are in constant flux. It is a fudge in which neither side can afford to lose face, and a series of compromises need to be made in order to keep the process ongoing.

Consider, for example, the non-compliance outcome-in-process (as discussed in Chapter 1), which, although envisioned to be a non-solution, is an important part of the Europeanisation process as the strong resistance to EU conditions can force the EU to reassess its approach to EU enlargement. An illustration is Serbia's unwillingness to comply with any of the EU's political ICTY cooperation conditions during the SAA negotiation process. The non-compliance in terms of the ICTY conditions was guided by and sparked the resurgence of nationalist politics. The initial reluctance of the EU to alter its conditions contributed to an identity divergence outcome-in-process in which Serbian politicians started questioning Serbia's European future. In response, the EU relied on the 'perverted conditionality' outcome-in-process to ensure Serbia would stay on a path towards EU integration. This 'outcome', which was a result of Serbia–EU tensions within the transitional justice policy field, had important impacts on LGBT politics as it meant that while the SAA conditionality on the ICTY was significantly softened, other controversial conditions, such as the anti-discrimination law, were taken off the agenda. It was only after this softening of conditions, which, in turn, aided the election of a pro-EU government in 2008 (marking the beginning of an identity convergence process), that conditionality could regain its normal form. As such, the anti-discrimination law became a condition *sine qua non* in the visa liberalisation process. Although the anti-discrimination conditionality was met with strong resistance, these tensions were overcome by the sizeable reward of visa-free travel which empowered the government to overcome nationalist opposition to the law.

However, the adoption of the anti-discrimination law represents nothing more than partial compliance with EU norms as its implementation remains lacking. The empirical material presented in Chapter 5 corroborated the often-observed implementation gap in Serbia. Whereas the Europeanisation literature often refers to political and institutional barriers to proper implementation of new legislation, I have highlighted the important of societal barriers to the implementation of anti-discrimination legislation. Drawing on my theory of the *attitudinal panopticon* (Slootmaeckers, 2022), I have argued that persistent societal homophobia creates visibility regimes that govern people who are different from the norm to self-regulate their actions and stop them from challenging the status quo by reporting injustices. The lack of social change observed in Serbia with relation to LGBT people, then, has become a disciplining environment in which people whose rights have been violated are prevented from seeking justice out of fear of further and more severe violations of their rights.

Going back to my earlier discussion on progress and the meaning of rights (no matter how important they are) more generally, I have demonstrated that although rights are an important aspect of the social justice project, we cannot rest on our laurels and assume that these laws and rights will generate social change over time. Indeed, the naive trust in the Myth of Rights (Scheingold, 2004) – the assumed direct link between legal change, rights and social change – that seems to be embedded within the Europeanisation literature obscures the fact that laws and rights are inherently embedded in a political and normative system. As such, legal change and rights not only require strong institutional support, but must also be accompanied by active work to transform political and normative systems. For laws to have an impact they need to be implemented, and for laws to be implemented social change is required. That is to say, for as long as the exercising of rights comes with high (perceived) political and social costs of increased visibility and the ensuing subjectification to disciplining forces (see Ahmed, 2017), we should not consider new rights a measure of progress in and of itself.

Through my analysis of the anti-discrimination legislation, I have made a case that our scholarly enquiry into the fundamental rights promotion should not follow the EU practice of limiting fundamental rights and even democracy to its institutional incarnations, but rather recognise that the so-called European norms gain their meaning through their embeddedness within the social fabric. Doing so, I argue we must challenge the overly institution-focused analysis of the implementation gap as reducing the norms and fundamental values to public policy measures and institutional change risks obscuring the social and cultural underpinnings of these norms.

The Belgrade Pride case study also demonstrated the importance of considering the relationality of policy issues and the flux nature of the process. Indeed, following the first ban on Belgrade Pride (i.e. non-compliance), the EU began to interpret Pride as a symbol of Serbia's Europeanness. With Pride becoming tied into the EU's 'fundamental values' policies and the Serbian government's need to reaffirm its commitment to European integration, Serbia engaged in a process of identity convergence. The government decided to support – not to say co-organise – Belgrade Pride in 2010 by explicitly linking it to Serbia's belonging in Europe. However, following extreme violence and anti-gay protests (which the state allowed to happen – i.e. partial compliance – see Chapter 1 and Figure 1.3), the government reverted to a process of identity divergence, using the extreme violence as an excuse to ban Pride for the next three years on security grounds, and thus 'postpone' dealing with it. This process of identity divergence took place at a moment in which Serbia and the EU were negotiating normative tensions on two fronts: both on LGBT issues as well as on the issue of Kosovo's status. In response to these multiple normative conflicts, the EU engaged in what has been labelled the 'hierarchy of tasks' outcome-in-process, prioritising its 'peace project' and regional stability over its so-called founding values. As long as Serbia made progress in the normalisation of relations with Kosovo, Serbia's non-compliance on Pride was 'tolerated'. It was only after the Kosovo issue was more or less 'resolved' that the EU reprioritised fundamental rights, and thus also Belgrade Pride. And while the increased EU pressure and (soft) conditionality on the issue was a key factor, it is not sufficient to explain why and how Belgrade Pride was organised in the following year. Indeed, the return of Belgrade Pride in 2014, and the government's re-engagement with Pride, is better explained as an instance of *tactical Europeanisation*. Indeed, internationally, the Serbian government used Pride as a tool to demonstrate Serbia's commitment to the European integration process by showing its alignment with the EU's 'pink agenda' (Ammaturo, 2015b), while domestically using Pride to emphasise the state's power and sovereignty. By emphasising the security of Pride and militarising it, Vučić also transformed Pride into a 'Ghost Pride' – i.e. a state-tolerated manifestation of Pride which takes place in a militarised 'transparent closet' (Kuhar, 2011) that keeps Pride's visibility strategies invisible and outside the public sphere, effectively undermining the very reforms and societal impact Pride pursues.

In summary, by emphasising the politics of the EU enlargement process and its relational and transnational nature, this book argued that one cannot understand Europeanisation by a mere analysis of the domestic impact of the EU enlargement process, but one should instead critically examine the relationship between the EU and a candidate country. The EU enlargement process, then, should be thought of as a political process in which the combination and imbrication of domestic and international politics produce outcomes that the dominant approaches in the Europeanisation literature cannot fully explain. Indeed, I have clearly shown that domestic responses to EU enlargement are not simply a product of domestic hegemonic struggles as these do not occur in isolation but are the result of the specific configuration of the different scales of the political integration process and their associated politics. Moreover, it has been highlighted that EU policies and/or norms cannot be viewed as given (or fixed), but that it is through their particular usage within a transnational context, and the interaction between domestic and international politics, that the meaning of these policies and/or norms are negotiated (re)defined and reinterpreted. Thus I have demonstrated the need for a more critical analysis of the civilisational politics embedded in the EU enlargement process that goes beyond institutional changes to included specific transnational configurations of politics and the complex (negotiated) outcomes they produce. These outcomes should forever take into account the people that are subject to the said policies and politics. Rights without material change for people remain empty, make-believe signifiers of progress. As scholars, we must recentre our attention on the people about whom we write, their experience and their realities, as progress in law without a change in their lived experience remains hypothetical.

Implications for the field of Europeanisation

The main contribution of this book to the EU enlargement literature is its reconceptualisation of Europeanisation. While supporting the need for more domestic-focused studies of the Europeanisation process, I argue that such increased focus on the domestic should not be at the expense of the international complexity of the EU enlargement process. As the EU enlargement process does not take place in a political vacuum, the analysis of the process cannot and should not be ignorant of its wider context. For example, the EU enlargement is not only a process by which new member states are admitted, but also plays an important role in the positioning of the EU within the wider international system as it produces the EU's international identity. As such, conditionality, and political conditionality in particular, is not a technocratic or neutral process; it is inherently political. As Sasse (2008, p. 855) previously argued, 'any component of the EU's democratic conditionality … is best understood as a social and political construct'. Thus, to really understand how the EU enlargement process affects candidate countries, one should not ask what the domestic impact is of the EU, but instead, bring under the spotlight the political nature of the process.

With that in mind, I have defined Europeanisation as a political process of *negotiated transitions*, which consists of transnational processes of: 1) construction, 2) diffusion, 3) contestation and translation, and 4) institutionalisation of formal and informal rules, procedures, policy paradigms, styles, 'ways of doing', and shared beliefs and norms which are in part constructed as part of the European policy processes and that, through the transactions of the political integration process, are further interpreted and (re)defined in order to be incorporated in the logic of domestic (national and subnational) discourse, political structures and public policies. This means that EU enlargement does not just entail formal negotiations, but that the content and meaning of the transformations demanded as part of the enlargement process are negotiated too. Both the EU and candidate countries are not only involved in formal negotiations that comprise the EU enlargement process, but in their relationship they are also continuously negotiating – and thus defining and redefining – the meaning of those values and norms that the EU claims to be its founding values.

To analyse these politics of Europeanisation, I argue that we need a reflexive approach to Europeanisation in which one does not only analyse how the EU promotes its norms but also how the resistance to these norms changes their meaning (for a similar call, see also Wiener, 2016). This book has provided an avenue to consider these politics of Europeanisation by developing an analytical framework that fundamentally takes Europeanisation to be a transnational and relational process – a multilayered normative struggle in which it is recognised that norms (and rules) are always contested and can therefore not be simply transferred to third parties. Norms need to be 'reinterpreted in the process so as to write out the tensions at the core of the integration process. [Thus, while] there may be competing norms within the EU ... these maybe especially come into tension if applied to a specific context' (Diez, 2013, pp. 202–203).

To illustrate, the current homonationalist historical moment has meant that the EU has begun presenting itself as being exceptionally LGBT-friendly which is contrasted with homophobic Others. This process, however, has also created the opportunity for Serbia to politicise LGBT rights for its own goals and engage in, what this book has labelled, *tactical Europeanisation*. Indeed, Serbia engaged in doublespeak: internationally recognising and showing adherence to the LGBT-friendly identity of the EU, while domestically engaging in political actions that are in line with an opposite Orthodox national identity. This, in turn, undermined the politicality of local LGBT activism. Such processes only become observable when considering Europeanisation through the presented transnational and relational conceptualisation.

By recognising that EU norms are not fixed, and are subject to a process of negotiations and reinterpretation, the new conceptualisation of Europeanisation also has strong implications for another often-present assumption within the EU enlargement literature. In fact, large parts of the Europeanisation literature not only engage in a top-down approach analysis of legal and institutional compliance, but do so in the assumption that formal compliance with rules and adoption of institutions will eventually lead to social change. This is not only problematic when we consider the barriers to implementation mentioned earlier, but there is an underlying expectation that the adoption of institutions will over time lead to an almost automatic 'socialisation' of EU norms among political elites. Just as the pathological turn within the Europeanisation scholarship criticises the EU for its outcome-focused analysis of domestic reforms (Mendelski, 2015, 2016), the presented research highlights that an outcome-focused research agenda remains equally ignorant of the translation processes that are part of the politics of Europeanisation. Consider, for example, the organisation of Pride parades which was not only negotiated within the multilayered normative struggle in terms of the timing of 'compliance', but also in terms of its meaning. Whereas Pride was originally a political tool of activists to transform Serbian society, through the Europeanisation process, it became an apolitical ritualised performance of the right to freedom of assembly. Hence, it is argued that one cannot and should not simply analyse if, how and when candidate countries have adopted certain laws or created institutions in line with EU requirements, but must also engage with the translation or reinterpretation of these laws, institutions and practices.

Empirically, my findings have echoed some of the previous findings of the Europeanisation via enlargement literature, but with the new theoretical framework, they also bring significant nuances and new questions to such debates. First, the book adds to the growing voices that are critical of the top-down approach to Europeanisation (see e.g. Alpan and Diez, 2014; Özdemir, 2014; Yılmaz and Soyaltın, 2014). Indeed, I have highlighted that both the adoption of the anti-discrimination framework and the organisation of Belgrade Pride are predominantly a product of the configurations of both domestic and international politics that occur within the enlargement process. This, however, raises important questions about the Europeanisation literature. For example, if domestic politics are key to understanding why, how and when certain policies are adopted as part of the EU enlargement process, can one still speak of 'transformative power Europe' and consider conditionality a driver of change?

I challenge such an EU-centric approach to Europeanisation as I have demonstrated that conditionality is better considered a facilitator of change rather than its driver. Although the role of conditionality in the adoption of the anti-discrimination framework and the organisation of Pride cannot and should not be discarded nor underestimated, this book contains a strong warning against overestimating the potential of conditionality or the influence of the EU on candidate countries more generally. Consider, for example, the role of the EU in the adoption process of the anti-discrimination law: although its pressure and conditionality were vital to the eventual adoption of the law, EU pressure only represents part of the story. Domestic civil society played a lead role in drafting the anti-discrimination law, pushing for the LGBT provisions of the law long before it became part of EU conditionality. Moreover, when the law finally did become part of conditionality, its adoption was mainly the result of a domestic shift in political narratives and power balance. Thus, while conditionality was an important factor, it served more as a facilitator than a driver of change as it provided the possibility for the government to overcome strong nationalist opposition to LGBT equality.

A similar observation could be made for the organisation of Pride. Although it is undeniable that the EU and the accession process have played a key role in the 'successful' Prides in 2010, 2014 and 2015, I have argued that a myopic view on these three Prides obscures the fact that the accession process has equally contributed to why Pride was banned for three consecutive years. The latter observation also supports the recent 'pathological turn' in the Europeanisation literature, which has argued that Europeanisation does not always lead to positive transformations but can also have 'pathological effect', reinforcing practices and politics which the EU enlargement process sought to eradicate (Mendelski, 2016).

Another important nuance relates to the lack of implementation of the anti-discrimination law. Whereas previous scholars have highlighted the lack of political will, public debate and institutional capacity as reasons for the limited implementation of laws, I have argued that we cannot simply analyse fundamental rights through public policy and institutions as there are important societal barriers to the implementation of laws. Indeed, a key problem is the lack of social conditions favourable for the implementation of the law. Not only is the general knowledge of discrimination legislation quite limited in Serbia, but more importantly LGBT people who have experienced discrimination are reluctant to report their cases to the relevant authorities, fearing the process might 'out' them. In other words, the persistence of homophobia within Serbia's societal structure acts as an attitudinal panopticon (Slootmaeckers, 2022), limiting the potentiality of the law for LGBT people as a means to combat discrimination.

This book then seeks to challenge the overly institution-focused analysis of the implementation gap and argues that by reducing the norms of anti-discrimination, and fundamental values more broadly, to public policy measures and institutional change, scholarship risks obscuring the social and cultural underpinnings of these norms. The vast Europeanisation literature has focused on a rather narrow understanding of the EU's impact on domestic politics, orienting itself towards changes in public policy, not in values and attitudes, and operates under the implicit assumption that (formal) compliance with EU rules and the adoption of institutions eventually leads to social change. However, such a linear view on progress ignores the possibility that the lack of social change in and of itself can become a disciplining environment in which people whose rights have been violated are prevented from seeking justice out of fear of further and more severe violations of their rights.

Implications for the field of international LGBT politics

Regarding the study of LGBT issues in a transnational context, the book has demonstrated that international pressure for LGBT equality is not an unalloyed good. As Ammaturo (2017, p. 93) has argued, connecting LGBT rights to the appealing idea of Europeanness is not a harmless operation with serious political and social implications. Not only can EU pressure for LGBT rights increase nationalist opponents' threat perception which, in turn, can lead to nationalist countermobilisations and even backlashes (Ayoub, 2014, 2016; Mole, 2011, 2016; O'Dwyer, 2012, 2018; Slootmaeckers and Touquet, 2016), it can also foreclose the politicality of LGBT activism. Whereas previous scholarship has argued that backlashes against LGBT rights can have a paradoxical impact in which 'waves of resistance are [in many cases] followed by some success' (Ayoub, 2016, p. 202), I have argued that such positive outcomes are far from given and that embedding LGBT politics in wider international (civilisational) politics can have serious political implications. I have shown that the EU's homocolonialist practice of what Rahman (2014, p. 281) calls 'pink testing', combined with domestic resistance to this, has had a harmful impact on local LGBT people and politics. For example, the violent opposition to Belgrade Pride in 2010 not only stopped it from happening for the next three years, but also depoliticised the event, potentially foreclosing further successes. Whereas the violence associated with Pride widened the gap between LGBT activist initiatives and LGBT people, the bans also pushed Pride into the human rights discourse. As such, Pride became an outcome, a form of activism voided of transformative politics. Whereas the indirect positive impact of backlashes can be the result of increased visibility of LGBT equality norms caused by the opposition (Ayoub, 2016), such visibility did not occur in the Serbian context. Indeed, by militarising Pride, a 'Ghost Pride' was created. This state-tolerated manifestation of Pride takes place in a militarised 'transparent closet' that keeps LGBT people's visibility strategies invisible and outside the public sphere, reinforcing traditional and nationalist conceptions of Serbian society.

These findings echo those of Stella (2007, 2012, 2013) who in the Russian context found that when Pride is organised by a small number of LGBT activists with international support, but without the involvement of the 'grassroots community', it may end up rendering the community it envisioned to empower invisible, while at the same time reinforcing the locally held assumption that homosexuality (as an identity) is a 'Western' import. This raises important questions about how we analyse LGBT rights and the way activism operates in different contexts. What does it mean for an activist practice, such as Pride, to move from one geotemporality to another? How does this shape LGBT politics?

Given that LGBT human rights are a political currency at the international level (Ammaturo, 2017), we must remain vigilant when analysing these politics. We cannot rely on laws and institutions as a measure of progress and must continuously ask what this 'progress' does for LGBT people. As queer scholars have argued that the granting of certain rights also has disciplining aspects, which in turn can depoliticise the LGBT movement (Ammaturo, 2017; Duggan, 2001; Stychin, 2000), it is important to not only analyse how new LGBT rights are adopted under international pressure, but also why they are adopted and how the adoption of these rights influences the politicality of the movement. As such, I argue for a more critical engagement with the globalisation of LGBT politics, as the symbolism of LGBT rights in international relations opens a space for reinterpretating these norms in such a way that they could become disciplining rather than liberating. Thus, it bears repeating there is a need for an analysis of international LGBT politics that takes at heart the queer politics of continually challenging, being critical, ceaselessly interrogating power, even after 'progress' or hard battles are won. So we must not only critically interrogate the symbolic nature of LGBT rights within international politics and local resistance to them, we must also engage with the domestic impact of international politics that goes beyond institutional changes to include the political transformations that result from such changes, in particular the new boundaries of exclusion created in the process.

In short, whereas a lot of scholarship on the international politics of LGBT rights focuses on the adoption of LGBT rights and celebrates legal and policy changes as a signal of progressive change, I argue for the continuous questioning of not only what these rights mean in terms of people's lived experiences, but also a constant questioning of 'Why?' – the political motivation for these changes. Without ignoring the material importance of legal changes, we cannot remain ignorant of the political motivations behind these changes and the ways in which these rights have been diffused. These questions remain important because these policies are inherently bound within arbitrary regulations of the human condition and experiences. If policies are adopted to avoid international scrutiny or critique, one can almost be certain that these new policies will be more likely to entrench existing hierarchies and power structures than to challenge them.

Implications for EU enlargement strategies and EU LGBT politics

Although the EU enlargement process has been described by some as 'the most successful democracy promotion policy ever implemented by an external actor' (Vachudova, 2014, p. 122), recent moves towards illiberalism and authoritarianism in some of the Central and Eastern European EU member states have demonstrated that such earlier positions might have been too optimistic. Democratic 'backsliding' has become a real concern in recent years and, more worryingly, it has been pointed out that these forms of backsliding 'are legitimated through the very institutions that democracy promotors have prioritized' (Bermeo, 2016, p. 6).

Indeed, as I have demonstrated throughout this book, institutions and practices are not sufficient to create normative change, or to allow the societal underpinnings of democracy and fundamental values to take root. In other words, if the EU wants to develop an EU enlargement process that reduces the possibilities of later democratic backsliding, it must acknowledge that how it engages in democracy promotion matters. Most importantly, the over-reliance on institutions as a measure for 'progress' is one of the core issues, as institutions can be made to work both in favour of and against democratic principles.

In other words, for as long as the EU operates such that the adoption of laws and institutions becomes an end in and of itself with the implicit assumption that these new institutions will eventually lead to social change, history will repeat itself. I therefore argue that rather than directing all its energy to the so-called socialisation of elites, the EU should ensure it actively involves the publics in its enlargement process to engage in actions and policies that enable social transformations and cultural shifts. Doing so would tackle the problem were the lack of social change itself becomes a barrier for the envisioned reforms.

Secondly, the EU should also become aware of the political process that underpins the enlargement process – in particular the identity process that underpins it. Given that norms and values play a role in how international identities are constructed, the possibility emerges for candidate countries to instrumentalise the symbolic nature of these norms and values to communicate Europeanness without having to actually produce positive change domestically. Consider for example the story with which I started this book: the appointment of Ana Brnabić as Prime Minister. Rather than taking this development at face value – as a sign of Serbia's progress with regard to LGBT rights – I see this appointment is a continuation of President Aleksandar Vučić's politics of tactical Europeanisation, in which LGBT issues like the Pride parade are used to speak to the EU's self-proclaimed LGBT-friendly identity without engaging with LGBT issues domestically. In fact, as I discuss in more details in the Epilogue, Brnabić has not only been a tool within Vučić's politics of tactical Europeanisation, she has also refused to engage with LGBT rights and has denied (or at best has been ignorant of) the lived experience of Serbian LGBT people. Most notably, while Brnabić became a parent (although without any legal rights) when her partner gave birth to a baby conceived through IVF in 2019, she did not intervene when one of her ministers introduced rules that would de facto prevent LGBT people from accessing fertility services.

To make EU enlargement a success and a process that can lead to meaningful change, the EU should move away from an outcome-focused analysis of reforms and adopt a process-focused analysis. If the EU understands and acknowledges 'how and why' reforms are undertaken and calls out symbolic gestures for what they are, the opportunities for candidate countries to instrumentalise these reforms for their own agenda will significantly reduce. While this requires changes within the EU enlargement process, it also requires the EU to move beyond using fundamental rights as a means to demark differences, and to engage with its own fundamental rights regime more intensely. Such a more honest fundamental rights policy requires the EU to 1) define more clearly what it considers to be its values and norms (beyond their institutional incarnations) and associated normative politics, and 2) establish real processes and enforcement mechanisms with real consequences to ensure member states compliance with said norms. Hence, the EU needs to develop a policy that engages more deeply with the content of the EU's normative regime, placing people rather than institutions at the centre, both within and outside its borders.

I want to conclude this book with a final critical remark on the way in which LGBT rights have been imagined within the EU at this point, and what it means for LGBT rights. While it is important to recognise that, as an institution, the EU has been able to produce a lot of important legal frameworks that have changed the material reality of some LGBT people, we must also keep asking the 'queer' questions. Whose existence has been recognised and under what conditions? Can we really claim there has been progress when those people transgressing heteronormative boundaries are still ridiculed, attacked, and pushed to oblivion? Though there is an importance to the legal recognition embedded within identity politics and strategic essentialism, I believe we must keep pushing for a more radical policy, push for an EU that moves beyond its institutional biases, moves beyond its neoliberal paradigms, to one that embraces the core of a social justice project and radically transforms systems to protect its most marginalised members first. I consciously avoid the word 'citizens' as I write this final paragraph, as the political fights for social justice should not be limited to a legal and illusional concept of belonging. I do so because the EU will never be a beacon of progress (whatever that is supposed to mean) if its politics are limited in its applications. If we are willing to condemn political homophobia elsewhere, but are unwilling to open borders to those that have fallen victim to state-directed violence, are we really a safe haven? Liberation is unconditional and transformative.

Thus, while I recognise the work that has been done within the EU to provide legal recognition to (some) LGBT people, I advocate for a more radical politics of queer liberation over LGBT equality. We need a political approach that is unconditional, transformative and forever aware of its own limitations – and, above all, while we might engage the state in these politics, we must remain forever sceptical of sovereign institutions as (self-proclaimed) agents of good.

Epilogue

With the speed of academic publishing always slower than we would like it to be, I want to take the time to reflect on some of the key events in Serbia that have happened since the end of my fieldwork. Though it is not my intention to provide a detailed overview of everything that has happened in Serbia since, I do want to highlight some of the key areas in which the processes identified throughout the book have persisted, and also some areas where clear signs of change can be observed. This attempt to pull the research into the present is a vital aspect of my relational and transnational approach to studying the Europeanisation of LGBT politics as all the so-called outcomes of this process are nothing more than outcome-in-process. They are an arbitrary endpoint of observation and require continuous updating.

So, where do things stand in Serbia? I hope after reading this book one would be less likely to assume that the appointment of Ana Brnabić as Prime Minister – the vignette with which I opened the book – is a sign of 'progress' and of a change in the Serbian approach to LGBT rights and politics. In line with what I have argued throughout the book, this appointment should be seen as a continuation of Vučić's tactical Europeanisation processes. He seeks to conceal himself and his autocratic tendencies (see Bieber, 2018) with a veil of LGBT friendliness that aims to misdirect attention from his real political goals – nationalist, illiberal and focused on traditional values. His political stance becomes incredibly clear when we consider his speech during the 4th Demographic Summit, which was held in Budapest in September 2021 under the overall summit theme of 'Family: The Key to Sustainability'. I will quote his speech at length, not only because the mere presence of Vučić at this summit speaks volumes about his real political affinities, but also because the content of the speech provides a unique insight into his political mind, and his views on how Serbia fits within the current political system. Immediately after three priests and a rabbi blessed the summit, while preaching the sanctity of marriage and the importance of family, Vučić took to the stage to start his address:

Dear friends, Katalin [Novák – Hungarian Minister for Families] is very much right saying that life is a question of survival, at least in Serbia and many other countries in the region. When we speak about demographic issues, it really became a question of survival, but it also is becoming one of the most important political issues ... I'm not going to speak about different measures how we started incentivising, how we are going to subsidise people who will have more kids. That is mainly what has already been done or we are going to increase and improve all financial terms for the families and kids in particular. I'm going to speak, and I'll do it as brief as it is possible, about politics, mindsets, and different opinions; if it is possible to have different opinions on this issue. But I will first of all try to depict the situation in the present day ... *We are facing a new, a sort of liberal political Marxism ... which is forcing us to listen to new theories which are going to change our lives. But changing our lives in a way that we are losing our life and losing possibility for our own survival.*

And today, if you analyse it, or let's say ten years ago, rule of law became the only issue that we were bothered with. Ok, rule of law is very important, no doubt, no question about it. But then, even in Europe, in our continent, it became a rule of logic jihadi war against those that are disobedient. Then – ok, it fulfilled its role – then we got climate change issues as the most important ... But is it really the most important question? Is it really more important than demographic issues? Is it really more important than the future of our countries, than the future of our nations? Is it really more important, or is there something more important than our kids, than our children? ... But nobody is discussing that. Nobody is discussing that ... It's not very fashionable, even not fancy, *if you want to speak about it and you have to always be wrapped in a way that someone from those Marxistic liberal circles would like to see you* ... You will know that I'm saying the truth ... because there are some other guys that are – I cannot say instructing the media – but still that are very good in creating media environment from which we cannot for which we cannot escape. We are entrapped in a way, and on the other hand we have to find solutions. That's why I'm profoundly grateful to you, because today we're going to hear a lot of great ideas, we're going to learn something. We come here to learn many things and then to introducing the measures in our country. I am not ashamed to say this; to the contrary I'm very glad that I'm here. I believe that unifying ourselves and not only speaking about our nations, speaking about our visions, about our ideas for the future, about creating the platform for certain survival of our countries that is something that we need to work on ...

I believe that it's high time to act and to react on our own hypocrisy, and to taking action which will lead us to the certain future and to the future that will keep our nations and other countries alive. (Aleksandar Vučić, 4th Demographic Summit, 23 September 2021, Budapest: emphases added)[1]

The reference to 'Marxistic liberal circles' is of particular interest as this seems to refer to the 'Western' approaches to liberal freedoms and what the right would often refer to as the 'woke' agenda, including LGBT rights, women's rights etc – an agenda which, according to Vučić, will lead to the demise of Serbia. He knows he cannot escape playing to the politics. In order to be able to advance his nationalistic, profamily politics in Serbia, he admits that he must do so 'wrapped in a way that someone from those Marxistic liberal circles would like to see' him. Vučić seems to have become an expert in presenting himself as the reformer to Europe – seemingly aligning with the EU's value system – while domestically maintaining politics that undermine any LGBT-friendly reform. The fact that he has been so successful is demonstrated by the gradual continuation of the EU accession negotiations with new chapters being opened, irrespective of the questionable status of rule of law and fundamental rights issues in Serbia and the EU's fundamental rights first approach.

This embrace of tactical Europeanisation has not been without consequences for LGBT people in Serbia. To illustrate my point, consider the track record of Ana Brnabić as Prime Minister. While I do not seek to deny the importance of representation and the potential impact Brnabić might have by virtue of being the Prime Minister, her politics and her approach to LGBT politics and equality have been far from supportive to LGBT people. Already in the immediate aftermath of her appointment, it became clear that Brnabić would do very little for LGBT people. Following the media attention she received as the first female/lesbian Prime Minister of Serbia, she stated that: 'Serbia is changing and changing fast, and if you will, I am part of that change, but I do not want to be branded "Serbia's gay PM"' (quoted in Wintour, 2017). When asked whether she would push for further reforms on LGBT rights, she said she believed Serbia would become more tolerant if economic security could be found for its citizens. Moreover, she explained that she does not think Serbia a homophobic country:

> I know that is one of the perceptions, and I understand attitudes are different in parts of Serbia … The citizens of Serbia have a right not to be portrayed by a loud [homophobic] minority. We can have a culture where we disagree, as long as there is tolerance and no violence. We all have different views and values, but I don't want to change people's thinking by law. (quoted in Wintour, 2017)

Whereas these statements might be a reflection of her own experience in Serbia – she comes after all from a relatively affluent family and holds a privileged position in Serbian society – the impact of this statement is not to be underestimated as it shows how unaware she is of the day-to-day lived experiences of LGBT people in Serbia. To further illustrate her detachedness from the wider LGBT population, consider the events of 2019. Brnabić made international headlines again as the first Prime Minister to have a child with a same-sex partner while in office (BBC News, 2019). Within a month of the birth, the Health Minister Zlatibor Lončar imposed new rules which meant that anyone with a 'history of homosexual relations during the last five years' would be banned from donating 'reproductive cells' for artificial insemination, in vitro fertilisation, or even for laboratory tests (Synovitz and Cosic, 2019). Despite the fact that this de facto bans LGBT people from being able to have children (when considering the rules with existing family law), Brnabić did not see any issues with these new rules and did not take any action to overturn them. In fact, she and her office refused to provide any comments. Whereas these are just snippets of her regime, what has become clear is that Brnabić remains disconnected and unconcerned with the everyday plight of LGBT people, apart from her yearly visit to the Belgrade Pride parade where she makes big (empty) statements about LGBT rights.

In the last year, the Serbian government started working on a new Same-Sex Civil Partnership Bill. While such a law would provide a much-needed and welcome recognition of same-sex couples in Serbia, one would be once again short-sighted to conclude that the fact that the government is preparing such a bill is a sign of any change of heart within the ruling party. In fact, following the 2020 parliamentary elections, the new bill is being proposed and developed by the newly appointed Minister for Human and Minority Rights and Social Dialogue, Gordana Čomić (formerly part of DS, and non-partisan since May 2020). The fact that a former member of the Democratic Party is proposing the same-sex partnership law is not without political meaning, as it once again creates political distance between the ruling party (SNS) and LGBT rights. It further allows Vučić to express his disagreement with the law without appearing to go against his own party. And indeed, in May 2021 Vučić declared that, as President, he would veto the law if it made it through Parliament, as he believes the new law goes against the constitution, which defines marriage as a heterosexual union (European Western Balkans, 2021).

When it comes to the Serbian government, it is clear that there is little interest in really engaging with LGBT rights and issues of anti-discrimination – not only through the accounts of events I mentioned above, but also through its general inaction regarding the implementation of the 2009 anti-discrimination legislation. For example, the government strategic documents (anti-discrimination strategy and action plan) were never implemented and never replaced when they expired. With regard to the judiciary, it must be noted that there have been some important final verdicts on cases of homophobic discrimination and hate crimes in more recent years. Yet the actions of the judiciary remain rather limited when it comes to hate crimes and discrimination cases. As I am writing this Epilogue, the Belgrade Pride

Info Centre had just been attacked again by a group of young men. Though this is the eleventh attack since its opening, none of the perpetrators have faced any consequences and no actions seem to have been taken by the authorities, despite the fact that there is ample CCTV footage and the Pride Info Centre has 24/7 police protection. As high-profile cases do not attract consequences, it does not come as a surprise that general victims of hate crime and discrimination remain reluctant to report their cases to the authorities (European Union Agency for Fundamental Rights, 2020).

Up to this point, everything might seem doom and gloom, but that is not how I want to finish this Epilogue. I want to take the last few paragraphs of *Coming In* to reflect on some of the positive developments that have happened in Serbia, more specifically the work that has been done by LGBT activists to respond to their political environment. First and foremost, since the end of my fieldwork, there have been several new NGOs within the Serbian landscape, many of which are increasingly turning their attention away from policy to community work. A noteworthy example is the new organisation Da Se Zna (To be known). Having experienced how the system fails victims of discrimination and hate crime, the founder established Da Se Zna in 2016 with the aim of mapping and documenting the violence committed against LGBT people. Since then, the organisation has grown significantly in capacity and their scope of activities. Today, they are 'primarily focused on strengthening the community through legal and psychological support, direct work with the community and conducting campaigns, but also on various advocacy activities aimed at relevant institutions and decision makers'.[2] While the support for victims of discrimination and hate crime provided by the association is vital to improving the implementation of the legal framework, I also want to draw attention to some of the campaigns they ran with the aim of producing wider social change. In one of these campaigns, they reclaimed an antiquated and parochial Serbian tradition through which members of the public used to place ads in newspapers to publicly shame people they felt wronged by. In a queer act of reclaiming, Da Se Zna used this technique to spread love instead of hate. They asked supportive parents, who were willing to publicly testify their support for their LGBT children, to place an ad in national and local newspapers to declare that they 'would never disown my son because he loves and lives with a person of the same sex'.[3] As result of this campaign an organisation for the parents of LGBT children was set up.

And some significant changes can be observed with regard to Belgrade Pride. As several key organisers of the event were forced into asylum, a new generation of activists got involved in its organisation. This new energy allowed Pride to become more engaged with LGBT people in Serbia. One of the key changes here has been the opening of the Belgrade Pride Centre in central Belgrade in 2017. Originally only funded for one month, the centre was reopened in 2018 and has been open ever since. It has developed into community space with different activities throughout the year. In 2019 Belgrade was chosen by the members of the European Pride Organisers Association to host EuroPride in 2022. Belgrade Pride had put in its bid with the aim of bringing EuroPride to Southeastern Europe and making Serbia the first country outside the European Economic Area to host the event, which it hoped would bring visibility to LGBT rights in the Western Balkans.

As this book went to press, EuroPride had just taken place in Belgrade. However, it proved to be a very different event than the organisers had hoped for. Being in Belgrade and observing the twists and turns of politics, I could not help but notice how the events of that week were in many ways haunted by the past politics of Pride in Belgrade. In the months before, Serbia witnessed levels of public homophobia that it had not seen since 2009. Four days before the event, EuroPride was banned in a way very similar to 2009, where it was not the event itself that was banned but rather the route. Once again security issues and tensions between Serbia and Kosovo were cited. In a last-minute U-turn, the government gave in to international pressure and allowed EuroPride to take place. However, we could not walk the streets, and the Minister of the Interior even said that his ban had remained in effect, and that protesters were only escorted from their gathering point in front of the constitutional court to Tašmajdan Park, the venue where the Pride concerts were held.

As I write, only days after EuroPride, it is too soon to make full sense of what happened or understand the politics of it, but two things are clear. First, the EuroPride week seemed to draw on every aspect of the history of Pride in Belgrade in one way or another, and this book provides key background for understanding what happened. Second, Vučić once again succeeded in instrumentalising the tools of tactical Europeanisation to have his cake and eat it too. But the defiance shown by activists to the state intimidation of that week suggests that LGBT politics in Serbia might be on the point of entering a qualitatively different stage – that is, if activists are able to tap in to this defiance and reconsider how they organise themselves.

Notes

1 Author's cleaned up transcription based on the recording of Vučić's speech available on: Budapest Demographic Summit IV, 2021. *Timeline*. [Online] Available at: <https://budapestidemografiaicsucs.hu/en/timeline> [Accessed 17 Apr. 2022].

2 See Da Se Zna, 2021 (Who are we) [Online] Available at: <https://dasezna.lgbt/en/who-we-are/> [Accessed 17 April 2022].

3 See SOGI Campaigns, 2016. Let it be … known: Serbia's award-winning campaign reclaims tradition to promote acceptance. [Online] Available at: <https://sogicampaigns.org/portfolio/let-it-be-known-serbias-award-winning-campaign-reclaims-tradition-to-promote-acceptance/> [Accessed 17 Apr. 2022].

Appendix: list of interviews

List of interviews in chronological order. Interviews are coded in accordance with their country/institution of origin, year and interview number. For example, the interview code SRB2014_7 stands for the seventh interview with a Serbian actor conducted in 2014.[1] The list also includes the name of the interviewee (unless they requested anonymity), the organisation they represent, and the date, location and type of interview.

Interview list

Interview **SRB2012_1** with anonymous representative of Gayten-LGBT, 18 October 2012, Dublin, face-to-face interview.

Interview **EP2012_1** with an anonymous official from European Parliament, 19 October 2012, Dublin, informal conversation.

Interview **SRB2012_2** with Jovanka Todorović, Labris, 20 October 2012, Dublin, face-to-face interview.

Interview **EP2013_1** with an anonymous official from European Parliament, 30 April 2013, Brussels, face-to-face interview.

Interview **EP2013_2** with Ulrike Lunacek, Member of European Parliament – Intergroup on LGBT rights, 15 May 2013, Belgium, telephone interview.

Interview **EP2013_3** with Sophie in 't Veld, Member of European Parliament – intergroup on LGBT rights, 23 May 2013, Belgium, telephone interview.

Interview **EC2013_1** with an anonymous official from European Commission (DG Enlargement), 29 May 2013, Brussels, face-to-face interview.

Interview **EP2013_4** with Michael Cashman, Member of European Parliament – Intergroup on LGBT rights, 06 June 2013, Brussels, face-to-face interview.

Interview EC2013_2 with an anonymous official from European Commission (DG Enlargement), 30 July 2013, Brussels, face-to-face interview.

Interview EC2013_3 with an anonymous official from European Commission (DG Enlargement), 24 October 2013, Zagreb, face-to-face interview.

Interview SRB2013_1 with Jovanka Todorović, Labris, 26 October 2013, Zagreb, face-to-face interview.

Interview EC2014_1 with an anonymous official from European Commission (DG Enlargement), 06 March 2014, Brussels, face-to-face interview.

Interview SRB2014_1 with Radica Hura, Independent Serbian Activist, 28 May 2014, Belgrade, face-to-face interview.

Interview SRB2014_2 with Marko Ilić, YiHR – Youth Initiative for Human Rights / Pride Organiser, 30 May 2014, Belgrade, face-to-face interview.

Interview SRB2014_3 with Jovanka Todorović, Labris, 30 May 2014, Belgrade, face-to-face interview.

Interview SRB2014_4 with anonymous activists from Siguran Puls Mladih (SPY), 31 May 2014, Belgrade, face-to-face interview.

Interview SRB2014_5 with Dragan Lončar, Gay Straight Alliance, 01 June 2014, Belgrade, face-to-face interview.

Interview SRB2014_6 with Ilija Milošović, IDAHO Belgrade, 01 June 2014, Belgrade, face-to-face interview.

Interview SRB2014_7 with Predrag Azdejković, Gay Lesbian Info Centre, 02 June 2014, Belgrade, face-to-face interview.

Interview SRB2015_1 with an anonymous official from Commissioner for the Protection of Equality, 16 April 2015, Belgrade, face-to-face interview.

Interview SRB2015_2 with Marko Ilić, National Democratic Institute / Pride Organiser, 17 April 2015, Belgrade, face-to-face interview.

Interview SRB2015_3 with Vladimir Veljković, Asocijacija DUGA / Former IGLYO board member, 19 April 2015, Belgrade, face-to-face interview.

Interview SRB2015_4 with Mladen Antonijević Priljeva, Forum for Ethnic Relations, 20 April 2015, Belgrade, face-to-face interview.

Interview SRB2015_5 with Tatjana Papić, Union University, Serbia / Belgrade Centre for Human Rights, 20 April 2015, Belgrade, face-to-face interview.

Interview SRB2015_6 with Boris Milićević, Serbian Socialist Party (SPS) / Gay Straight Alliance, 21 April 2015, Belgrade, face-to-face interview.

Interview SRB2015_7 with Gordana Mitrović, Hestija, 21 April 2015, Belgrade, face-to-face interview.

Interview SRB2015_8 with an anonymous official from Legal and Judicial Reform Programme, 22 April 2015, Belgrade, face-to-face interview.

Interview SRB2015_9 with anonymous officials from Ministry of Foreign Affairs of the Republic of Serbia, 23 April 2015, Belgrade, face-to-face interview.

Interview SRB2015_10 with Agata Milan Đurić, Gayten-LGBT / employee Ombudsman, 23 April 2015, Belgrade, face-to-face interview.

Interview SRB2015_11 with Zorica Mršević, Institute of Social Sciences / Former deputy Ombudsman, 24 April 2015, Belgrade, face-to-face interview.

Interview SRB2015_12 with Mina Pejić/Božović, Independent Serbian Activist, 24 April 2015, Belgrade, face-to-face interview.

Interview SRB2015_13 with Nebojša Otović, Gay Straight Alliance, 26 April 2015, Belgrade, face-to-face interview.

Interview SRB2015_14 with Radica Hura, Independent Serbian Bisexual Activist, 27 April 2015, Belgrade, face-to-face interview.

Interview SRB2015_15 with an anonymous official from Office for Cooperation with Civil Society, 27 April 2015, Belgrade, face-to-face interview.

Interview SRB2015_16 with Dušan Maljković, Centre for Queer Studies, 28 April 2015, Belgrade, face-to-face interview.

Interview SRB2015_17 with Goran Miletić, Civil Rights Defenders, 29 April 2015, Belgrade, face-to-face interview.

Interview SRB2015_18 with Marko Karadzić, Former State Secretary of the Minister for Human and Minority Rights, 29 April 2015, Belgrade/ DC, Skype interview.

Interview SRB2015_19 with Aleksandar Prica, Asocijacija DUGA, 30 April 2015, Sabać, face-to-face interview.

Interview SRB2015_20 with Sandra Ilić, Asocijacija DUGA, 30 April 2015, Sabać, face-to-face interview.

Interview SRB2015_21 with anonymous representative of Diversity Champions Serbia, 01 May 2015, Belgrade, face-to-face interview.

Interview SRB2015_22 with Aleksandar Stričević, Independent Serbian Activist / former activist from Gay Straight Alliance, 02 May 2015, Belgrade, face-to-face interview.

Interview SRB2015_23 with an anonymous official from Delegation of the EU to Serbia, 06 May 2015, Belgrade, face-to-face interview.

Interview SRB2015_24 with Jovanka Todorović, Labris, 06 May 2015, Belgrade, face-to-face interview.

Interview SRB2015_25 with Milena Vasić, YUCOM – Lawyers' Committee for Human Rights, 06 May 2015, Belgrade, face-to-face interview.

Interview SRB2015_26 with anonymous officials from Dutch Embassy, 07 May 2015, Belgrade, face-to-face interview.

Interview SRB2015_27 with anonymous official from the Ombudsman – Protector of Citizens, 08 May 2015, Belgrade, face-to-face interview.

Interview SRB2015_28 with anonymous official from Serbia's European Integration Office, 08 May 2015, Belgrade, face-to-face interview.

Interview SRB2015_29 with Milan Pantenić, a former activist from Gay Straight Alliance, 09 May 2015, Belgrade, face-to-face interview.

Interview SRB2015_30 with Igor Vojvodić, a former activist from Gay Straight Alliance, 10 May 2015, Belgrade, face-to-face interview.

Interview SRB2015_31 with Lazar Pavlović, Gay Straight Alliance, 10 May 2015, Belgrade, face-to-face interview.

Interview SRB2015_32 with Milan Antonijević, YUCOM – Lawyers' Committee for Human Rights, 11 May 2015, Belgrade, face-to-face interview.

Interview SRB2015_33 with Milos Đajić, DS – Democratic Party, President of the Committee of Human Rights and cooperation with NGOs, 12 May 2015, Belgrade, face-to-face interview.

Interview SRB2015_34 with Danica Todorov, Deputy Provincial Ombudsman, 13 May 2015, Novi Sad, face-to-face interview.

Interview SRB2015_35 with anonymous representative of Ižađi, 13 May 2015, Novi Sad, face-to-face interview.

Interview SRB2015_36 with an anonymous official from the Ministry of Justice, 14 May 2015, Belgrade, face-to-face interview.

Interview SRB2015_37 with Uroš Kosanović, Independent Serbian Activist, 15 May 2015, Belgrade, face-to-face interview.

Interview SRB2015_38 with Dragana Todorović, Labris, 18 May 2015, Belgrade, face-to-face interview.

Interview SRB2015_39 with Anita Mitić, Youth Initiative for Human Rights, 18 May 2015, Belgrade, face-to-face interview.

Interview SRB2015_40 with anonymous representative of Gayten-LGBT, 18 May 2015, Belgrade, face-to-face interview.

Interview SRB2015_41 with Aleksandar Vasilijević, Head of the Department for Organisation, Prevention and Community Policing, 19 May 2015, Belgrade, face-to-face interview.

Interview SRB2015_42 with Saša Gajin, Center for Advanced Legal Studies, 19 May 2015, Belgrade, face-to-face interview.

Interview EC2015_1 with an anonymous official from European Commission (DG Near), 26 May 2015, Brussels, face-to-face interview.

Interview SRB2015_43 with an anonymous official from Democratic Party of Serbia, 11 September 2015, Belgrade, face-to-face interview.

Interview SRB2015_44 with anonymous officials from LDP – Liberal Democratic Party, 12 September 2015, Belgrade, face-to-face interview.

Interview SRB2015_45 with Miloš Urošević, Women in Black, 14 September 2015, Belgrade, face-to-face interview.

Interview SRB2015_46 with Vladan Glišić, Dveri, 17 September 2015, Belgrade, face-to-face interview.

Interview SRB2015_47 with Nevena Petrušić, Former Commissioner for the Protection of Equality, 21 September 2015, Nis, face-to-face interview.

Interview SRB2015_48 with an anonymous activist from Duga Niš, 21 September 2015, Nis, face-to-face interview.

Interview SRB2015_49 with an anonymous official from National Democratic Institute, 22 September 2015, Belgrade, face-to-face interview.

Interview SRB2015_50 with Gordana Čomić, DS – Democratic Party, 22 September 2015, Belgrade, face-to-face interview.

Interview SRB2015_51 with Predrag Azdejković, Gay Lesbian Info Centre / Organiser Trans* Pride, 23 September 2015, Belgrade, face-to-face interview.

Interview SRB2015_52 with Slobodan (Boban) Stojanović, Belgrade Pride, 23 September 2015, Belgrade, face-to-face interview.

Interview SRB2015_53 with Nikola Milovasljević, a former activist from Gay Straight Alliance, 24 September 2015, Belgrade, face-to-face interview.

Interview SRB2015_54 with Aleksandar Stojaković, Centre for Queer Studies, 24 September 2015, Belgrade, face-to-face interview.

Interview SRB2015_55 with Branko Ružić, SPS – Serbian Socialist Party, 25 September 2015, Belgrade, face-to-face interview.

Interview SRB2015_56 with anonymous officials from Norwegian Embassy, 25 September 2015, Belgrade, face-to-face interview.

Interview SRB2015_57 with Maja Mičić, YiHR – Youth Initiative for Human Rights / Former Pride Organiser, 30 October 2015, London/Belgrade, Skype interview.

Interview SRB2015_58 with an anonymous official from United States Agency for International Development, 06 November 2015, London/Belgrade, Skype interview.

Interview SRB2015_59 with an anonymous official from Ministry without Portfolio responsible for EU Integration, 12 November 2015, London/Belgrade, mail interview.

Interview SRB2015_60 with Goran Miletić, Civil Rights Defenders, 04 December 2015, London/Belgrade, mail interview.

Interview SRB2016_1 with Nevena Petrušić, Former Commissioner for the Protection of Equality, 21 September 2016, London/Belgrade, mail interview.

Interview SRB2016_2 with an anonymous official from Commissioner for the Protection of Equality, 23 September 2016, London/Belgrade, mail interview.

Interview SRB2016_3 with an anonymous official from Judicial Academy, 05 October 2016, London/Belgrade, Skype interview.

Interview **SRB2016_4** with an anonymous official from Academy of Criminalistic and Police Studies, 19 October 2016, London/Belgrade, mail interview.

Interview **SRB2016_5** with an anonymous official from UN Office in Serbia (OHCHR), 07 November 2016, London/Belgrade, Skype interview.

Interview **SRB2016_6** with an anonymous official from OSCE office in Serbia, 01 December 2016, London/Belgrade, mail interview.

Interview **EC2016_1** with an anonymous official from European Commission (DG Near), 05 December 2016, Brussels, face-to-face interview.

Note

1 Further explanation of codes: EP = European Parliament, EC = European Commission; SRB = Serbia. The delegation of the EU to Serbia is coded as a Serbian actor as it is distinct from the institutions in Brussels.

References

Ahmed, S., 2007. 'You end up doing the document rather than doing': Diversity, race equality and the politics of documentation. *Ethnic and Racial Studies*, 30(4), pp. 590–609.

Ahmed, S., 2017. *Living a Feminist Life*. Durham, NC: Duke University Press.

Aleksić, M. ed., 2015. *PrEUgovor – Report on Progress of Serbia in Chapters 23 and 24*. [online] Belgrade Centre for Security Policy. Available at: <https://bezbednost.org/en/publication/coalition-preugovor-report-on-progress-of-serbia-in-chapters-23-and-24-2/> [Accessed 15 Aug. 2022].

Alpan, B. and Diez, T., 2014. The devil is in the 'domestic'? European integration studies and the limits of Europeanization in Turkey. *Journal of Balkan and Near Eastern Studies*, 16(1), pp. 1–10.

Altman, D. and Symons, J., 2016. *Queer Wars: The New Global Polarization over Gay Rights*. Cambridge: Polity.

Ames, L. M., 2004. Beyond gay Paree: What does the enlargement of the European Union mean for same-sex partners. *Emory International Law Review*, 18, pp. 503–554.

Ammaturo, F. R., 2015a. Spaces of Pride: A visual ethnography of Gay Pride parades in Italy and the United Kingdom. *Social Movement Studies*, 15(1), pp. 19–40.

Ammaturo, F. R., 2015b. The 'pink agenda': Questioning and challenging European homonationalist sexual citizenship. *Sociology*, 49(6), pp. 1151–1166.

Ammaturo, F. R., 2017. *European Sexual Citizenship: Human Rights, Bodies and Identities*. London: Palgrave Macmillan.

Ammaturo, F. R. and Slootmaeckers, K., 2020. *The Politics of Rainbow Maps*. [online] LSE Engenderings. Available at: <https://blogs.lse.ac.uk/gender/2020/05/28/the-politics-of-rainbow-maps/> [Accessed 9 Oct. 2020].

Anastasijević, D., 2009. Right-wing threats scrap Serbian Gay-Pride parade. *Time* [online] 23 Sep. Available at: <http://content.time.com/time/world/article/0,8599,1925715,00.html> [Accessed 15 Aug. 2022].

Andrić, G., 2015. Serbian ombudsman pressed on friend's suicide. Balkan Insight [online] 23 Apr. Available at: <www.balkaninsight.com/en/article/suicide-case-pulled-out-in-campaign-against-serbian-ombudsman> [Accessed 15 Aug. 2022].

Antonijević, M., Golubović, K., Stjelja, I., Vujić, K., Grujić, N., Vasić, Z., Krstev, M., Pokusevski, D., Bogdanović, M., Radić, M., Raicević, V. and Kurti, V., 2014. *Equality – Regulation and Reality*. Belgrade: YUCOM – Lawyers' Committee for Human Rights.

202   *References*

Arandarenko, M. and Nojkovic, A., 2008. *The Labour Market in Serbia: Overview*. Thessaloniki: Center for Democracy and Reconciliation in Southeast Europe.

Archer, R., 2014. *Where Have All the fascists Gone? Belgrade Pride 2014*. [online] Balkans in Europe Policy Blog. Available at: <www.suedosteuropa.uni-graz.at/biepag/node/94> [Accessed May 2016, no longer available].

Armstrong, E. A. and Crage, S. M., 2006. Movements and memory: The making of the Stonewall myth. *American Sociological Review*, 71(5), pp. 724–751.

Ayoub, P. M., 2013. Cooperative transnationalism in contemporary Europe: Europeanization and political opportunities for LGBT mobilization in the European Union. *European Political Science Review*, 5(2), pp. 279–310.

Ayoub, P. M., 2014. With arms wide shut: Threat perception, norm reception, and mobilized resistance to LGBT rights. *Journal of Human Rights*, 13(3), pp. 337–362.

Ayoub, P. M., 2016. *When States Come Out: Europe's Sexual Minorities and the Politics of Visibility*. New York: Cambridge University Press.

Ayoub, P. M. and Chetaille, A., 2020. Movement/countermovement interaction and instrumental framing in a multi-level world: Rooting Polish lesbian and gay activism. *Social Movement Studies*, 19(1), pp. 21–37.

Ayoub, P. M. and Paternotte, D., 2014a. Challenging borders, imagining Europe: Transnational LGBT activism in a new Europe. In: N. A. Naples and J. B. Mendez, eds. *Border Politics: Social Movements, Collective Identities, and Globalization*. New York: New York University Press. pp. 230–257.

Ayoub, P. M. and Paternotte, D. eds., 2014b. *LGBT Activism and the Making of Europe: A Rainbow Europe?* London: Palgrave Macmillan.

Ayoub, P. and Paternotte, D., 2020. Europe and LGBT rights: A conflicted relationship. In: M. J. Bosia, S. M. McEvoy and M. Rahman, eds. *The Oxford Handbook of Global LGBT and Sexual Diversity Politics*. New York: Oxford University Press. pp. 153–169.

B92, 2009a. Anti-discrimination bill arrives in parliament. *B92* [online] 18 Mar. Available at: <www.b92.net/eng/news/politics.php?yyyy=2009&mm=03&dd=18&nav_id=57898> [Accessed 15 Aug. 2022].

B92, 2009b. Government sticks to its new draft law. *B92* [online] 15 Mar. Available at: <www.b92.net/eng/news/politics.php?yyyy=2009&mm=03&dd=15&nav_id=57837> [Accessed 15 Aug. 2022].

B92, 2011a. Belgrade Mayor: I would ban Pride Parade. *B92* [online] 3 Oct. Available at: <www.b92.net/eng/news/politics.php?yyyy=2011&mm=10&dd=03&nav_id=76670> [Accessed 15 Aug. 2022].

B92, 2011b. Court: 2009 Pride parade ban unconstitutional. *B92* [online] 30 Dec. Available at: <www.b92.net/eng/news/society.php?yyyy=2011&mm=12&dd=30&nav_id=78051> [Accessed 15 Aug. 2022].

B92, 2011c. Elections played role in canceling of gay parade. *B92* [online] 10 Oct. Available at: <www.b92.net/eng/news/politics.php?yyyy=2011&mm=10&dd=10&nav_id=76794> [Accessed 15 Aug. 2022].

B92, 2012a. Holding of gay Pride parade still uncertain. *B92* [online] 29 Sep. Available at: <www.b92.net/eng/news/society.php?yyyy=2012&mm=09&dd=29&nav_id=82413> [Accessed 15 Aug. 2022].

B92, 2012b. Serbian authorities decide to ban gay parade. *B92* [online] 3 Oct. Available at: <www.b92.net/eng/news/politics.php?yyyy=2012&mm=10&dd=03&nav_id=82473> [Accessed 15 Aug. 2022].

B92, 2013. PM says gay parade 'good for country' – but he won't attend. *B92* [online] 24 Sep. Available at: <www.b92.net/eng/news/politics.php?yyyy=2013&mm=09&dd=24&nav_id=87764> [Accessed 15 Aug. 2022].

B92, 2014a. Srbija pokazala da poštuje zakon. *B92* [online] 28 Sep. Available at: <www.b92.net/info/vesti/index.php?yyyy=2014&mm=09&dd=28&nav_category=11&nav_id=905084> [Accessed 8 Dec. 2021].

B92, 2014b. Vucic: I will not attend Pride Parade, it is my choice. *B92* [online] 25 Sep. Available at: <www.b92.net/eng/news/society.php?yyyy=2014&mm=09&dd=25&nav_id=91712> [Accessed 15 Aug. 2022].

B92 and Tanjug, 2010. Gay rights activist joins Socialists. *B92* [online] 14 Dec. Available at: <www.b92.net/eng/news/politics.php?yyyy=2010&mm=12&dd=14&nav_id=71503> [Accessed 15 Aug. 2022].

Bache, I., Bulmer, S. and Gunay, D., 2012. Europeanization: A critical realist perspective. In: T. Exadaktylos and C. M. Radaelli, eds. *Research Design in European Studies: Establishing Causality in Europeanization*. Basingstoke: Palgrave Macmillan. pp. 64–84.

Balkan Inside, 2013. Serbia, Pride parade cancelled, all gatherings banned. [online] Balkan Inside, 27 Sep. Available at: <www.balkaninside.com/serbia-pride-parade-cancelled-all-gatherings-banned>. [Accessed 6 May 2016, no longer available].

Balkan Insight, 2013. Serbian President: Prepare for Gay Pride 2014 now. [online] Sep. Available at: <www.balkaninsight.com/en/article/nikolic-calls-for-preparations-for-2014-gay-pride> [Accessed 15 Aug. 2022].

Balkan Insight, 2014a. Belgrade Pride 2014: Live blog. [online] Sep. Available at: <www.balkaninsight.com/en/article/belgrade-pride-2014-live-blog> [Accessed 15 Aug. 2022].

Balkan Insight, 2014b. Serbia rightists urge PM to scrap gay march. [online] May. Available at: <www.balkaninsight.com/en/article/serbia-rightists-calls-on-authorities-to-cancel-belgrade-gay-pride> [Accessed 15 Aug. 2022].

Balkanist, 2013. Midnight Pride: Belgrade's unauthorized Pride parade (VIDEO). [online] 28 Sep. Available at: <http://balkanist.net/belgrade-unathorized-pride-parade/>.

Barlovac, B., 2011. Belgrade gays protest over stabbing incident. Balkan Insight [online] 19 Oct. Available at: <www.balkaninsight.com/en/article/belgrade-gays-protest-over-stabbing-lesbian> [Accessed 15 Aug. 2022].

Bauman, Z., 1991. *Modernity and Ambivalence*. Cambridge: Polity.

Bauman, Z., 1993. *Postmodern Ethics*. Oxford: Blackwell.

BBC News, 2004. Kosovo rioters burn Serb churches. [online] 18 Mar. Available at: <http://news.bbc.co.uk/1/hi/world/europe/3525168.stm> [Accessed 15 Aug. 2022].

BBC News, 2011. Serbia bans gay Pride parade citing violence fears. [online] 1 Oct. Available at: <www.bbc.co.uk/news/world-europe-15134182> [Accessed 15 Aug. 2022].

BBC News, 2017a. Serbia to have first gay prime minister as Ana Brnabic is chosen. [online] 16 Jun. Available at: <www.bbc.co.uk/news/world-europe-40297480> [Accessed 1 Mar. 2019].

BBC News, 2017b. Serbia–Kosovo train row escalates to military threat. [online] 15 Jan. Available at: <www.bbc.co.uk/news/world-europe-38630152> [Accessed 15 Aug. 2022].

BBC News, 2019. Ana Brnabic: Gay partner of Serbian PM gives birth. [online] 20 Feb. Available at: <www.bbc.co.uk/news/world-europe-47312826> [Accessed 29 Dec. 2021].

BBC News, 2021. EU declared 'LGBT freedom zone' in response to Poland's 'LGBT-free zones'. [online] 11 Mar. Available at: <www.bbc.co.uk/news/world-europe-56366750> [Accessed 13 Apr. 2021].

Belgrade Pride 2009 Organising Committee, 2009. *Pride March 2009 is Banned*. [online] Available at: <www.minoritycentre.org/news/Pride-march-2009-banned> [Accessed 6 Oct. 2016, no longer available].

Bermeo, N., 2016. On democratic backsliding. *Journal of Democracy*, 27(1), pp. 5–19.

Beta, 2009. 'Parada ponosa' u Beogradu na leto. *B92* [online] 28 Apr. Available at: <www.b92.net/info/vesti/index.php?yyyy=2009&mm=04&dd=28&nav_category=12&nav_id=357862> [Accessed 15 Aug. 2022].

Beta and Večernje Novosti, 2010. Čiplić: Naći će se treći poverenik. *B92* [online] 1 Mar. Available at: <www.b92.net/info/vesti/index.php?yyyy=2010&mm=03&dd=01&nav_id=414716> [Accessed 8 Jun. 2016].

Bieber, F., 2002. Nationalist mobilization and stories of Serb suffering: The Kosovo myth from 600th anniversary to the present. *Rethinking History*, 6(1), pp. 95–110.

Bieber, F., 2003. The Serbian opposition and civil society: Roots of the delayed transition in Serbia. *International Journal of Politics, Culture, and Society*, 17(1), pp. 73–90.

Bieber, F., 2015. The Serbia–Kosovo Agreements: An EU success story? *Review of Central and East European Law*, 40(3–4), pp. 285–319.

Bieber, F., 2018. The rise (and fall) of Balkan stabilitocracies. *Horizons: Journal of International Relations and Sustainable Development*, 10, pp. 176–185.

Bieber, F., Galijas, A. and Archer, R., 2014. *Debating the End of Yugoslavia*. Abingdon: Routledge.

Bilić, B., 2016a. Europe ♥ Gays? Europeanisation and Pride parades in Serbia. In: B. Bilić, ed. *LGBT Activism and Europeanisation in the Post-Yugoslav Space: On the Rainbow Way to Europe*. London: Palgrave Macmillan. pp. 117–153.

Bilić, B., 2016b. Europeanization, LGBT activism, and non-heteronormativity in the post-Yugoslav space: An introduction. *Southeastern Europe*, 40(1), pp. 1–12.

Bilić, B. ed., 2016c. *LGBT Activism and Europeanisation in the Post-Yugoslav Space: On the Rainbow Way to Europe*. London: Palgrave Macmillan.

Bilić, B., 2016d. Whose Pride? LGBT 'community' and the organization of Pride parades in Serbia. In: K. Slootmaeckers, H. Touquet and P. Vermeersch, eds. *The EU Enlargement and Gay Politics*. London: Palgrave Macmillan. pp. 203–220.

Bilić, B. and Stubbs, P., 2016. Beyond EUtopean promises and disillusions: A conclusion. In: B. Bilić, ed. *LGBT Activism and Europeanisation in the Post-Yugoslav Space: On the Rainbow Way to Europe*. London: Palgrave Macmillan. pp. 231–248.

Binnie, J. and Klesse, C., 2012. Solidarities and tensions: Feminism and transnational LGBTQ politics in Poland. *European Journal of Women's Studies*, 19(4), pp. 444–459.

Blagojević, J., 2011. Between walls: Provincialisms, human rights, sexualities and Serbian public discourses on EU integration. In: R. Kulpa and J. Mizielińska, eds. *De-centring Western Sexualities: Central and Eastern European Perspectives.* Farnham: Ashgate. pp. 27–41.

Blić, 2010. Nezavisni kandidat za poverenika za manjine nepodoban. Blić [online] 20 Feb. Available at: <www.blic.rs/vesti/politika/nezavisni-kandidat-za-poverenika-za-manjine-nepodoban/7dg3m0j> [Accessed 15 Aug. 2022].

Bogdanović, M., 2012. Kako sam napravila Prajd 2010 [How I made Pride 2010]. *Optimist* [online] Sep. Available at: <http://en.gsa.org.rs/2012/10/how-i-made-pride-2010/ [Accessed 15 Aug. 2022]>.

Bojić, B., 2009. Skandalozno: Amfilohiju sude zbog gej parade?! Press Online [online] 24 Sep. Available at: <www.novinar.de/2009/09/24/skandalozno-amfilohiju-sude-zbog-gej-parade.html> [Accessed 15 Aug. 2022].

Börzel, T. A., 2013. When Europeanization hits limited statehood: The Western Balkans as a test case for the transformative power of Europe. In: A. Elbasani, ed. *European Integration and Transformation in the Western Balkans: Europeanization or Business as Usual?* Abingdon: Routledge. pp. 173–184.

Börzel, T. A. and Pamuk, Y., 2012. Pathologies of Europeanisation: Fighting corruption in the southern Caucasus. *West European Politics*, 35(1), pp. 79–97.

Börzel, T. A. and Risse, T., 2003. Conceptualizing the domestic impact of Europe. In: K. Featherstone and C. M. Radaelli, eds. *The Politics of Europeanization.* Oxford: Oxford University Press. pp. 57–89.

Börzel, T. A. and Risse, T., 2007. Europeanization: The domestic impact of EU politics. In: K. E. Jørgensen, M. Pollack and B. Rosamond, eds. *Handbook of European Union Politics.* London: SAGE. pp. 483–504.

Bosia, M. J., 2014. Strange fruit: Homophobia, the state, and the politics of LGBT rights and capabilities. *Journal of Human Rights*, 13(3), pp. 256–273.

Bosia, M. J., 2015. To love or to loathe: Modernity, homophobia, and LGBT rights. In: M. L. Picq and M. Thiel, eds. *Sexualities in World Politics: How LGBTQ Claims Shape International Relations.* Abingdon: Routledge. pp. 38–53.

Bosia, M. J. and Weiss, M. L., 2013. Political homophobia in comparative perspective. In: M. L. Weiss and M. J. Bosia, eds. *Global Homophobia: States, Movements, and the Politics of Oppression.* Urbana: University of Illinois Press. pp. 1–29.

Bourdieu, P., 1985. The genesis of the concepts of habitus and field. *Sociocriticism*, 2(2), pp. 11–24.

Bourdieu, P., 1989. Social space and symbolic power. *Sociological Theory*, 7(1), pp. 14–25.

Bourdieu, P. and Wacquant, L. J. D., 1992. The purpose of reflexive sociology (the Chicago Workshop). In: *An Invitation to Reflexive Sociology.* Chicago: University of Chicago Press. pp. 60–215.

Bowden, B., 2014. To rethink standards of civilisation, start with the end. *Millennium – Journal of International Studies*, 42(3), pp. 614–631.

Bracewell, W., 2000. Rape in Kosovo: Masculinity and Serbian nationalism. *Nations and Nationalism*, 6(4), pp. 563–590.

Bracke, S., 2012. From 'saving women' to 'saving gays': Rescue narratives and their dis/continuities. *European Journal of Women's Studies*, 19(2), pp. 237–252.

Brosig, M., 2010. The challenge of implementing minority rights in Central Eastern Europe. *Journal of European Integration*, 32(4), pp. 393–411.

Brown, W., 2006. *Regulating Aversion: Tolerance in the Age of Identity and Empire*. Princeton, NJ: Princeton University Press.

Browne, K., 2007. A party with politics? (Re)making LGBTQ Pride spaces in Dublin and Brighton. *Social & Cultural Geography*, 8(1), pp. 63–87.

Bull, H., 1977. *The Anarchical Society: A Study of Order in World Politics*. Basingstoke: Palgrave Macmillan.

Bulmer, S., 2007. Theorizing Europeanization. In: P. Graziano and M. Vink, eds. *Europeanization: New Research Agendas*. Basingstoke: Palgrave. pp. 46–58.

Burawoy, M., 1998. The extended case method. *Sociological Theory*, 16(1), pp. 4–33.

Butterfield, N., 2016. Professionalization in sexual politics and activism in Croatia in the 2000s. *Southeastern Europe*, 40(1), pp. 54–80.

Carter, D., 2004. *Stonewall: The Riots that Sparked the Gay Revolution*. New York: St Martin's Griffin.

Catholic News Agency, 2021. *Poland objects to EU declaring itself 'LGBT freedom zone'*. [online] Catholic News Agency. Available at: <www.catholicnewsagency.com/news/246849/poland-objects-to-eu-declaring-itself-lgbt-freedom-zone> [Accessed 13 Apr. 2021].

CeSID, 2013. *Public Opinion Survey Report: Public Perceptions of Discrimination in Serbia*. Belgrade: Commissioner for the Protection of Equality. [online] Available at: <www.undp.org/serbia/publications/citizens-attitudes-discrimination-serbia> [Accessed 15 Aug. 2022].

Chetaille, A., 2011. Poland: Sovereignty and sexuality in post-socialist times. In: M. Tremblay, D. Paternotte and C. Johnson, eds. *The Lesbian and Gay Movement and the State: Comparative Insights Into a Transformed Relationship*. Farnham: Ashgate. pp. 119–133.

Christians, L.-L., 2011. *2011 Expert Workshops on the Prohibition of Incitement to National, Racial or Religious Hatred – Annex Serbia*. [online] Available at: <www.ohchr.org/Documents/Issues/Expression/ICCPR/Vienna/Annexes/Serbia.pdf> [Accessed 15 Aug. 2022].

Clark, J. N., 2008. *Serbia in the Shadow of Milosevic: The Legacy of Conflict in the Balkans*. London: I. B. Tauris.

Cohen, C. J., 1997. Punks, bulldaggers, and welfare queens: The radical potential of queer politics? *GLQ: A Journal of Lesbian and Gay Studies*, 3(4), pp. 437–465.

Commissioner for the Protection of Equality, 2016. *Regular Annual Report of the Commissioner for Protection of Equality for 2015*. Belgrade: Commissioner for the Protection of Equality.

Connell, R. W., 2005. *Masculinities*. 2nd ed. Cambridge: Polity.

Cooper-Cunningham, D., 2021. The international politics of sex: Visual activism in response to Russian state homophobia. PhD dissertation, University of Copenhagen.

Council of Europe, 2012. *Secretary General Jagland 'surprised and disappointe' about ban of 'Belgrade Pride'*. [online]. Available at: <https://wcd.coe.int/ViewDoc.jsp?p=&id=1983785&Site=DC&BackColorInternet=F5CA75&BackColorIntranet=F5CA75&BackColorLogged=A9BACE&direct=true> [Accessed 15 Aug. 2022].

Council of the European Union, 2010. *Toolkit to Promote and Protect the Enjoyment of all Human Rights by Lesbian, Gay, Bisexual and Transgender (LGBT) People.* Available at: <https://data.consilium.europa.eu/doc/document/ST-11179-2010-INIT/en/pdf> [Accessed 15 Aug. 2022].

Council of the European Union, 2012. *EU Strategic Framework and Action Plan on Human Rights and Democracy.* Luxembourg: European Union.

Council of the European Union, 2013. *Guidelines to Promote and Protect the Enjoyment of all Human Rights by Lesbian, Gay, Bisexual, Transgender and Intersex (LGBTI) Persons.* Available at: <https://data.consilium.europa.eu/doc/document/ST-11492-2013-INIT/en/pdf> [Accessed 15 Aug. 2022].

Crouch, C. and Marquand, D. eds., 1992. *Towards Greater Europe? A Continent Without an Iron Curtain.* Oxford: The Political Quarterly.

Currier, A., 2010. Political homophobia in postcolonial Namibia. *Gender & Society,* 24(1), pp. 110–129.

Czernielewska, M., Paraskevopoulos, C. J. and Szlachta, J., 2004. The regionalization process in Poland: An example of 'Shallow' Europeanization? *Regional & Federal Studies,* 14(3), pp. 461–495.

Davydova, D., 2012. Baltic Pride 2010: Articulating sexual difference and heteronormative nationalism in contemporary Lithuania. *Sextures,* 2(2), pp. 32–46.

Decker, K., Harley, G. and Svircev, S., 2014. *Serbia Judicial Functional Review: Main Report.* Washington, DC: World Bank – Multi-Donor Trust Fund for Justice Sector Support in Serbia [online]. Available at: <http://documents.worldbank.org/curated/en/912041468333616786/pdf/940140WP0v20P10ort0Final0Version0EN.pdf> [Accessed 15 Aug. 2022].

Delanty, G., 2006. Borders in a changing Europe: Dynamics of openness and closure. *Comparative European Politics,* 4(2), pp. 183–202.

Delatolla, A., 2020. Sexuality as a standard of civilization: Historicizing (homo) colonial intersections of race, gender, and class. *International Studies Quarterly,* 64(1), pp. 148–158.

Dépelteau, F. 2015. Relational sociology, pragmatism, transactions and social fields. *International Review of Sociology,* 25(1), pp. 45–64.

Deutsche Welle, 2013. EU sets date for Serbia membership talks. Deutsche Welle [online] 18 Dec. Available at: <www.dw.com/en/eu-sets-date-for-serbia-membership-talks/a-17304630> [Accessed 15 Aug. 2022].

Deutsche Welle, 2014. German gay rights activist critically injured in Belgrade assault. Deutsche Welle [online] 13 Sep. Available at: <www.dw.de/german-gay-rights-activist-critically-injured-in-belgrade-assault/a-17920121> [Accessed 15 Aug. 2022].

Diez, T., 2004. Europe's Others and the return of geopolitics. *Cambridge Review of International Affairs,* 17(2), pp. 319–335.

Diez, T., 2005. Constructing the self and changing others: Reconsidering 'Normative Power Europe'. *Millennium – Journal of International Studies,* 33(3), pp. 613–636.

Diez, T., 2006. The paradoxes of Europe's borders. *Comparative European Politics,* 4(2–3), pp. 235–252.

Diez, T., 2013. Normative power as hegemony. *Cooperation and Conflict,* 48(2), pp. 194–210.

Diez, T., Stetter, S. and Albert, M., 2006. The European Union and border conflicts: The transformative power of integration. *International Organization*, 60(3), pp. 563–593.

Dioli, I., 2009. Back to a nostalgic future: The queeroslav utopia. *Sextures*, 1(1), pp. 24–42.

Dioli, I., 2012. Labour, LGBT* rights, and Europe. Discourses in Italy and Serbia. PhD dissertation, University of Bologna.

Djurić, M., 2001. *Under Attack in Yugoslavia: Gay Rights, Democracy.* [online] The Gully. Available at: <www.thegully.com/essays/gaymundo/010723yu_gay_djuric.html> [Accessed 15 Aug. 2022].

Donnelly, J., 1998. Human rights: A new standard of civilization? *International Affairs*, 74(1), pp. 1–23.

Downes, M., 2004. *Police Reform in Serbia: Towards the Creation of a Modern and Accountable Police Service.* Belgrade: Law Enforcement Department OSCE Mission to Serbia and Montenegro. [online] Available at: <www.osce.org/serbia/18310?download=true> [Accessed 15 Aug. 2022].

Drezgić, R., 2010. Religion, politics and gender in the context of nation-state formation: The case of Serbia. *Third World Quarterly*, 31(6), pp. 955–970.

Duberman, M., 1993. *Stonewall.* New York: Plume.

Duggan, L., 2001. *The Twilight of Equality? Neoliberalism, Cultural Politics, and the Attack on Democracy.* Boston, MA: Beacon Press.

Duggan, M., 2010. Politics of Pride: Representing relegated sexual identities in Northern Ireland. *Northern Ireland Legal Quarterly*, 61(2), pp. 163–178.

Economides, S. and Ker-Lindsay, J., 2015. 'Pre-Accession Europeanization': The case of Serbia and Kosovo. *JCMS: Journal of Common Market Studies*, 53(5), pp. 1027–1044.

Edwards, J. A., 2015. Bringing in earthly redemption: Slobodan Milosevic and the national myth of Kosovo. *Advances in the History of Rhetoric*, 18(1), pp. 187–204.

Eichler, M., 2008. Gender and nation in the Soviet/Russian transformation. In: Y. Abu-Laban, ed. *Gendering the Nation-State: Canadian and Comparative Perspectives.* Toronto: University of British Columbia Press. pp. 46–59.

Eigenmann, L., 2022. 'This is a union of values': The rise of the LGBTI rights norm as part of the EU's identity construction. *Social Politics: International Studies in Gender, State & Society*, 29(1), pp. 95–117.

Ejdus, F. and Božović, M., 2019. Europeanisation and indirect resistance: Serbian police and Pride parades. *International Journal of Human Rights*, 23(4), pp. 493–511.

Ejdus, F. and Subotić, J., 2014. Kosovo as Serbia's sacred space: Governmentality, pastoral power, and sacralization of territories. In: G. Ognjenović and J. Jozelić, eds. *Politicization of Religion, the Power of Symbolism.* New York: Palgrave Macmillan. pp. 159–184.

Elbasani, A. ed., 2013a. *European Integration and Transformation in the Western Balkans: Europeanization or Business as Usual?* Abingdon: Routledge.

Elbasani, A., 2013b. Europeanization travels to the Western Balkans: Enlargement strategy, domestic obstacles and diverging reforms. In: A. Elbasani, ed. *European*

Integration and Transformation in the Western Balkans: Europeanization or Business as Usual? Abingdon: Routledge. pp. 3–21.

Eleveld, K., 2009. White House condemns Uganda Bill. *Advocate* [online] 12 Dec. Available at: <www.advocate.com/news/daily-news/2009/12/12/white-house-condemns-uganda-bill> [Accessed 15 Aug. 2022].

Emirbayer, M., 1997. Manifesto for a relational sociology. *American Journal of Sociology*, 103(2), pp. 281–317.

European Commission, 2005a. *Commission Staff Working Paper – Annex to the Communication from the Commission on the Preparedness of Serbia and Montenegro to Negotiate a Stabilisation and Association Agreement with the European Union.* Brussels: European Union. [online]. Available at: <https://eur-lex.europa.eu/legal-content/EN/TXT/HTML/?uri=CELEX:52005SC0478&from=EN> [Accessed 27 Jul. 2021].

European Commission, 2005b. Communication from the Commission on the Preparedness of Serbia and Montenegro to Negotiate a Stabilisation and Association Agreement with the European Union {SEC(2005) 478}. Brussels: European Commission. [online]. Available at: <https://eur-lex.europa.eu/legal-content/EN/TXT/PDF/?uri=CELEX:52005DC0476&from=EN> [Accessed 27 Jul. 2021].

European Commission, 2006. *Enlargement Strategy and Main Challenges 2006–2007.* Brussels: European Union.

European Commission, 2007. *Enlargement Strategy and Main Challenges 2007–2008.* Brussels: European Union. [online]. Available at: <https://eur-lex.europa.eu/legal-content/EN/ALL/?uri=CELEX:52007DC0663> [Accessed 15 Aug. 2022].

European Commission, 2009. *Serbia 2009 Progress Report.* Brussels: European Union.

European Commission, 2010. *Serbia 2010 Progress Report.* Brussels: European Union.

European Commission, 2011. *Enlargement Strategy and Main Challenges 2011–2012.* Brussels: European Union.

European Commission, 2013a. *Enlargement Strategy and Main Challenges 2013–2014.* Available at: <https://eur-lex.europa.eu/legal-content/EN/TXT/?uri=CELEX%3A52013DC0700&qid=1659268952128> [Accessed 15 Aug. 2022].

European Commission, 2013b. *Serbia 2013 Progress Report.* Brussels: European Union.

European Commission, 2014. *Serbia 2014 Progress Report.* Brussels: European Union.

European Council, 1994. European Council Meeting on 9 and 10 December 1994 in Essen: Presidency Conclusions. [online] *europarl.europa.eu.* Essen. Available at: <www.europarl.europa.eu/summits/ess1_en.htm> [Accessed 15 Aug. 2022].

European Parliament, 2014. *European Parliament resolution of 13 March 2014 on Launching Consultations to Suspend Uganda and Nigeria from the Cotonou Agreement in View of Recent Legislation Further Criminalising Homosexuality.* Brussels: European Parliament. [online]. Available at: <www.europarl.europa.eu/doceo/document/TA-7-2014-0254_EN.html> [Accessed 15 Aug. 2022].

European Parliament, 2016. *2015 Progress Report on Serbia: European Parliament Resolution of 4 February 2016 on the 2015 Report on Serbia (2015/2892(RSP)).* [online] Strassbourg. Available at: <www.europarl.europa.eu/doceo/document/TA-8-2016-0046_EN.html> [Accessed 15 Aug. 2022].

European Union Agency for Fundamental Rights, 2020. *A Long Way to Go for LGBTI Equality*. Luxembourg: Publications Office of the European Union.

European Western Balkans, 2021. Vučić says he will not sign the same-sex unions law, his justification raises suspicion. European Western Balkans [online] 6 May. Available at: <https://europeanwesternbalkans.com/2021/05/06/vucic-says-he-will-not-sign-the-same-sex-unions-law-his-justification-raises-suspicion/> [Accessed 29 Dec. 2021].

Eyben, R., 2010. Hiding relations: The irony of 'effective aid'. *European Journal of Development Research*, 22(3), pp. 382–397.

Fagan, A. and Sircar, I., 2015. *Europeanization of the Western Balkans: Environmental Governance in Bosnia-Herzegovina and Serbia*. London: Palgrave.

Falkner, G. and Treib, O., 2008. Three worlds of compliance or four? The EU-15 compared to new member states. *Journal of Common Market Studies*, 46(2), pp. 293–313.

Featherstone, K., 2003. Introduction: In the name of 'Europe'. In: K. Featherstone and C. M. Radaelli, eds. *The Politics of Europeanization*. Oxford: Oxford University Press. pp. 3–26.

Ficchi, L., 2011. Candidate countries facing a binding charter of fundamental rights: What's new. In: G. di Federico, ed. *The EU Charter of Fundamental Rights: From Declaration to Binding Instrument*. New York: Springer. pp. 109–121.

Fonet, Beta and Tanjug, 2010. Interior minister calls for peaceful Pride parade. *B92* [online] 9 Oct. Available at: <www.b92.net/eng/news/society.php?yyyy=2010&mm=10&dd=09&nav_id=70191> [Accessed 15 Aug. 2022].

Freyburg, T. and Richter, S., 2010. National identity matters: The limited impact of EU political conditionality in the Western Balkans. *Journal of European Public Policy*, 17(2), pp. 263–281.

Füle, Š., 2012. *Statement by Commissioner Füle on Belgrade 2012 Pride Parade Ban*. [online] European Commission. Available at: <http://ec.europa.eu/archives/commission_2010–2014/fule/headlines/news/2012/10/20121004_en.htm> [Accessed 15 Aug. 2022].

Füle, Š., 2014. *Statement of Commissioner Füle on Belgrade Pride Parade*. [online] European Commission. Available at: <http://europa.eu/rapid/press-release_STATEMENT-14–289_en.htm> [Accessed 15 Aug. 2022].

Galbreath, D., 2003. The politics of European integration and minority rights in Estonia and Latvia. *Perspectives on European Politics and Society*, 4(1), pp. 35–53.

Garcia, M., 2011. Serbian woman stabbed for LGBT shirt. *Advocate* [online] 17 Oct. Available at: <www.advocate.com/news/daily-news/2011/10/17/serbian-woman-stabbed-lgbt-shirt> [Accessed 15 Aug. 2022].

Gaweda, B., 2021. Europeanization, democratization, and backsliding: Trajectories and framings of gender equality institutions in Poland. *Social Politics: International Studies in Gender, State & Society*, 28(3), pp. 629–655.

Gay Straight Alliance, 2007. *We'll Do Fine with a Little Help From Growing Group of Our Friends: Report on the LGBT Human Rights in Serbia in 2007*. Belgrade. [online]. Available at: <http://en.gsa.org.rs/wp-content/uploads/2012/09/GSA-report-2007.pdf> [Accessed 15 Aug. 2022].

Gay Straight Alliance, 2010. *Prejudices Exposed: Homophobia in Serbia 2010.* Belgrade: Gay Straight Alliance.

Gay Straight Alliance, 2011. *Step by Step: Report on Human Rights Status of LGBT Persons in Serbia 2010.* Belgrade: Gay Straight Alliance.

Gay Straight Alliance, 2014. *Court of Appeal Gave the Final Verdict – Dragan Marković Palma Guilty for Discrimination of LGBT Population.* [online]. Available at: <http://en.gsa.org.rs/2014/07/court-of-appeal-gave-the-final-verdict-dragan-markovic-palma-guilty-for-discrimination-of-lgbt-population/> [Accessed 15 Aug. 2022].

George, A. L. and Bennett, A., 2005. *Case Studies and Theory Development in the Social Sciences.* Cambridge, MA: MIT Press.

Georgievski, D., 2013. *Civil Society Condemns Attacks on Equality Commissioner Nevena Petrušić.* [online] One World Platform for Southeast Europe. Available at: <www.oneworldsee.org/content/civil-society-condemns-attacks-equality-commissioner-nevena-petrušić> [Accessed May 2017, no longer available].

Glenn, J. K., 2004. From nation-states to member states: Accession negotiations as an instrument of Europeanization. *Comparative European Politics,* 2(1), pp. 3–28.

GLIC, 2013. Prekinite da preko leđa LGBT populacije uslovljavate Srbiju. *GayEcho* [online] 1 Mar. Available at: <http://gayecho.com/glic/?p=584#.V5XegGWvJ5i> [Accessed 15 Aug. 2022].

Gligorijević, J., 2011. Neslaganje oko parade i ponosa. *Vreme.* [online] 25 Aug. Available at: <www.vreme.com/cms/view.php?id=1007671> [Accessed 15 Aug. 2022].

Gordon, N. and Pardo, S., 2015. Normative Power Europe and the power of the local. *Journal of Common Market Studies,* 53(2), pp. 416–427.

Gordy, E. D., 1999. *Culture of Power in Serbia: Nationalism and the Destruction of Alternatives.* University Park: Pennsylvania State University Press.

Gould, J. A. and Moe, E., 2015. Nationalism and the Struggle for LGBTQ Rights in Serbia, 1991–2014. *Problems of Post-communism,* 62(5), pp. 273–286.

Grabbe, H., 2001. How does Europeanization affect CEE governance? Conditionality, diffusion and diversity. *Journal of European Public Policy,* 8(6), pp. 1013–1031.

Grabbe, H., 2003. Europeanization goes east: Power and uncertainty in the EU accession process. In: K. Featherstone and C. M. Radaelli, eds. *The Politics of Europeanization.* Oxford: Oxford University Press. pp. 303–327.

Grabbe, H., 2006. *The EU Transformative Power: Europeanization through Conditionality in Central and Eastern Europe.* New York: Palgrave Macmillan.

Graff, A., 2006. We are (not all) homophobes: A report from Poland. *Feminist Studies,* 32(2), pp. 434–449.

Greenberg, J., 2006. Nationalism, masculinity and multicultural citizenship in Serbia. *Nationalities Papers,* 34(3), pp. 321–341.

Grosse, T. G., 2010. Social dialogue during enlargement: The case of Poland and Estonia. *Acta Politica,* 45(1–2), pp. 112–135.

GSA Info Centre, 2011. *GSA Meets Serbian Government Representatives.* [online] Available at: <http://en.gsa.org.rs/2011/10/gsa-meets-serbian-government-representatives/> [Accessed 15 Aug. 2022].

Guzina, D., 2003. Socialist Serbia's narratives: From Yugoslavia to a greater Serbia. *International Journal of Politics, Culture, and Society IJPS*, 17(1), pp. 91–111.

Harley, A., 2010. Belgrade Pride unaffected as anti-gay protesters battle against police. *UK Gay News* [online] 10 Oct. Available at: <www.ukgaynews.org.uk/Archive/10/Oct/1004.htm> [Accessed May 2017, no longer available].

Haughton, T., 2007. When does the EU make a difference? Conditionality and the accession process in Central and Eastern Europe. *Political Studies Review*, 5(2), pp. 233–246.

Haughton, T., 2011. Half full but also half empty: Conditionality, compliance and the quality of democracy in Central and Eastern Europe. *Political Studies Review*, 9(3), pp. 323–333.

Higashino, A., 2004. For the sake of "peace and security"? The role of security in the European Union enlargement eastwards. *Cooperation and Conflict*, 39(4), pp. 347–368.

Hillion, C., 2013. *Enlarging the European Union and Deepening its Fundamental Rights Protection.* [online] European Policy Analysis. Swedish Institute for European Policy Studies. Available at: <www.sieps.se/en/publications/2013/enlarging-the-european-union-and-deepening-its-fundamental-rights-protection-201311epa/> [Accessed 15 Aug. 2022].

Hofferberth, M. and Weber, C., 2015. Lost in translation: A critique of constructivist norm research. *Journal of International Relations and Development*, 18(1), pp. 75–103.

Hudes, K., 1984. Coordination of Paris and London club reschedulings. *New York University Journal of International Law and Politics*, 17, pp. 553–571.

Huszka, B., 2017. Human rights on the losing end of EU enlargement: The case of Serbia. *Journal of Common Market Studies*, 8(4), p. 365.

Igrutinović, D., 2015. Tanks, truncheons, testosterone: A panicky reconstruction of masculinity in the Serbian media after the Pride parade. In: T. Rosic Ilic, J. Koteska and J. Ljumovic, eds. *Representation of Gender Minority Groups in Media: Serbia, Montenegro, and Macedonia. Belgrade*: Faculty of Media and Communications. pp. 63–80.

Igrutinović, D., Sremac, S. and van den Berg, M., 2015. Pride parades and/or prayer processions: Contested public Space in Serbia #Belgrade Pride 2014. *Journal of Empirical Theology*, 28(2), pp. 204–225.

ILGA-Europe, 2016. *Annual Review of the Human Rights Situation of Lesbian, Gay, Bisexual, Trans and Intersex People in Europe 2016.* Brussels: ILGA-Europe. [online]. Available at: <https://ilga-europe.org/files/uploads/2022/04/annual-review-2016.pdf> [Accessed 15 Aug. 2022].

InSerbia, 2013a. No regrets over the ban of Pride parade, elections not needed – Vucic. [online] 30 Sep. Available at: <http://inserbia.info/today/2013/09/no-regrets-over-the-ban-of-pride-parade-elections-not-needed-vucic/> [Accessed May 2017, no longer available].

InSerbia, 2013b. Serbia: Belgrade Pride Week and Parade 2014 on May 25? InSerbia [online] 5 Oct. Available at: <http://inserbia.info/today/2013/10/serbia-belgrade-pride-week-and-parade-2014-on-may-25/> [Accessed May 2017, no longer available].

InSerbia, 2014a. Belgrade Pride parade canceled. InSerbia [online] 17 May. Available at: <http://inserbia.info/today/2014/05/belgrade-pride-parade-canceled/> [Accessed May 2017, no longer available].

InSerbia, 2014b. Belgrade Pride parade [live]. InSerbia [online] 28 Sep. Available at: <http://inserbia.info/today/2014/09/belgrade-pride-parade-live/> [Accessed May 2017, no longer available].

InSerbia, 2015. Why is Serbia's Ombudsman 'Enemy of the State', 'Killer', 'Shame for Serbia', …? InSerbia [online] Apr. Available at: <http://inserbia.info/today/2015/04/why-is-serbias-ombudsman-enemy-of-the-state-killer-shame-for-serbia/> [Accessed May 2017, no longer available].

Intergroup on LGBT Rights, 2011. *Belgrade Pride Banned: Members of the European Parliament Express Deep Regret.* [online]. Available at: <https://lgbti-ep.eu/2011/09/30/belgrade-pride-banned-meps-express-deep-regret/> [Accessed 15 Aug. 2022].

Intergroup on LGBT Rights, 2012. *Belgrade Pride Banned Again for 2012.* [online]. Available at: <https://lgbti-ep.eu/2012/10/03/belgrade-pride-banned-again-for-2012/> [Accessed 15 Aug. 2022].

Intergroup on LGBT Rights, 2014. *LGBTI Intergroup MEP heading to Belgrade Pride.* [online] Available at: <https://lgbti-ep.eu/2014/09/26/lgbti-intergroup-mep-heading-to-belgrade-pride/> [Accessed 15 Aug. 2022].

Irinej, Kopilovic, A., Zilkic, A., Vrbovski, S., Cete-Semesi, I., Dolinski, A. and Asiel, I., 2009. *Zajedničko Saopštenje Predstavnikâ Tradicionalnih Crkava i Verskih Zajednica Povodom Predloga Zakona o Zabrani Diskriminacije.* spc.rs. [online]. Available at: <www.novinar.de/2009/03/06/zajednicko-saopstenje-predstavnika-tradicionalnih-crkava-i-verskih-zajednica-povodom-predloga-zakona-o-zabrani-diskriminacije.html?lang=lat> [Accessed 15 Aug. 2022].

Irvine, J. A. and Lilly, C. S., 2007. Boys must be boys: Gender and the Serbian Radical Party, 1991–2000. *Nationalities Papers*, 35(1), pp. 93–120.

Jackson, P. T. and Nexon, D. H., 1999. Relations before states: Substance, process and the study of world politics. *European Journal of International Relations*, 5(3), pp. 291–332.

Jackson, P. T. and Nexon, D. H., 2019. Reclaiming the social: Relationalism in anglophone international studies. *Cambridge Review of International Affairs*, 32(5), pp. 582–600.

Janjić, D., 2015. Smear campaign against the Serbian ombudsman. *Osservatoria Balkani e Causaso Transeuropa* [online] 7 May. Available at: <www.balcanicaucaso.org/eng/Areas/Serbia/Smear-campaign-against-the-Serbian-Ombudsman-161389> [Accessed 15 Aug. 2022].

Jerosimić, A., 2008. *Human Rights in Serbia 2007: Legal Provisions and Practice Compared to International Human Rights Standards.* Belgrade: Belgrade Centre for Human Rights.

Johnson, D. N., 2012. We are waiting for you: The discursive (de)construction of Belgrade Pride 2009. *Sextures*, 2(2), pp. 6–31.

Jovanović, M., 2013. Silence or condemnation: The Orthodox Church on homosexuality in Serbia. *Družboslovne razprave*, 29(73), pp. 79–95.

Judah, T., 2008. *Kosovo: What Everyone Needs to Know?* Oxford: Oxford University Press.

Kacarska, S., 2012. Europeanisation through mobility: Visa liberalisation and citizenship regimes in the Western Balkans. CITSEE Working Paper 2012/21. Available at: <www.pure.ed.ac.uk/ws/files/12810156/CITSEE_WORKING_PAPER_2012_21.pdf> [Accessed 15 Aug. 2022].

Kahlina, K., 2015. Local histories, European LGBT designs: Sexual citizenship, nationalism, and 'Europeanisation' in post-Yugoslav Croatia and Serbia. *Women's Studies International Forum*, 49, pp. 73–83.

Kauppi, N., 2003. Bourdieu's political sociology and the politics of European integration. *Theory & Society*, 32(5/6), pp. 775–789.

Kauppi, N., 2018. *Toward a Reflexive Political Sociology of the European Union.* Cham: Palgrave Macmillan.

Keck, M. E. and Sikkink, K., 1998. *Activists Beyond Borders.* Ithaca, NY: Cornell University Press.

Kimmel, M. S., 1987. The contemporary 'crisis' of masculinity in historical perspective. In: H. Brod, ed. *The Making of Masculinities: The New Men's Studies.* London: Allen & Unwin. pp. 121–154.

Kim-Puri, H. J., 2005. Conceptualizing gender-sexuality-state-nation. *Gender & Society*, 19(2), pp. 137–159.

King Jr, M. L., 2010 [1968]. *Where Do We Go from Here: Choas or Community?* Boston, MA: Beacon Press.

Kirchick, J., 2010. Battle in Belgrade: Is Serbia really ready to join the European Union? *Foreign Policy* [online] 11 Oct. Available at: <https://foreignpolicy.com/2010/10/11/battle-in-belgrade/> [Accessed 15 Aug. 2022].

Koldinská, K., 2009. Institutionalizing intersectionality: A new path to equality for new member states of the EU? *International Feminist Journal of Politics*, 11(4), pp. 547–563.

Kollman, K. and Waites, M., 2009. The global politics of lesbian, gay, bisexual and transgender human rights: An introduction. *Contemporary Politics*, 15(1), pp. 1–17.

Korica, B., 2012. Banning of gay pride may damage Serbia's European Union chances. *Gay Star News* [online] 5 Oct. Available at: <www.gaystarnews.com/article/banning-gay-pride-may-damage-serbia's-european-union-chances051012> [Accessed 15 Aug. 2022].

Kostovicova, D., 2006. Civil society and post-communist democratization: Facing a double challenge in post-Milošević Serbia. *Journal of Civil Society*, 2(1), pp. 21–37.

Kostovicova, D., 2014. When enlargement meets common foreign and security policy: Serbia's Europeanisation, visa liberalisation and the Kosovo policy. *Europe–Asia Studies*, 66(1), pp. 67–87.

Kovačević, A. and Jelovac, B., 2010. *Intervju: Ivica Dačić Ministar Policije.* [online] Akademedia Srbija. Available at: <www.akademediasrbija.com/index.php?option=com_content&view=article&id=1529:intervju-ivica-daim-ministar-policije&catid=38:cat-komentari-vesti&Itemid=54> [Accessed May 2017, no longer available].

Kovács, M. and Kabachnik, P., 2001. Shedding light on the quantitative Other: the EU's discourse in the Commission opinions of 1997. In: J. Böröcz and M.

Kovács, eds. *Empire's New Clothes: Unveiling EU Enlargement.* Telford: Central Europe Review. pp. 147–195.

Kristoffersson, M., van Roozendaal, B. and Poghosyan, L., 2016. European integration and LGBTI activism: Partners in realising change? In: K. Slootmaeckers, H. Touquet and P. Vermeersch, eds. *The EU Enlargement and Gay Politics: The Impact of Eastern Enlargement on Rights, Activism and Prejudice.* London: Palgrave. pp. 45–68.

Krizsan, A., 2009. From formal adoption to enforcement. Post-accession shifts in EU impact on Hungary in the equality policy field. *European Integration Online Papers (EIoP)*, 13(2), pp. 1–18.

Kuhar, R., 2011. The heteronormative panopticon and the transparent closet of the public space in Slovenia. In: R. Kulpa and J. Mizielińska, eds. *De-centring Western Sexualities: Central and Eastern European Perspectives.* Farnham: Ashgate. pp. 149–166.

Kuhar, R., 2013. In the name of hate: Homophobia as a value. *Southeastern Europe*, 37(1), pp. 1–16.

Kuhar, R. and Paternotte, D. eds., 2017. *Anti-gender Campaigns in Europe: Mobilizing Against Equality.* London: Rowman & Littlefield International.

Kuhar, R. and Švab, A., 2008. Homophobia and violence against gays and lesbians in Slovenia. *Revija za sociologiju*, 39(4), pp. 267–281.

Kulpa, R., 2014. Western leveraged pedagogy of Central and Eastern Europe: Discourses of homophobia, tolerance, and nationhood. *Gender, Place Culture: A Journal of Feminist Geography*, 21(4), pp. 431–448.

Kulpa, R. and Mizielińska, J. eds., 2011. *De-centring Western Sexualities: Central and Eastern European Perspectives.* Farnham: Ashgate.

Kunz, R. and Maisenbacher, J., 2017. Women in the neighbourhood: Reinstating the European Union's civilising mission on the back of gender equality promotion? *European Journal of International Relations*, 23(1), 122–144.

Kurepa, T., 2010. *Parada ponosa ili prilagodjavanje 'političke volje'.* [online]. Available at: <https://progresivnamisao.wordpress.com/2014/04/14/parada-ponosa-ili-prilagodavanje-politicke-volje/> [Accessed 15 Aug. 2022].

Kuus, M., 2004. Europe's eastern expansion and the reinscription of otherness in East-Central Europe. *Progress in Human Geography*, 28(4), pp. 472–489.

Kuus, M., 2005. Multiple Europes: Boundaries and margins in European Union enlargement. *Geopolitics*, 10(3), pp. 567–570.

Kuus, M., 2007. Something old, something new: Eastness in European Union enlargement. *Journal of International Relations and Development*, 10(2), pp. 150–167.

Labris and Gayten-LGBT, 2001. Saopstenje Organizatora: Povodom Brutalnog Nasilja Izvrsenog Nad Gradjankama I Gradjanima Na Gej-Lezbejskoj Paradi U Beogradu. *B92* [online] 1 Jul. Available at: <www.b92.net/specijal/gay-parada/gay-saop.phtml> [Accessed 15 Aug. 2022].

Lambevski, A., 2009. Querying (sexual) citizenships. *Sextures*, 1(1), pp. 1–6.

Lennox, C. and Waites, M., 2013. Human rights, sexual orientation and gender identity in the Commonwealth: From history and law to developing activism and transnational dialogues. In: *Human Rights, Sexual Orientation and Gender Identity in the Commonwealth Struggles for Decriminalisation and Change.* London: School of Advanced Studies, University of London. pp. 1–59.

Lombardo, E. and Forest, M., 2012. *The Europeanization of Gender Equality Policies: A Discursive-Sociological Approach.* Basingstoke: Palgrave Macmillan.

Luciani, L., 2021. Where the personal is (geo)political: Performing queer visibility in Georgia in the context of EU association. *Problems of Post-communism* (early view).

Mahony, H., 2006. EU 'deeply wrong' on Serbia, prime minister says. *EU Observer* [online] 19 Jun. Available at: <https://euobserver.com/news/21899> [Accessed 15 Aug. 2022].

Makarychev, A. and Medvedev, S., 2015. Biopolitics and power in Putin's Russia. *Problems of Post-communism*, 62(1), pp. 45–54.

Malová, D. and Dolný, B., 2008. The Eastern enlargement of the European Union: Challenges to democracy? *Human Affairs*, 18(1), pp. 67–80.

Manners, I., 2002. Normative Power Europe: A contradiction in terms? *Journal of Common Market Studies*, 40(2), pp. 235–258.

Manners, I., 2013. Assessing the decennial, reassessing the global: Understanding European Union normative power in global politics. *Cooperation and Conflict*, 48(2), pp. 304–329.

Manners, I. and Whitman, R., 2003. The 'difference engine': Constructing and representing the international identity of the European Union. *Journal of European Public Policy*, 10(3), pp. 380–404.

Marinković, L., 2015. Community Post: At least 2 people beaten up for being gay in Belgrade in the last 2 weeks. BuzzFeed [online] 17 Apr. Available at: <www.buzzfeed.com/lazaralazara/at-least-2-people-beaten-up-for-being-gay-in-belgr-6qjt> [Accessed 15 Aug. 2022].

Marjanović, S., 2013. *Policijska saznanja: Huligani pčelama i osama napadaju Paradu ponosa?!* [online] Blić. Available at: <www.blic.rs/vesti/drustvo/policijska-saznanja-huligani-pcelama-i-osama-napadaju-paradu-ponosa/yst3vqj> [Accessed 15 Aug. 2022].

Marko, D., 2013. *Media Reforms in Turbulent Times: The Role of Media Assistance in the Establishment of Independent Media Institutions in Serbia. Working Paper Series on International Media Assistance in the Western Balkans, Working Paper, prepared in the framework of the Regional Research Promotion Programme in the Western Balkans RRPP.* Sarajevo: Analitika – Center for Social Research.

Marko, D., 2015. The role of media assistance in the establishment of public service broadcasting in Serbia. *International Journal of Digital Television*, 6(3), pp. 293–309.

Massari, M., 2005. Do all roads lead to Brussels? Analysis of the different trajectories of Croatia, Serbia-Montenegro and Bosnia-Herzegovina. *Cambridge Review of International Affairs*, 18(2), pp. 259–273.

McKay, T. and Angotti, N., 2016. Ready rhetorics: Political homophobia and activist discourses in Malawi, Nigeria, and Uganda. *Qualitative Sociology*, 39(4), pp. 397–420.

Mendelski, M., 2015. The EU's pathological power: The failure of external rule of law promotion in South Eastern Europe. *Southeastern Europe*, 39(3), pp. 318–346.

Mendelski, M., 2016. Europeanization and the rule of law: Towards a pathological turn. *Southeastern Europe*, 40(3), pp. 346–384.

Meredith, L., 2013. The future of EU enlargement. *LSE Ideas* [live event], 26 November, London.

Merlingen, M., 2007. Everything Is Dangerous: A Critique of 'Normative Power Europe'. *Security Dialogue*, 38(4), pp. 435–453.

Mićić, M., 2014. *Application of Fair Trial Principle in Judicial System of Serbia*. Belgrade: Youth Initiative for Human Rights.

Mijačić, D., 2010. *Support to the Implementation of Anti-discrimination Legislation and Mediation in Serbia: An Independent Evaluation Report*. Belgrade: United Nations Development Programme Serbia.

Mikuš, M., 2011. 'State Pride': Politics of LGBT rights and democratisation in 'European Serbia'. *East European Politics & Societies*, 25(4), pp. 834–851.

Mikuš, M., 2015. 'Faggots won't walk through the city': Religious nationalism and LGBT Pride parades in Serbia. In: S. Sremac and R. R. Ganzevoort, eds. *Religious and Sexual Nationalisms in Central and Eastern Europe: Gods, Gays, and Governments*. Leiden: Brill. pp. 15–32.

Milanović Hrašovec, I., 2010. Diskriminacija Zakona o zabrani diskriminacije. *Vreme* [online] 25 Feb. Available at: <www.vreme.com/cms/view.php?id=915613> [Accessed 15 Aug. 2022].

Milićević, A. S., 2006. Joining the war: Masculinity, nationalism and war participation in the Balkans war of secession, 1991–1995*. *Nationalities Papers*, 34(3), pp. 265–287.

Milićević, B., Sarić, N., Pavlović, L., Bogdanović, M., Đukic, V., Ćirilović, N., Madzarević, L., Gajišin, V. and Lazić, V., 2009. *No Retreat No Surrender: Report on Human Rights Status of GLBT Persons in Serbia 2009*. Belgrade: Gay Straight Alliance. [online]. Available at: <http://en.gsa.org.rs/wp-content/uploads/2012/08/GSA-report-2009.pdf> [Accessed 15 Aug. 2022].

Miller, R., 2010. Gay pride shows Serbia's progress. *Guardian* [online] 11 Oct. Available at: <www.theguardian.com/commentisfree/2010/oct/11/gay-pride-serbia-progress> [Accessed 15 Aug. 2022].

Mizielińska, J. and Kulpa, R., 2011. 'Contemporary peripheries': Queer studies, circulation of knowledge and East/West divide. In: R. Kulpa and J. Mizielińska, eds. *De-centring Western Sexualities: Central and Eastern European Perspectives*. Farnham: Ashgate. pp. 11–26.

Mladjenovic, L., 2001. Notes of a feminist lesbian during wartime. *European Journal of Women's Studies*, 8(3), pp. 381–391.

Mole, R., 2011. Nationality and sexuality: Homophobic discourse and the 'national threat' in contemporary Latvia. *Nations and Nationalism*, 17(3), pp. 540–560.

Mole, R., 2016. Nationalism and homophobia in Central and Eastern Europe. In: K. Slootmaeckers, H. Touquet and P. Vermeersch, eds. *The EU Enlargement and Gay Politics: The Impact of Eastern Enlargement on Rights, Activism and Prejudice*. London: Palgrave Macmillan. pp. 99–122.

Morus, C. M., 2007. Slobo the Redeemer: The rhetoric of Slobodan Milosevic and the construction of the Serbian 'people'. *Southern Communication Journal*, 72(1), pp. 1–19.

Mos, M., 2013. Conflicted Normative Power Europe: The European Union and sexual minority rights. *Journal of Contemporary European Research*, 9(1), pp. 78–93.

Mos, M., 2014. Of gay rights and Christmas ornaments: The political history of sexual orientation non-discrimination in the Treaty of Amsterdam. *Journal of Common Market Studies*, 52(3), pp. 632–649.

Mos, M., 2018. The fight of the Religious Right in Europe: Old whines in new bottles. *European Journal of Politics and Gender*, 1(3), pp. 325–343.

Mos, M., 2020. Ambiguity and interpretive politics in the crisis of European values: Evidence from Hungary. *East European Politics*, 36(2), pp. 267–287.

Moss, K., 2017. Russia as the saviour of European civilization: Gender and the geopolitics of traditional values. In: R. Kuhar and D. Paternotte, eds. *Anti-gender Campaigns in Europe: Mobilizing against Equality*. London: Rowman & Littlefield International. pp. 194–214.

Muller, P., 2000. L'analyse cognitive des politiques publiques: Vers une sociologie politique de l'action publique. *Revue francaise de science politique*, 50(2), pp. 189–207.

Nagel, J., 1998. Masculinity and nationalism: Gender and sexuality in the making of nations. *Ethnic and Racial Studies*, 21(2), pp. 242–269.

Nancheva, N., 2007. What are norms good for? Ethnic minorities on Bulgaria's way to Europe. *Journal of Communist Studies and Transition Politics*, 23(3), pp. 371–395.

National Democratic Institute, 2015. *NDI Poll on LGBTI Issues in the Balkans is a Call to Action*. [online]. Available at: <www.ndi.org/LGBTI_Balkans_poll> [Accessed 24 Jun. 2016].

Nenadović, M., 2012. Enlargement anno 2012. In: H. Swoboda, E. Stetter and J. M. Wiersma, eds. *EU Enlargement Anno 2012: A Progressive Engagement*. Brussels: European Union. pp. 21–34.

Neuman Stanivukovi, S., 2012. Croatia as the 28th EU member state: How did we get here and where should we go from now? *Papiers d'actualité / Current Affairs in Perspective* [online]. Available at: <www.fondation-pierredubois.ch/images/stories/papiers_dactualit/no1_2012_croatia.pdf> [Accessed 15 Aug. 2022].

Nicolaïdis, K. and Howse, R., 2002. 'This is my EUtopia …': Narrative as power. *Journal of Common Market Studies*, 40(4), pp. 767–792.

Nielsen, C. A., 2013a. Stronger than the state? Football hooliganism, political extremism and the Gay Pride parades in Serbia. *Sport in Society*, 16(8), pp. 1038–1053.

Nielsen, C. A., 2013b. The cyclical farce of Serbian Gay Pride. Balkan Insight [online] 7 Oct. Available at: <www.balkaninsight.com/en/article/the-cyclical-farce-of-serbian-gay-pride> [Accessed 2 Aug. 2021].

Noutcheva, G., 2009. Fake, partial and imposed compliance: The limits of the EU's normative power in the Western Balkans. *Journal of European Public Policy*, 16(7), pp. 1065–1084.

Nozar, W., 2012. The 100% union: The rise of chapters 23 and 24. In: H. Swoboda, E. Stetter and J. M. Wiersma, eds. *EU Enlargement Anno 2012: A Progressive Engagement*. Brussels: European Union. pp. 87–96.

Nuñez-Mietz, F. G., 2019. Resisting human rights through securitization: Russia and Hungary against LGBT rights. *Journal of Human Rights*, 18(5), pp. 1–21.

Obama, B., 2014. *Statement by the President on the Anti-Homosexuality Bill in Uganda*. [online] The White House. Available at: <www.whitehouse.gov/the-press-office/2014/02/16/statement-president-anti-homosexuality-bill-uganda> [Accessed 15 Aug. 2022].

Oberschall, A., 2000. The manipulation of ethnicity: From ethnic cooperation to violence and war in Yugoslavia. *Ethnic and Racial Studies*, 23(6), pp. 982–1001.

Obradović-Wochnik, J., 2009. Knowledge, acknowledgement and denial in Serbia's responses to the Srebrenica massacre. *Journal of Contemporary European Studies*, 17(1), pp. 61–74.

Obradović-Wochnik, J., 2013. *Ethnic Conflict and War Crimes in the Balkans: The Narratives of Denial in Post-conflict Serbia*. London: I. B. Taurus.

Obradović-Wochnik, J. and Wochnik, A., 2014. Invalid Ballots and the "crisis of representative democracy": Re-inventing protest at the 2012 Serbian elections. *East European Politics & Societies*, 28(4), pp. 808–835.

O'Dwyer, C., 2010. From conditionality to persuasion? Europeanization and the rights of sexual minorities in post-accession Poland. *Journal of European Integration*, 32(3), pp. 229–247.

O'Dwyer, C., 2012. Does the EU help or hinder gay-rights movements in post-communist Europe? The case of Poland. *East European Politics*, 28(4), pp. 332–352.

O'Dwyer, C., 2018. *Coming out of communism: The emergence of LGBT activism in Eastern Europe*. New York: New York University Press.

O'Dwyer, C. and Schwartz, K. Z. S., 2010. Minority rights after EU enlargement: A comparison of antigay politics in Poland and Latvia. *Comparative European Politics*, 8(2), pp. 220–243.

Olsen, J. P., 2002. The many faces of Europeanization. *Journal of Common Market Studies*, 40(5), pp. 921–952.

OSCE, 2015. *Training of Judges on Anti-discriminatory Legislation*. [online] OSCE. Available at: <www.osce.org/node/85512> [Accessed May 2016, no longer available].

Özdemir, B., 2014. The role of the EU in Turkey's legislative reforms for eliminating violence against women: A bottom-up approach. *Journal of Balkan and Near Eastern Studies*, 16(1), pp. 119–136.

Panke, D., 2012. Process tracing: Testing multiple hypotheses with a small number of cases. In: T. Exadaktylos and C. M. Radaelli, eds. *Research Design in European Studies: Establishing Causality in Europeanization*. Basingstoke: Palgrave Macmillan. pp. 125–140.

Parliamentary Assembly of the Council of Europe, 2002. *CoE Parliamentary Assembly Opinion No. 239 on the Federal Republic of Yugoslavia's Application for Membership of the Council of Europe*. [online]. Available at: <https://assembly.coe.int/nw/xml/XRef/Xref-XML2HTML-en.asp?fileid=17039&lang=en> [Accessed 9 Dec. 2021].

Parsons, C., 2010. How – and how much – are sociological approaches to the EU distinctive? *Comparative European Politics*, 8(1), pp. 143–159.

Paternotte, D. and Kuhar, R., 2017. The anti-gender movement in comparative perspective. In: R. Kuhar and D. Paternotte, eds. *Anti-gender Campaigns in Europe: Mobilizing Against Equality*. London: Rowman & Littlefield International. pp. 253–276.

Paternotte, D. and Tremblay, M., 2015. Introduction: Investigating lesbian and gay activism. In: D. Paternotte and M. Tremblay, eds. *The Ashgate Research Companion to Lesbian and Gay Activism*. Abingdon: Routledge. pp. 1–12.

Pavasović Trošt, T. and Kovacevic, N., 2013. Football, hooliganism and nationalism: The reaction to Serbia's gay parade in reader commentary online. *Sport in Society*, 16(8), pp. 1054–1076.

Pavasović Trošt, T. and Slootmaeckers, K., 2015. Religion, homosexuality and nationalism in the Western Balkans: The role of religious institutions in defining the nation. In: S. Sremac and R. R. Ganzevoort, eds. *Religious and Sexual Nationalisms in Central and Eastern Europe: Gods, Gays, and Governments*. Leiden: Brill. pp. 154–180.

Pederson, T., 2009. *Serbia: Pride Parade Cancelled as Government Loses Nerve*. [online] WikiLeaks. Available at: <https://wikileaks.org/plusd/cables/09BELGRADE1080_a.html> [Accessed 15 Aug. 2022].

Perica, V., 2002. *Balkan Idols: Religion and Nationalism in Yugoslav States*. Oxford: Oxford University Press.

Perunović, A., 2015. The state of exception and security discourses: Belgrade's Pride parades on the 'no man's land'. In: T. Rosic Ilic, J. Koteska and J. Ljumovic, eds. *Representation of Gender Minority Groups in Media: Serbia, Montenegro, and Macedonia*. Belgrade: Faculty of Media and Communications. pp. 81–92.

Petrović, I., 2014. Vučić: Napad na nekoga ko je različit je sramota. Deutsche Welle [online] 15 Sep. Available at: <www.dw.de/vučić-napad-na-nekoga-ko-je-različit-je-sramota/a-17922174> [Accessed 15 Aug. 2022].

Petrović, V., 2011. *Human Rights in Serbia 2010: Legal Provisions and Practice Compared to International Human Rights Standards*. Belgrade: The Belgrade Centre for Human Rights. [online]. Available at: <www.bgcentar.org.rs/bgcentar/eng-lat/wp-content/uploads/2013/04/Human-Rights-in-Serbia-A-Comprehensive-Report-for-2010-in-Serbian-and-English-2011..pdf> [Accessed 15 Aug. 2022].

Petrušić, N., 2011. *Regular Annual Report for 2010: Commissioner for Protection of Equality*. Belgrade: Commissioner for Protection of Equality.

Petrušić, N. ed., 2012. *Regular Annual Report for 2011: Commissioner for Protection of Equality*. Translated by B. Janjic. Belgrade: Commissioner for Protection of Equality. [online]. Available at: <http://ravnopravnost.gov.rs/wp-content/download/2011%20Regular%20Annual%20Report.pdf> [Accessed 15 Aug. 2022].

Petrušić, N. ed., 2013. *Review of Court Decisions of the Courts in Republic of Serbia in the Area of Protection Against Discrimination*. Belgrade: Commissioner for Protection of Equality. [online]. Available at: <http://ravnopravnost.gov.rs/wp-content/download/review_of_court_decisions_of_the_courts_in_republic_of_

serbia_in_the_area_of_protection_against_discrimination.pdf> [Accessed 15 Aug. 2022].

Petrušić, N., 2014. *Regular Annual Report of the Commission for the Protection of Equality for 2013*. Belgrade: Commissioner for Protection of Equality.

Pond, E., 2013. Serbia reinvents itself. *Survival*, 55(4), pp. 7–30.

Poppe, A. E., Leininger, J. and Wolff, J., 2019. Beyond contestation: Conceptualizing negotiation in democracy promotion. *Democratization*, 26(5), pp. 777–795.

Prozorov, S., 2011. The other as past and present: Beyond the logic of 'temporal othering' in IR theory. *Review of International Studies*, 37(3), pp. 1273–1293.

Puar, J. K., 2007. *Terrorist Assemblages: Homonationalism in Queer Times*. Durham, NC: Duke University Press.

Puar, J. K., 2013a. Homonationalism as assemblage: Viral travels, affective sexualities. *Jindal Global Law Review*, 4(2), pp. 23–43.

Puar, J. K., 2013b. Rethinking homonationalism. *International Journal of Middle East Studies*, 45(2), pp. 336–339.

Qin, Y., 2016. A relational theory of world politics. *International Studies Review*, 18(1), pp. 33–47.

Qin, Y., 2018. *A Relational Theory of World Politics*. Cambridge: Cambridge University Press.

Radaelli, C. M., 2003. The Europeanization of public policy. In: K. Featherstone and C. M. Radaelli, eds. *The Politics of Europeanization*. Oxford: Oxford University Press. pp. 27–56.

Radaelli, C. M., 2004. Europeanisation: Solution or problem? *European Integration Online Papers (EIoP)*, 8(16). Available at: <https://papers.ssrn.com/sol3/papers.cfm?abstract_id=601163> [Accessed 15 Aug. 2022].

Radaelli, C. M. and Pasquier, R., 2007. Conceptual issues. In: P. Graziano and M. P. Vink, eds. *Europeanization: New Research Agendas*. Basingstoke: Palgrave. pp. 35–45.

Rahman, M., 2014. Queer rights and the triangulation of Western exceptionalism. *Journal of Human Rights*, 13(3), pp. 274–289.

Ramet, S. P., 2007. The denial syndrome and its consequences: Serbian political culture since 2000. *Communist and Post-communist Studies*, 40(1), pp. 41–58.

Ramet, S. P., 2011. Serbia's corrupt path to the rule of law: An introduction. In: O. Listhaug, S. P. Ramet and D. Dulic, eds. *Civic and Uncivic Values: Serbia in the Post-Milosevic Era*. Budapest: CEU Press. pp. 3–20.

Rao, R., 2020. *Out of Time: The Queer Politics of Postcoloniality*. Oxford: Oxford University Press.

Rawłuszko, M., 2021. And if the opponents of gender ideology are right? Gender politics, Europeanization, and the democratic deficit. *Politics & Gender*, 17(2), pp. 301–323.

Rechel, B., 2008. What has limited the EU's impact on minority rights in accession countries? *East European Politics & Societies*, 22(1), pp. 171–191.

Renkin, H. Z., 2009. Homophobia and queer belonging in Hungary. *Focaal*, 2009(53), pp. 20–37.

Renkin, H. Z., 2013. Perverse frictions: Pride, dignity, and the Budapest LGBT march. *Ethnos: Journal of Anthropology*, 80(3), pp. 409–432.

Rettman, A., 2010. EU ambassador to attend gay pride in Serbia. *EU Observer* [online] 6 Oct. Available at: <https://euobserver.com/lgbti/30979> [Accessed 15 Aug. 2022].

Rhodes-Kubiak, R., 2015. *Activist Citizenship and the LGBT Movement in Serbia: Belonging, Critical Engagement, and Transformation*. New York: Palgrave.

Risse, T., Cowles, M. G. and Caporaso, J., 2001. Europeanization and domestic change: Introduction. In: M. G. Cowles, J. Caporaso and T. Risse, eds. *Transforming Europe: Europeanization and Domestic Change*. Ithaca, NY: Cornell University Press. pp. 1–20.

Ristić, M., 2014a. Pride 2014: Belgrade holds parade amid heavy security. Balkan Insight [online] 28 Sep. Available at: <www.balkaninsight.com/en/article/belgrade-holds-gay-pride-amid-heavy-security> [Accessed 15 Aug. 2022].

Ristić, M., 2014b. Serbia urged to protect gays after brutal attack. Balkan Insight [online] 15 Sep. Available at: <www.balkaninsight.com/en/article/serbia-urged-to-protect-gays-after-brutal-attack> [Accessed 15 Aug. 2022].

Roseneil, S. and Stoilova, M., 2011. Heteronormativity, intimate citizenship and the regulation of same-sex sexualities in Bulgaria. In: R. Kulpa and J. Mizielińska, eds. *De-centring Western Sexualities: Central and Eastern European Perspectives*. Farnham: Ashgate. pp. 167–190.

Rosić Ilić, T., 2015. Belgrade Pride parade 2014: Tabloidization and parody of the process of EU integration. *European Journal of Social Sciences Education and Research*, 5(1), pp. 19–24.

Rumelili, B., 2004. Constructing identity and relating to difference: Understanding the EU's mode of differentiation. *Review of International Studies*, 30(1), pp. 27–47.

Russell-Omaljev, A., 2016. *Divided We Stand: Discourses on Identity in 'First' and 'Other' Serbia*. Stuttgart: ibidem.

Sasse, G., 2008. The politics of EU conditionality: The norm of minority protection during and beyond EU accession. *Journal of European Public Policy*, 15(6), pp. 842–860.

Saurugger, S., 2012. Beyond non-compliance with legal norms. In: T. Exadaktylos and C. M. Radaelli, eds. *Research Design in European Studies: Establishing Causality in Europeanization*. Basingstoke: Palgrave Macmillan. pp. 105–124.

Saxon, D., 2006. Exporting justice: Perceptions of the ICTY among the Serbian, Croatian, and Muslim communities in the former Yugoslavia. *Journal of Human Rights*, 4(4), pp. 559–572.

Schäuble, M., 2009. Contested masculinities: Discourses on the role of Croatian combatants during the 'Homeland War'; (1991–1995). In: C. Eifler and R. Seifert, eds. *Gender Dynamics and Post-conflict Reconstruction*. Frankfurt am Main: Peter Lang. pp. 169–198.

Scheingold, S. A., 2004. *The Politics of Rights: Lawyers, Politics, and Political Change*. Ann Arbor, MI: University of Michigan Press.

Schimmelfennig, F. and Sedelmeier, U., 2005a. Introduction: Conceptualizing the Europeanization of Central and Eastern Europe. In: U. Sedelmeier, ed. *The*

Europeanization of Central and Eastern Europe. Ithaca, NY: Cornell University Press. pp. 1–28.

Schimmelfennig, F. and Sedelmeier, U. eds., 2005b. *The Europeanization of Central and Eastern Europe.* Ithaca, NY: Cornell University Press.

seebiz.eu, 2010. *Ivica Dačić: Nisam ja odlučio da bude Parada ponosa, vi ste to birali 5. oktobra.* [online] Kapital. Available at: <http://kapital.rs/vesti/2010/10/ivica-dacic-nisam-ja-odlucio-da-bude-parada-ponosa/> [Accessed May 2016, no longer available].

Seifert, R., 2009. Armed conflict, post-war reconstruction and gendered subjectivities. In: C. Eifler and R. Seifert, eds. *Gender Dynamics and Post-conflict Reconstruction.* Frankfurt am Main: Peter Lang. pp. 21–45.

Shevtsova, M., 2020. Fighting 'Gayropa': Europeanization and instrumentalization of LGBTI rights in Ukrainian public debate. *Problems of Post-communism,* 67(6), pp. 500–510.

Shevtsova, M., 2021. *LGBTI Politics and Value Change in Ukraine and Turkey: Exporting Europe?* Abingdon: Routledge.

Simo, A., 2001. Violence stops Yugoslavia Gay Pride. The Gully [online] 5 Jul. Available at: <www.thegully.com/essays/gaymundo/010705gay_yugoslavia.html> [Accessed 15 Aug. 2022].

Sky News, 2014. Serbia election: Progressive Party 'wins poll'. Sky News [online] 16 Mar. Available at: <https://news.sky.com/story/serbia-election-progressive-party-wins-poll-10413493> [Accessed 15 Aug. 2022].

Sloat, A., 2005. The rebirth of civil society: The growth of women's NGOs in Central and Eastern Europe. *European Journal of Women's Studies,* 12(4), pp. 437–452.

Slootmaeckers, K., 2017. The litmus test of Pride: Analysing the emergence of the Belgrade 'Ghost' Pride in the context of EU accession. *East European Politics,* 33(4), pp. 517–535.

Slootmaeckers, K., 2019. Nationalism as competing masculinities: Homophobia as a technology of othering for hetero- and homonationalism. *Theory and Society,* 48(2), pp. 239–265.

Slootmaeckers, K., 2020. Constructing European Union identity through LGBT equality promotion: Crises and shifting othering processes in the European Union enlargement. *Political Studies Review,* 18(3), pp. 346–361.

Slootmaeckers, K., 2022. Unpacking normative resonance: The attitudinal panopticon and the implementation gap of LGBT rights in Serbia. *Social Politics: International Studies in Gender, State & Society,* 29(1), pp. 1–23.

Slootmaeckers, K. and O'Dwyer, C., 2018. Europeanization of attitudes towards homosexuality: Exploring the role of education in the transnational diffusion of values. *Innovation: The European Journal of Social Science Research,* 31(4), pp. 406–428.

Slootmaeckers, K. and Sircar, I., 2018. Marrying European and domestic politics? The marriage referendum in Croatia and value-based Euroscepticism. *Europe–Asia Studies,* 70(3), pp. 321–344.

Slootmaeckers, K. and Touquet, H., 2016. The co-evolution of EU's Eastern enlargement and LGBT politics: An ever gayer Union? In: K. Slootmaeckers, H. Touquet and P. Vermeersch, eds. *The EU Enlargement and Gay Politics: The Impact of Eastern Enlargement on Rights, Activism and Prejudice*. London: Palgrave. pp. 19–44.

Slootmaeckers, K., Touquet, H. and Vermeersch, P., 2016a. Introduction: EU enlargement and LGBT rights – beyond symbolism? In: K. Slootmaeckers, H. Touquet and P. Vermeersch, eds. *The EU Enlargement and Gay Politics: The Impact of Eastern Enlargement on Rights, Activism and Prejudice*. London: Palgrave. pp. 1–16.

Slootmaeckers, K., Touquet, H. and Vermeersch, P. eds., 2016b. *The EU Enlargement and Gay Politics: The Impact of Eastern Enlargement on Rights, Activism and Prejudice*. London: Palgrave Macmillan.

Smismans, S., 2010. The European Union's fundamental rights myth. *Journal of Common Market Studies*, 48(1), pp. 45–66.

Smith, K. E., 2001. The EU, human rights and relations with third countries: 'Foreign policy' with an ethical dimension? In: K. E. Smith and M. Light, eds. *Ethics and Foreign Policy*. Cambridge: Cambridge University Press. pp. 185–203.

Smith, K. E., 2005. The outsiders: The European neighbourhood policy. *International Affairs*, 81(4), pp. 757–773.

Stahl, B., 2011. Perverted Conditionality: The Stabilisation and Association Agreement between the European Union and Serbia. *European Foreign Affairs Review*, 16(4), pp. 465–487.

Stahl, B., 2013. Another 'strategic accession'? The EU and Serbia (2000–2010). *Nationalities Papers*, 41(3), pp. 447–468.

Stakić, I., 2011. Homophobia and hate speech in Serbian public discourse: How nationalist myths and stereotypes influence prejudices against the LGBT minority. *Equal Rights Review*, 7, pp. 44–65.

Stakić, I., 2015. Securitization of LGBTIQ minority in Serbian far-right discourses: A post-structuralist perspective. *Intersections: East European Journal of Society and Politics*, 1(1), pp. 183–206.

Stein, M., 2012. *Rethinking the Gay and Lesbian Movement*. New York: Routledge.

Stella, F., 2007. The right to be different? Sexual citizenship and its politics in post-Soviet Russia. In: *Gender, Equality and Difference During and After State Socialism*. Basingstoke: Palgrave Macmillan. pp. 146–166.

Stella, F., 2012. The politics of in/visibility: Carving out queer space in Ul'yanovsk. *Europe–Asia Studies*, 64(10), pp. 1822–1846.

Stella, F., 2013. Queer space, Pride, and shame in Moscow. *Slavic Review*, 72(3), pp. 458–480.

Stjelja, I., Todorović, K., Todorović, D. and Todorović, J., 2014. *Hate Crimes: Actions of State Authorities in Cases of Attacks Against LGBT Persons in Serbia*. Belgrade: Labris.

Stojaković, A., 2014. *Parada Ponosa i LGBT populacija*. Belgrade: Centar za kvir studije. [online]. Available at: <www.lgbti-era.org/one-stop-shop/pride-parades-and-lgbt-population> [Accessed 15 Aug. 2022].

Stojanović, D., 2010a. Official: Anti-gay riots send wrong message to EU. *NBC News* [online] 11 Oct. Available at: <www.nbcnews.com/id/39617475/ns/world_news-europe/t/official-anti-gay-riots-send-wrong-message-eu/> [Accessed 15 Aug. 2022].

Stojanović, D., 2010b. Serb police clash with anti-gay rioters. *AP News* [online] 10 Oct. Available at: <https://apnews.com/article/c22f64ecee724b20b893afc471126ddf> [Accessed 2 Aug. 2021].

Stojanović, D., 2011. *On Kosovo, Raspberries and Gay Pride*. [online] Peščanik. Available at: <http://pescanik.net/on-kosovo-raspberries-and-gay-pride/> [Accessed 15 Aug. 2022].

Stojčić, M., 2014. Summary and final examination. In: A. Stojakovic, ed. *Parada Ponosa i LGBT populacija*. Belgrade: Centar za kvir studije. pp. 131–144.

Stojčić, M. and Petrović, D., 2016. *Homofobija i internalizovana homofobija u Srbiji: Kvalitativno instrazivanje*. Belgrade: Centre for Queer Studies. [online]. Available at: <www.lgbti-era.org/one-stop-shop/homophobia-and-internalized-homophobia-serbia-qualitative-research> [Accessed 15 Aug. 2022].

Stojković, B., 2003. *Transversal Study Cultural Policy and Cultural Diversity: National Report Serbia*. Strasbourg: Council of Europe. [online]. Available at: <https://rm.coe.int/0900001680929f53> [Accessed 15 Aug. 2022].

Štulhofer, A. and Rimac, I., 2009. Determinants of homonegativity in Europe. *Journal of Sex Research*, 46(1), pp. 24–32.

Stychin, C. F., 2000. 'A stranger to its laws': Sovereign bodies, global sexualities, and transnational citizens. *Journal of Law and Society*, 27(4), pp. 601–625.

Subotić, J., 2011. Europe is a state of mind: Identity and Europeanization in the Balkans. *International Studies Quarterly*, 55(2), pp. 309–330.

Subotić, J. and Carey, H. F., 2014. The European Union, the ICTY, and the challenge of Europeanization in Serbia. In: H. F. Carey, ed. *European Institutions, Democratization, and Human Rights Protection in the European Periphery*. Lanham, MD: Lexington Books. pp. 289–315.

Süleymanoğlu-Kürüm, R. and Cin, F. M. eds., 2021. *Feminist Framing of Europeanisation: Gender Equality Policies in Turkey*. London: Palgrave Macmillan.

Swimelar, S., 2016. The struggle for visibility and equality: Bosnian LGBT rights. In: K. Slootmaeckers, H. Touquet and P. Vermeersch, eds. *The EU Enlargement and Gay Politics: The Impact of Eastern Enlargement on Rights, Activism and Prejudice*. London: Palgrave Macmillan. pp. 175–202.

Swimelar, S., 2019. Nationalism and Europeanization in LGBT rights and politics: A comparative study of Croatia and Serbia. *East European Politics and Societies: And Cultures*, 33(3), pp. 603–630.

Swimelar, S., 2020. LGBT rights in Bosnia: The challenge of nationalism in the context of Europeanization. *Nationalities Papers*, 48(4), pp. 768–790.

Synovitz, R. and Cosic, G., 2019. Lesbian PM or not, Serbia blocks gays' path to parenthood. *Radio Free Europe* [online] 22 Aug. Available at: <www.rferl.org/a/lesbian-pm-or-not-serbia-blocks-gays-path-to-parenthood/30123813.html> [Accessed 29 Dec. 2021].

Szulc, L., 2018. *Transnational Homosexuals in Communist Poland*. London: Palgrave Macmillan.

Szulecka, J. and Szulecki, K., 2013. Analysing the Rospuda River controversy in Poland: Rhetoric, environmental activism, and the influence of the European Union. *East European Politics*, 29(4), pp. 397–419.

Tanjug, 2009. Anti-discrimination law changes next week. *B92* [online] 5 Mar. Available at: <www.b92.net/eng/news/politics.php?yyyy=2009&mm=03&dd=05&nav_id=57600> [Accessed 15 Aug. 2022].

Tanjug, 2010. Minister announces gay parade for 2010. *B92* [online] 18 Jan. Available at: <www.b92.net/eng/news/society.php?yyyy=2010&mm=01&dd=18&nav_id=64557> [Accessed 15 Aug. 2022].

Tansey, O., 2007. Process tracing and elite interviewing: A case for non-probability sampling. *PS Political Science and Politics*, 40(4), pp. 765–772.

Tatham, A. F., 2009. *Enlargement of the European Union*. Alphen aan den Rijn, The Netherlands: Kluwer Law International.

Thiel, M., 2022. *The European Union's International Promotion of LGBTI Rights: Promises and Pitfalls*. Abingdon: Routledge.

Thoreson, R. R., 2014. *Transnational LGBT Activism: Working for Sexual Rights Worldwide*. Minneapolis: University of Minnesota Press.

Todorović, J., 2013. *Annual Report on the Position of the LGBTIQ Population in Serbia for 2012*. Belgrade: Labris.

Todorović, J., 2015. *Annual Report on the Position of the LGBTIQ Population in Serbia for 2014*. Belgrade: Labris.

Trauner, F., 2009. From membership conditionality to policy conditionality: EU external governance in South Eastern Europe. *Journal of European Public Policy*, 16(5), pp. 774–790.

UN News Service, 2013. *Serbia: UN Rights Office Urges Protection of Gay Rights After Pride Parade is Cancelled*. [online]. Available at: <www.un.org/apps/news/story.asp?NewsID=46153#.WCBKsXecaCX> [Accessed 15 Aug. 2022].

Upchurch, M., 2006. State, labour and market in post-revolution Serbia. *Capital & Class*, 30(2), pp. 1–30.

Vachudova, M. A., 2008. Tempered by the EU? Political parties and party systems before and after accession. *Journal of European Public Policy*, 15(6), pp. 861–879.

Vachudova, M. A., 2014. EU leverage and national interests in the Balkans: The puzzles of enlargement ten years on. *Journal of Common Market Studies*, 52(1), pp. 122–138.

Väyrynen, T., 2013. Keeping the trauma of war open in the male body: Resisting the hegemonic forms of masculinity and national identity in visual arts. *Journal of Gender Studies*, 22(2), pp. 137–151.

Vermeersch, P., 2004. Minority policy in Central Europe: Exploring the impact of the EU's enlargement strategy. *Global Review of Ethnopolitics*, 3(2), pp. 3–19.

Vermeersch, P., 2007. A minority at the border: EU enlargement and the Ukrainian minority in Poland. *East European Politics & Societies*, 21(3), pp. 475–502.

Wæver, O., 1996. European security identities. *Journal of Common Market Studies*, 34(1), pp. 103–132.

Wallace, W., 1992. From twelve to twenty-four? The challenges to the EC posed by the revolutions in Eastern Europe. In: C. Crouch and D. Marquand, eds. *Towards Greater Europe? A Continent Without an Iron Curtain*. Oxford: The Political Quarterly. pp. 34–51.

Webb, J., 2018. Resolving contestation through discursive engagement: Towards the contextual diffusion of EU rule of law norms? *Southeast European and Black Sea Studies*, 18(3), pp. 401–418.

Weeks, J., 2015. Gay liberation and its legacies. In: D. Paternotte and M. Tremblay, eds. *The Ashgate Research Companion to Lesbian and Gay Activism*. Abingdon: Routledge. pp. 45–57.

Weiss, M. L. and Bosia, M. J. eds., 2013. *Global Homophobia: States, Movements, and the Politics of Oppression*. Urbana: University of Illinois Press.

Wendt, A., 1994. Collective identity formation and the international state. *American Political Science Review*, 88(2), pp. 384–396.

Wiener, A., 2007a. Contested meanings of norms: A research framework. *Comparative European Politics*, 5(1), pp. 1–17.

Wiener, A., 2007b. The dual quality of norms and governance beyond the state: Sociological and normative approaches to 'interaction'. *Critical Review of International Social and Political Philosophy*, 10(1), pp. 47–69.

Wiener, A., 2016. Contested compliance: Interventions on the normative structure of world politics. *European Journal of International Relations*, 10(2), pp. 189–234.

Wilkinson, C., 2014. Putting 'traditional values' into practice: The rise and contestation of anti-homopropaganda laws in Russia. *Journal of Human Rights*, 13(3), pp. 363–379.

Williams, A., 2004. *EU Human Rights Policies: A Study in Irony*. Oxford: Oxford University Press.

Wintour, P., 2017. Ana Brnabić: 'I do not want to be branded Serbia's gay PM'. *Guardian* [online] 28 Jul. Available at: <www.theguardian.com/world/2017/jul/28/ana-brnabic-serbia-prime-minister-interview> [Accessed 29 Dec. 2021].

Wockner, R., 2009. *Serbian Gay Pride Parade Cancelled After Threats*. [online] QX. Available at: <www.qx.se/english/11794/serbian-gay-pride-parade-canceled-after-threats> [Accessed 15 Aug. 2022].

Woll, C. and Jacquot, S., 2010. Using Europe: Strategic action in multi-level politics. *Comparative European politics*, 8(1), pp. 110–126.

Woodcock, S., 2004. Globalization of LGBT identities: Containment masquerading as salvation or why lesbians have less fun. In: M. Frunza, and T.-E. Vacarescu, eds. *Gender and the (Post) East–West Divide*. Cluj-Napoca, Romania: Limes Publishing House. pp. 171–188.

Woodcock, S., 2009. Gay Pride as violent containment in Romania: A Brave New Europe. *Sextures*, 1(1), pp. 7–23.

Yılmaz, G. and Soyaltın, D., 2014. Zooming into the 'domestic' in Europeanization: Promotion of fight against corruption and minority rights in Turkey. *Journal of Balkan and Near Eastern Studies*, 16(1), pp. 11–29.

Youngs, R., 2004. Normative dynamics and strategic interests in the EU's external identity. *Journal of Common Market Studies*, 42(2), pp. 415–435.

YUCOM, 2009. Withdrawal of the anti-discrimination law. *Pescanik* [online] 5 Mar. Available at: <http://pescanik.net/withdrawal-of-the-anti-discrimination-law/> [Accessed 15 Aug. 2022].

YUCOM, 2015. *Promoting mechanisms for the prevention of hate speech.* [online] YUCOM Lawyers' Committee for Human Rights. Available at: <http://en.yucom.org.rs/promoting-mechanisms-for-the-prevention-of-hate-speech/> [Accessed 15 Aug. 2022].

Žarkov, D., 2002. Srebrenica trauma: Masculinity, military and national self-image in Dutch daily newspapers. In: C. Cockburn and D. Žarkov, eds. *The Postwar Moment: Militaries, Masculinities and International Peacekeeping.* London: Lawrence & Wishart. pp. 183–203.

Zielonka, J., 2013. Europe's new civilizing missions: The EU's normative power discourse. *Journal of Political Ideologies*, 18(1), pp. 35–55.

Zimmermann, L., 2016. Same same or different? Norm diffusion between resistance, compliance, and localization in post-conflict states. *International Studies Perspectives*, 17(1), pp. 98–115.

Zimmermann, L., 2017. *Global Norms with a Local Face: Rule-of-Law Promotion and Norm-Translation.* Cambridge: Cambridge University Press.

Zivković, M., 2011. *Serbian Dreambook: National Imaginary in the Time of Milosevic.* Bloomington: Indiana University Press.

Zwingel, S., 2012. How do norms travel? Theorizing international women's rights in transnational perspective. *International Studies Quarterly*, 56(1), pp. 115–129.

Zwingel, S., 2017. Women's rights norms as content-in-motion and incomplete practice. *Third World Thematics: A TWQ Journal*, 2(5), pp. 675–690.

Index

EU authorised representative for GPSR:
Easy Access System Europe, Mustamäe tee 50,
10621 Tallinn, Estonia
gpsr.requests@easproject.com

www.ingramcontent.com/pod-product-compliance
Lightning Source LLC
Chambersburg PA
CBHW052001270326
41929CB00015B/2739